MOPAR
THE PERFORMANCE YEARS

MARTYN L. SCHORR

671 Press

For my son, Stuart, daughter, Collier,
and my wife and best friend, Sharon.

The information in this book is true and complete to the best of our knowledge. All recommendations
are made without any guarantee on the part of the author or publisher, who also disclaim any liability
incurred in connection with the use of this data or specific details.

We recognize, further, that some words, model names, and designations mentioned herein
are the property of the trademark holder. We use them for identification purposes only.
This is not an official publication.

Version History
671 Press edition published July 2009
Originally published as three volumes of the Quicksilver Supercars series:
Mopar: The Performance Years Volume 1, ISBN 0-940346-09-5;
Volume 2, ISBN 0-940346-17-6;
and *Volume 3*, ISBN 0-940346-22-2

Schorr, Martyn L.
Mopar: The Performance Years

ISBN   0-9821733-1-8
ISBN-13 978-0-9821733-1-2

Design, layout, and scanning by Tom Heffron

671 Press logo design by Micah Edel

Contents

Introduction

From the early 1960s through the mid-1970s, Dodge and Plymouth supercars and ponycars defined "ultimate performance" on the street, drag strips, and NASCAR's high-speed tracks. *Mopar: The Performance Years* represents a compilation of the best of three volumes covering these years. The books were published originally as part of the Quicksilver Supercar Series. Out of print for more than two decades, original individual editions of the books are coveted by collectors and rarely come up for sale. Not content to let collectors have all the fun, we've brought them back to provide a unique window into muscle car history.

This book chronicles Mopar's participation in this "era of excessive force," using original factory technical materials and period photography of both prototype and production vehicles. Everything from mini (273-340) to maxi (383-413-426-440) Wedge and Hemi cars are featured as they originally looked and performed when brand new.

I was editor of *Hi-Performance CARS* magazine, and editorial director of the Magnum Automotive Group during Dodge and Plymouth's golden performance years. I had the good fortune to be at the right place at the right time, which afforded me access to the hottest cars, racers, factory engineers, and all the people directly involved with racing and performance programs. We created this nostalgic Mopar tribute by working with original factory documents, notes taken at press previews, and during road testing and interviews with engineers and racers. Photos were shot at racetracks, Chrysler's Chelsea Proving Grounds, and on the street. The interviews and road tests were originally conducted for use in *Hi-Performance CARS* as well as other Magnum publications like *SPEED and SUPER/STOCK, SUPERCAR & FX,* and *SUPERCAR* test annuals.

In addition to period photography of production cars, this book showcases rare pre-production vehicles. Check out the '65 Dodge 426 Hemi Coronet Hardtop—announced but never produced; the

Street Hemi didn't make it into production until the 1966 model year! I also made a number of trips from my home in the suburbs to my office in New York City in a two-door '65 Coronet 426 Hemi sedan prototype. It had been raced by David Pearson and Scott Harvey in the Trans-Canada Rally and then shipped to me for street testing.

I had the opportunity to test-drive Mopar exotica at the Chrysler Proving Grounds and on the streets of New York City. For a week in 1964, I borrowed a clone of the Ramchargers' lightweight *Candy-Matic* Dodge, powered by a radical Stage III 426 Wedge--and I had a ball at local street racing haunts! I've also experienced riding shotgun (sitting on a makeshift seat) with Al Eckstrand in the legendary altered-wheelbase, Hilborn-injected Golden Commandos' Hemi Plymouth on Chelsea's drag strip. I discovered how less could be more after making some runs in the Golden Commandos' *Goldfish* Barracuda that won F/Stock at the 1965 NHRA Nationals. Those really were the good old days!

It's all captured here along with the straight scoop on high-performance engine development and Chrysler Engineering drag test reports on 340, 383, 426, and 440 cubic-inch Plymouths. And we've got everything you've always wanted to know about the aerodynamics of the Charger Daytona and Super-bird "winged warriors."

Vintage Mopar supercars and ponycars are historically significant automobiles that represent Chrysler, Dodge, and Plymouth's finest hours and the "golden years" of high-performance motoring in America. Enjoy this look back at the way things were.

Martyn L. Schorr

Publisher's Note

Regarding Mopar's musclecar era of the 1960s and 1970s, there is no shortage of lavish, hard-cover books with color photographs. They suffer, however, from the fact that they were written and composed in recent times; *Mopar: The Performance Years* instead conveys impressions formed without the revisionist hindsight that colors other books on the subject. Instead, it presents these cars, engines, events, and people honestly, as they were seen by contemporary observers. In that, it provides a unique and valuable perspective that is sure to transport the reader back to an exciting time in automotive history.

Peter Bodensteiner
Founder and Partner, 671 Press

THE HEMI REVOLUTION

A four-letter word creates havoc in the world of racing and high-performance

The classic '53 Dodge Red Ram Hemi engine displacing 241 cubic inches and packed with unreal performance potential. In September 1953 the factory ran a four-door Dodge sedan at Bonneville with a variety of engines from 183 to 305 cubic inches. It ran at over 101 mph for 48 hours. It broke the '53 Red Ram record for the 10-mile run at over 108 mph.

THERE WERE three different versions of the old series Hemi: the Chrysler, the DeSoto, and the Dodge. There were four different sizes of the Chrysler: 301, 331, 354, and 392 cubic inches. The De-Soto version came in five different sizes: 276, 291, 330, 341, and 345 cubic inches. There were also five different sizes of the Dodge engine: 241, 260, 270, 315, and 325 cubic inches. There were two basic valve train layouts used on all these engines. One was a single rocker shaft, and the other had double rocker shafts (two-per-head). The double-rocker version is the true Hemi cylinder head and the better of the two designs. Also, each of the three versions, Chrysler, De-Soto, and Doge, had two basic blocks. One block was standard and the other was a raised-block design.

In many cases valve sizes other than the ones stated were used. The ones shown are the most commonly used. These engines also come with hydraulic lifters on the milder engines and mechanical lifters on the higher output versions.

Most of these engines were offered in two-barrel, four-barrel dual-quad versions. The 1958 dual-quad 392 Chrysler had an advertised rating of 380 hp. These engines have no interchangeable pieces with the new-style Hemi (426). They also can be easily identified from the new 426 Hemi by the fact that they (the 301-392 Hemi) have the distributor located at the rear of the engine, while the 426 Hemi has the distributor at the front. Also because of the number of different blocks, the interchangeability between the various old Hemi engines

would be limited.

Dodge's performance evolution started when division engineers scaled down the Firepower design for the 1953 models. The new Dodge Red Ram engine was very similar to the Chrysler in general layout—had the same oversquare stroke/bore ratio, stiff compact block with beefy bulkheads, and lots of crankpin overlap on the crankshaft, and the Hemi heads with inclined valves and dual rocker shafts were adapted. The Dodge version was smaller and lighter. This was quite an accomplishment in view of the complex head castings required with the domed chambers and inclined valves.

And, performance increase over the 230-inch Six was fantastic. The Red Ram had 3-7/16 x 3¼-inch bore and stroke (241 cubic inches), and was rated at 140

An early Chrysler Hemi with short stack fuel injectors mounted on home-made tube manifolding. Setup with Scott injection was quite popular during the late-Fifties and early-Sixties.

When it came to making groundshaking power, the Hemi was the only choice for many years. With rocker covers off you can see the dual rocker shafts and "mouse trap" valve spring assemblies.

Stock, top, and modified heads for the Red Ram Dodge Hemi as prepared by factory engineers back in 1953 for use in a record-breaking Salt Flats engine.

DODGE 1955 RED RAM HEMI ENGINES

	RED RAM	SUPER RED RAM
Displacement	270 cubic inches	270 cubic inches
Horsepower	175	183/193
Compression Ratio	7.6-to-1	7.6-to-1
Oil pressure	40-65 psi	40-65 psi
Intake Valve	1.72-inch	1.75-inch
Exhaust Valve	1.47-inch	1.41-inch
Cam Lift	.360/.364-inch	.360/.364-inch
Valve Springs	Single	Dual
Cam Duration	244 degrees	244 degrees
Carburetion	Stromberg Two-Barrel	Stromberg Two-Barrel Carter Four-Barrel
Exhaust	Single	Dual

NOTE: Dual exhausts and four-barrel carburetor increased the output from 183 to 193 horsepower and were part of optional Power Pack.

hp at 4,400 rpm with 7.1-to-1 compression and a two-throat carburetor. 0-60 mph times immediately dropped to the neighborhood of 15 seconds. Dodge engineers were highly encouraged by the unexpected performance and fuel economy of the little V-8—so much so, in fact, that arrangements were made to attack the Class C stock car records at Bonneville (for engines between 183 and 305 cubic inches). The runs were made in September, 1953, using brand new '54 models—a sedan and a convertible—to attack closed car and open body records simultaneously. The '54 engines had 7.5-to-1 compression and 150 horses.

Drivers Danny Eames, Jimmy Jackson and others set new records from the standing-start kilometer up to four days. Best speed for the sedan was 108.6 mph for 10 kilos, with a top of 97.66 mph for the convertible (top down) over 200 kilos. The sedan broke the 15-year-old records of 107+ mph set by Ab Jenkins' supercharged Cord in 1937, and the new records proved that the Dodges were getting their advertised 150 hp. Betty Skelton turned a two-way average of 105.88 mph at Daytona Beach in a '54 Dodge to win the NASCAR Class II.

About this time a number of people were beginning to see important performance possibilities in the Red Ram. Dodge engineers bored a '54 block ⅛-inch (260 cubic inches), raised compression to 8.5, ported the heads, and went to a 280-degree cam and four Zenith carbs on log manifolds. Result: 245 hp at 5,600 rpm! This bomb was wrapped in the "Fire Arrow" dream car.

Betty Skelton put this one around the Chrysler test track at 143.4 mph! Tony Campana built up a Red Ram for the Dean Van Lines 1955 Indianapolis car, based on the 270 inch '55 block. He used ported heads, huge valves, Hilborn fuel injection, roller cam and mag ignition, and came up with 310 hp at 7,200 rpm on alcohol! Driver Jimmy Bryan got it around the Indy oval at 140 mph on nitro; but oiling troubles kept them from qualifying.

The years between 1955 and 1957 saw Detroit up to its ears in professional stock car racing. Dodge was no exception. The horsepower race was in full swing by then and the mass market was demanding more and more performance in all classes of cars. Dodge decided to jump in during the 1955 season, and by

Continued

Dodge sponsored Don Garlits for many years and always made sure that Dodge decals were on the 392-inch Chrysler Hemis. This is the Swamp Rat VI which Garlits campaigned with an old-style motor even though the 426 Hemi was available.

Two factory engineers assemble the lower end of one of the Bonneville motors in a "clean room" at Chrysler Engineering.

If one 392-inch Hemi is good, then two must be better! It's hard to imagine trying to harness that much horsepower and torque. Long after the new series Hemi came into being, the popular choice for fuel dragster use was the tried and true "old fashioned" Hemi.

that fall they were rolling full speed with a new line of '56s.

The big news was introduction of the famous D-500 series of sports-luxury cars. This was actually a package that could be ordered on any Dodge body. In addition to a hopped-up engine it included a beefed-up automatic transmission (optional), heavy-duty springs and shocks, beefed driveline and heavy-duty brakes. The big '56 engine had a stroked crankshaft to give 315 cubic inches. D-500 engines had 9.25-to-1 compression (compared with 8.0 standard), big four-barrel carb, dual exhausts and a high-lift 252-degree cam with solid lifters, and were rated 260 hp at 4,800 rpm. This engine could get the 3,800-pound '56 Dodge up to 60 mph in less than nine seconds and hit 83-84 mph speeds on the strip.

It's interesting how that number 500 got into the model designation. This was supposed to represent the number of identical examples of a given model that had to be produced and distributed to the public to make it eligible to run in NASCAR's Grand National stock division. As it turned out, NASCAR rules were considerably more lenient. Manufacturers were permitted to use special over-the-counter factory equipment on these basic cars (it didn't need to be installed on the assembly line). So the 500-car stipulation didn't mean much.

In the case of the D-500, Dodge even published a separate designation of D-500-1 for its racing model! This had *dual* four-barrel carbs on a log-type manifold, hotter solid-lifter cam, and was rated 295 hp at 5,200 rp.m The chassis had heavy-duty hubs and wheels, stiffer

springs and shocks, heavy-duty differential in a Chrysler rear axle and other special parts. They were all-out *racing* cars ... and relatively few were ever sold to the public.

Danny Eames won his Daytona class with ease on a flying mile average of 130.58 mph and standing-mile speed of 81 mph. And on the NASCAR oval tracks later in the season Lee Petty did very nicely against the new Ford and Chevy V8s and big Chrysler 300-Bs. It was a terrific start for the famous D-500 series.

We saw more of the same in 1957. Another 1/16-inch bore gave 325 cubic inches on the *little* Dodge block (it originally started at 241 cubic inches), and this put the D-500's rating up to 285 hp at 4,800. A special optional D-500A kit included the former dual four-barrel carburetion system, a hotter cam and hot ignition for a rating of 310 hp. And for the 1957 racing season Dodge engineers decided to throw caution to the winds. It was OK'd with NASCAR to factory-install the 354 cubic inch Chrysler 300-B engine in '57 Dodges. They called them D-501 packages. With 340 hp on tap at 5,200 rpm, this combo got the job done. Their best two-way average on a very bad Daytona Beach was 129.75 mph. Unfortunately the combo never really got tracking on the NASCAR ovals ... and before the carbs could be debugged the A.M.A. anti-racing declaration hit like a bombshell in June, 1957, putting a sudden stop to *all* domestic racing development almost overnight.

This wasn't the end of the D-500 series; but it was the end of any exciting news in the performance field for quite a long time.

CHRYSLER 300 HEMI SERIES

Model	Displacement	Horsepower	Torque	Bore & Stroke	Compression	Carburetion
1955 C-300	331	300 @ 5,200	345 @ 3,200	3.81 x 3.63	8.50-to-1	Dual-quads
1956 300-B Optional	354	340 @ 5,200 355 @ 5,200	385 @ 3,400 405 @ 3,400	3.94 x 3.63	9.0-to-1 10.0-to-1	Dual-quads
1957 300-C Optional	392	375 @ 5,200 390 @ 5,400	420 @ 4,000 430 @ 4,200	4.00 x 3.90	9.25-to-1 10.0-to-1	Dual-quads
1958 300-D Optional	392	380 @ 5,200 390 @ 5,200	435 @ 3,600 435 @ 3,600	4.00 x 3.90	10.0-to-1	Dual-quads Fuel-injection

Old Hemis may be heavy, but for sheer torque and horsepower they are really hard to beat. And, with the right camming and carburetion, they still make dynamite street rod engines.

MOPAR HEMI GUIDE

ENGINE	YEAR	BORE X STROKE	BLOCK	CRANK	VALVE SIZE
CHRYSLER					
301	1955	3.63 x 3.63	Standard	B	H
331	1951-'56	3.81 x 3.63	Standard	B	G
354	1956-'57	3.94 x 3.63	Standard	B	F G
392	1957-'58	4.00 x 3.90	Raised Block	A	F
DESOTO					
276	1952-'54	3.80 x 3.80	Standard	C	H
291	1955	3.78 x 3.80	Standard	C	H
330	1956	3.72 x 3.80	Raised Block	E	G
341	1957	3.72 x 3.34	Raised Block	B	G
345	1957	3.63 x 3.34	Raised Block	B	G
DODGE					
241	1953-'55	3.44 x 3.25	Standard	D	J
260	1955	3.56 x 3.25	Standard	D	J
270	1955	3.63 x 3.25	Standard	D	J
315	1956	3.63 x 3.80	Raised Block	B	H
325	1957-'58	3.69 x 3.80	Raised Block	B	H

	CRANK			VALVE SIZE	
	Main Journal Diameter	Rod Bearing Diameter		Intake Valve	Exhaust Valve
A	3.69	2.38	F	2.00	1.75
B	2.50	2.25	G	1.94	1.75
C	2.38	2.06	H	1.84	1.50
D	2.38	1.94	J	1.72	1.47

EVOLUTION OF THE WEDGE

Thanks to racing-oriented engineers, in-house racing groups like the Ramchargers and Golden Commandos, the new 413 and 426 Wedges become the engines to beat

This is the 413-426-inch Wedge that that revolutionized Super/Stock drag racing during the early-Sixties. In 1963 this engine could be had from the factory with 13.5-to-1 compression and all the goodies you needed to go racing and win.

Popping the hood on this Chrysler 300 reveals an awesome array of plumbing complete with dual four-barrel carburetors and incredible power for a luxury/sports-style vehicle.

THE FIRST sign that Chrysler was coming out from under the rock was when the unique ram induction manifolds were brought out in 1960. These consisted of 30-inch ducts between the valve port and a plenum chamber under a four-barrel, one for each bank. (The carb for the right bank was over the left-bank rocker cover, with the passages looping across the engine—and vice versa.) The natural acoustic pressure pulsations bouncing back and forth through these passages would literally *supercharge* the cylinder and *ram* fuel-air in under a pressure when the rpm and passage length were matched. Chrysler chose the long 30-inch length to provide the major boost at 2,800 rpm for maximum passing acceleration on the highway. Those 413-cube ram-inducted '60 Chryslers had so much mid-range torque that the kickdown gear in the transmission was rarely needed.

Dodge also adopted the ram manifolds in 1960. In 1961 they offered them in two versions, the original long ram tubes tuned at 2,800 rpm and a special short ram setup that had passage walls in the manifold castings cut back to give a shorter effective tuning length for major boost above 4,000 rpm. (The long passages would actually reduce power somewhat above 4,400.) The short rams were for racing.

But these intake manifolds were only a small part of the Dodge performance story in 1961. It was fast becoming obvious to Dodge that a super-performance model capable of winning Top Stock Eliminator on the strips was needed if Dodge ever hoped to grab a bigger share of the youth market. The Dodge people were only too well aware that engineering and tooling these special cars for limited production was prohibitively expensive. They didn't feel they could afford it. So they figured out a loophole. There was nothing in the stock class rules to prevent a manufacturer from selecting various pieces of special speed equipment for his engine, then merely certifying it as "factory equipment for dealer installation and putting a factory part number on it. This made the stuff "stock" in the eyes of drag strip tech committees and saved Dodge the cost and trouble of making the parts and installing them on a factory assembly line.

It worked. Dodge certified the 413 Chrysler Dodges—with dozens of combinations of pistons from Jahns and Forgedtrue (up to 13-to-1). intake manifolds plus a triple two-throat from Weiand and camshafts and valve gear parts from Iskenderian and Howard. You could hand-build a *racing* version of the 413 Chrysler engine (with even bigger-than-stock exhaust valves) and it would be legally stock in your '61 Dodge. Performance went up accordingly. Dodge engineers put a rating of 410 hp at 5.400 rpm on the 413 engine with high-compression Forgedtrue pistons, short ram manifolds. factory RC-92 cam (292 degree duration) and dual-point ignition.

This program was not completed until the summer of 1961. so there wasn't much chance for the new deal to show its stuff on the strips that season. However the famous Ramchargers Club of Detroit threw together a '61 Dodge coupe and took it to NHRA's National Champion-

ships They were plagued with shifting trouble from the new heavy-duty Chrysler three-speed; but driver Al Eckstrand managed a trial run at 13.03 seconds and 110 mph. Shifting goofed them in the Super/Stock eliminations: but Eckstrand did beat Stock Eliminator Don Nicholson's 409 Chevy in a grudge match!

NHRA officials knew this couldn't go on. Trying to check and certify the Stock class winners at Indy in 1961 was a nightmare. There was such a confusing array of factory and California equipment on the engines (Dodge wasn't the only company that was doing this) that tech inspectors hardly knew what was "stock" and what wasn't. So they came up with a new rule for 1962: All Stock class entries had to be produced on a factory assembly line. with all basic equipment installed on the line (except for the usual ignition, exhaust headers. etc.). Otherwise the car would run in a new Factory Experimental class.

Dodge was floored by the new NHRA rule. It meant running in the FX division or spending money they couldn't afford on an assembly line racing car. Fortunately they decided to forge ahead with a new factory high-performance model and

Don Garlits took Top Fuel Eliminator at the NHRA Winternationals in 1963 with his Swamp Rat V powered by a factory-supplied Dodge 426-inch Wedge. He ran over 186 mph in 8.26 seconds to take the title.

This may not be the hot setup for the quarter-mile, but long ram runners with four-barrel carbs are the ultimate in status. Goodies like this still pop up at wap meets and Mopar car shows.

The Pace Car for the 1963 Indy 500 was this Chrysler 300-J powered by a dual-quad 413-incher rated at 390 hp.

CHRYSLER 300 WEDGE SERIES

Model	Displacement	Horsepower	Torque	Bore x Stroke	Compression	Carburetion
1959/300-E	413	380 @ 5,000	450 @ 3,600	4.18 x 3.75	10.0-to-1	Dual-quads
1969/300-F Short-Ram	413	375 @ 5,000 400 @ 5,200	495 @ 2,800 465 @ 3,600	4.18 x 3.75	10.10-to-1	Dual-quads
1961/300-G Short-Ram	413	375 @ 5,000 400 @ 5,200	495 @ 2,800 465 @ 3,600	4.18 x 3.75	10.10-to-1	Dual-quads
1962/300-H Short-Ram	413	380 @ 5,200 405 @ 5,400	450 @ 3,600 473 @ 3,600	4.18 x 3.75	10.10-to-1 11.0-to-1	Dual-quads
1963/300-J	413	390 @ 4,800	485 @ 3,600	4.18 x 3.75	9.60-1o-1	Dual-quads
1964/300-K Short-Ram	413	360 @ 4,800 390 @ 4,800	470 @ 3,200 485 @ 3,600	4.18 x 3.75	10.0-to-1 9.60-to-1	Four-barrel Dual-quads
1965/300-L	413	360 @ 4,800	470 @ 3,200	4.18 x 3.75	10.10-to-1	Four-barrel

scheduled it for the spring of 1962. They decided to call it the Ramcharger 413, after the group that had done much to put Dodge on the racing map.

The engine is based on the 413 block. But there are special head castings with much larger ports and larger 1.88-inch exhaust valves; new aluminum dual four-barrel manifold with a short 15-inch ram length to tune at 5,500 rpm; 300-degree cam with heavy-duty valve gear good for 6,500 rpm; forged pistons of 11-to-1 compression (or 13.5-to-1 optional), beefed lower end, and beautiful new streamlined cast iron exhaust headers that split the flow from the alternate-firing cylinders 3 and 4 on the left bank. The 1963 versions of this engine came through with the blocks bored .060-inch to 426 cubic inches and much-improved lubrication systems. New 1963 ratings are 415 hp at 5,600 rpm with 11-to-1 compression and 425 hp with 13.5-to-1.

The displacement of the 1963 Ramcharger engine was increased to 426 cubic inches. In addition, many engineering improvements have been incorporated and engines are available with either 11-to-1 or 13.5-to-1 compression.

SHORT RAM INTAKE MANIFOLD

The one-piece aluminum short ram (15-inch) manifold is fitted with two four-barrel carburetors. This manifold is tuned to give increased output in the higher speed ranges (above 4,000 rpm). The manifold has generous tapered branches which are designed with ports to match the port areas in the new cylinder heads.

Two four-barrel carburetors, Model AFB-3447 SA are used. These incorporate a hand choke instead of automatic. The two air cleaners are high-capacity and unsilenced.

CYLINDER HEADS AND VALVES

The cylinder heads are internally-similar to the standard heads previously used. However, port areas are larger and the heat cross-over passage has been eliminated. The deck structure has also been strengthened for more positive head gasket sealing. The cylinder head gasket is made from stainless steel.

The new intake valves used with the heads are 2.08-inch in diameter and streamlined for higher air flow. The exhaust valves are ¼-inch larger than standard or 1.88-inch in diameter.

To improve oil economy, Teflon intake valve stem oil seals have been incorporated into the 1963 engines. To accommodate this seal, the intake valve guide diameter is reduced from .640 to .525-inch for a distance of .375-inch from the top of the guide.

COMPRESSION RATIO SPECIFICATIONS

Combustion Chamber Volume Minimum 81 cc: Maximum 86 cc (To reduce the volume of the combustion chamber 1 cc, .005-inch must be milled from the head surface. The cylinder head surface finish should be 100-120 micro-inches. For each 0.010-inch removed from the cylinder head 0.012-inch must be removed from the intake side of the head.)

Distance from top of the lower flat of piston to the block deck.

Comp. Ratio 11-to-1
Minimum	.0155
Maximum	.0455

Comp. Ratio 13.5-to-1
Minimum	.018
Maximum	.043

Both the intake and exhaust valves have a single wide bead spring retainer lock which is stronger than the multiple bead lock. Dual valve springs are used with both the intake and exhaust valves. A flat wound steel damper is also fitted to the outer spring to eliminate harmonics.

ROCKER ARMS AND OTHER VALVE GEAR

The heavy-duty rockers are cast malleable iron incorporating a lash adjusting screw with a lock nut. Pushrods are ⅜-inch in diameter steel tubing with .083-inch wall thickness and hardened inserts in each end.

The camshaft specifications are as follows: .509-inch lift at the valve, intake opening 33 degrees BTC; Closing 87 degrees ABC; exhaust opening 78 degrees BBC; closing 42 degrees ATC; Overlap 75 degrees; duration 300 degrees for both intake and exhaust.

This camshaft is ground with a low taper to minimize tappet to cam loading stresses and should be used only with flat face tappets. The lifters are of the flat face design and are of special material compatible to the camshaft. These lifters have .001-inch more diametrial or side clearance than standard to eliminate any possibility of "hang up" at high speeds causing valve float.

CYLINDER BLOCK

The cylinder block is fitted with selected bearing caps for maximum strength. The cylinder bores are notched for the 1⅞-inch exhaust valve clearance.

PISTONS

The 11-to-1 ratio standard and the optional 13.5-to-1 pistons are forged aluminum. They increase thermal effi-

1962 HIGH-PERFORMANCE ENGINES

CUBIC INCHES	BORE	STROKE	HORSEPOWER	TORQUE	COMPRESSION	INDUCTION
361	4.120	3.380	305 @ 4800	395 @ 3000	9.00	FOUR-BARREL
383	4.250	3.380	305 @ 4600	410 @ 2400	10.00	TWO-BARREL
413	4.190	3.750	340 @ 4600	470 @ 2800	10.00	FOUR-BARREL

1963 HIGH-PERFORMANCE ENGINES

CUBIC INCHES	BORE	STROKE	HORSEPOWER	TORQUE	COMPRESSION	INDUCTION
383	4.250	3.380	305 @ 4600	410 @ 2400	10.00	TWO-BARREL
383	4.250	3.380	330 @ 4600	425 @ 2800	10.00	FOUR-BARREL
383	4.250	3.380	360 @ 4800	470 @ 3200	10.10	FOUR-BARREL
383	4.250	3.380	390 @ 4800	485 @ 3600	9.60	DUAL-QUAD
413	4.190	3.750	340 @ 4600	470 @ 2800	10.00	FOUR-BARREL
426	4.250	3.750	415 @ 5600	470 @ 4400	11.00	DUAL-QUAD
426	4.250	3.750	425 @ 5600	480 @ 4400	13.50	DUAL-QUAD

ciency for higher output but, require the highest octane gasoline available.

The 13.5-to-1 ratio pistons are practical for *only* limited application. Wide open throttle bursts must be limited to 15 seconds to prevent engine damage. These pistons also require high clearance, have no pin offset, and no bimetal thermal correction. They will be noisier than standard, particularly when cold.

PISTON RINGS

The top compression rings are chrome-plated, high-strength cast-iron. The lower oil control rings are of cast-iron construction. Standard intermediate rings are retained.

CONNECTING RODS

The connecting rods for the 426 engine have been redesigned to insure satisfactory performance under the additional power output.

CRANKSHAFT

The crankshaft has hardened journals and shot-peened fillets. Tri-metal heavy-duty bearings are used. The main bearings for 1963 have been redesigned with wider .180-inch oil grooves for improved oil flow to the connecting rod bearings.

LUBRICATION

The engine oil pan has special baffles to prevent oil sloshing at high speeds. The passages in the oil pump pick-up-pipe oil-strainer, and the galley to the pump have been enlarged, to increase the oil pump capacity at high speeds.

IGNITION DISTRIBUTOR

A dual-point centrifugal advance distributor is used in the new 426 engine. No vacuum advance is used. The centrifugal advance is calibrated for 24 degrees, crankshaft advance at 2,000 engine rpm. With the 10 degrees basic timing total advance is 34 degrees.

EXHAUST MANIFOLD

Bolted to the four-bolt square flange of the manifolds are 3-inch exhaust pipes. These pipes drop down beneath the car and where they turn out toward the side of the car, they are capped by four bolt square covers, which can be removed for competition.

EXHAUST SYSTEM

The exhaust manifolds are of streamlined high capacity with 3-inch outlets and made out of cast iron.

One-piece aluminum short ram manifold is tuned to really turn-on over 4,000 rpm. With large ports and 15-inch runners, manifold is useless at low rpm on the street.

ENGINE SPECIFICATIONS

11-to-1 Compression Ratio	13.5-to-1 Compression Ratio
415 hp @ 5,600 rpm	425 hp @ 5,600 rpm
470 ft./lbs. @ 4,400 rpm	480 ft./lbs. @ 4,400 rpm

Type	.90°V
Number of Cylinders	.8
Bore	.4,250-inch.
Stroke	.3.750 inch.
Piston Displacement	.426 cubic inches
Compression Ratio (Std)	.11-to-1
(Optional)	.13.5-to-1

This is the engine compartment of a stone-stock '64 Plymouth. Revamped 426 Wedge for 1964 had a top compression ratio of 12.5-to-1.

WEDGES, RAMCHARGERS AND RECORDS!

The Ramchargers organize, the Dragmasters turn a Lancer
into a killer FX-er and the performance die is cast

Bud Faubel, in one of his early "ummarked" Honker Dodges, blasts off the line at the NHRA Indy Nationals. Engine is ram-quad 413-incher.

CAPSULE COMMENTS

THE performance programs of the Chrysler divisions haven't been as extensive as those at GM and Ford because of tight budgets and lack of production facilities. But things are looking up for 1962. They are taking full advantage of one gimmick the other companies have barely touched as yet: instead of engineering and producing all their own speed equipment, they are selecting certain pieces of California equipment from the hot rod industry and giving them *factory-certified approval* for dealer installation in the field. This makes the stuff just as legal as factory-built parts in the eyes of the competition officials and yet they do not have to design, engineer, test or produce them. It works very nicely.

This is where most of the 1962 improvements come from.

The 361-cube engine, rated 305 horsepower, will be the hottest thing you can order on a 1962 off the assembly line. But the 383 and 413 cube blocks are being continued as over-the-counter operations. All the 1961 carburetion options are also being continued—including single four-barrel, dual four-barrels in line on a log-type manifold, and the well-known Sonoramic dual quad ram carburetion. One setup uses long ram tubes that *tune* at 2,800 rpm for torque, while the competition type has short rams and gives about 20 horsepower more above 4,000 rpm. In addition Dodge is approving Edelbrock and Weiand triple two-throat manifolds for use on the big V8 (though these would probably not give as much horsepower as the dual quad on the ram tubes).

1962 HIGH-PERFORMANCE ENGINES

CUBIC INCHES	BORE	STROKE	HORSEPOWER	TORQUE	COMPRESSION	INDUCTION
361	4.120	3.380	305 @ 4800	395 @ 3000	9.00	FOUR-BARREL
383	4.250	3.380	305 @ 4600	410 @ 2400	10.00	TWO-BARREL
413	4.190	3.750	340 @ 4600	470 @ 2800	10.00	FOUR-BARREL

Factory tube headers and ram-tuned quads highlight the factory-built drag racing engine. Anyone could buy one by simply checking off the right boxes on the order sheet!

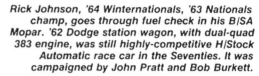

Rick Johnson, '64 Winternationals, '63 Nationals champ, goes through fuel check in his B/SA Mopar. '62 Dodge station wagon, with dual-quad 383 engine, was still highly-competitive H/Stock Automatic race car in the Seventies. It was campaigned by John Pratt and Bob Burkett.

And there's more. Dodge lists the Chrysler 300 cylinder heads, with the large 1.74-inch exhaust valves, as optional equipment now. And—perhaps best of all—you can now legally use dome-top Forged True pistons to give 12-to-1 compression ratio. The Dodge and Plymouth competition engines had been handicapped in the past by having only 10-to-1 available. Camshafts are being continued unchanged. The solid-lifter job with 284 degrees duration is the one usually chosen with the short rams. A new model, RC-92, solid-lifter cam, with 292 degrees duration, has recently been added. There are no factory-built cast exhaust headers for the big Chrysler V8 as yet that will fit the small Dodge-Plymouth chassis. (The Chrysler 300 headers can't squeeze in.) But, specialty headers are legal in the stock classes—and Hedman sells a beautiful set for this engine.

All in all, there appears to be some real potential here. As far as I know only one car had the new stuff at Indianapolis, a '61 Dodge coupe entered by the "Ramchargers" club of Detroit, a group of young Chrysler engineers. This thing really honked. They were turning ets in the mid-13's consistently and 108-109 mph. But the three-speed floorshift transmission was giving trouble and they hung up Second gear on both their elimination runs. (the O/SS class runs on Saturday and top stock eliminator on Monday). They managed to trim Don Nicholson's 409 Chevy on one grudge run, though. ●

DRAGMASTER DOES IT!

Dode Martin and Jim Nelson of Dragmaster shoehorn a 413-inch Ramcharger motor into a compact Dodge Lancer, creating a killer A/FX racer. The engine adds 430 extra pounds and, when combined with a three-speed T-85 close-ratio box with Hurst shifter, wails to the tune of 113 mph in 12.68 seconds. Goodies include Dragmaster headers, 4340 ChromeMoly steel torsion bars, Police Car driveshaft, rear end and brakes and a Mallory Mini-Mag. Dragmaster's Dodge Dart Six dragster is still being campaigned.

Dode Martin poses with Hilborn-injected Dragmaster Dart rail. George Parkinson wrenched and drove the Golden Lancer, one of the premier FX cars. Action shot taken at Pomona drag strip.

THE RAM TRUCK

Disc jockey Dick Boynton and wife, Mary, raised quite a few eyebrows with their 413-inch RamCharger pickup truck. B/FX truck looks a bit strange in the staging lanes, dwarfing conventional stockers.

THE DODGE D-100 half-ton pickup was never intended to exceed 100 miles-per-hour. It is a 122-inch-wheelbase utility vehicle, and racing was the last thing that its designers thought of when they produced it. To say the least, it is an offbeat race car, and that is one of the things that attracted Dick Boynton to it.

Boyton, director of news and sports programs for radio station KDEO in San Diego, California, is an enthusiastic drag racer who has had considerable success in stock cars. When he hit upon turning the D-100 into a drag race machine, the experts predicted failure. But with the help of Dragmaster's Jim Nelson, who has proven that Dodge engines can win on the drag strip, the boxy truck was transformed into a winner.

Boynton calls it the Ram Truck, and almost everthing is against its being competitive. It weighs 3,900 pounds, has 70 percent of the weight concentrated on the front wheels, and an almost total lack of streamlining.

What does it take to make it go? The Slant Six engine and three-speed manual transmission were discarded. In their place is a stock 413-cubic-inch, 420-horsepower Ram Charger V-8 and a three-speed TorqueFlite automatic transmission.

For maximum traction, the rear tires are 9.00 x 15-inch M&H Racemaster street slicks, with nine inches of rubber width on the road. The stock limited-slip differential carries a 4.89-to-1 gear ratio, and there are special exhaust headers built by Horsepower Engineering of Pasadena. Traction Master torque reaction arms help prevent rear wheel hop during maximum acceleration. Because the D-100 was never intended to go so fast, it was necessary to alter the front end alignment from factory specifications.

Boynton races the Ram Truck in NHRA's B/Factory Experimental category, and says that the spectators get a terrific kick out of seeing the truck pursue its winning ways against potentially faster cars.

How fast has he gone? So far he has driven the standing quarter-mile in 12.95 seconds at 110.80 mph. Boynton says that the Ram Truck is still in the developmental stage, that he can improve these figures as he gains more experience.

Everyone loves a winner and the truck bears the names of four dealers—Boulevard Dodge, San Diego; Carl Burger Dodge, La Mesa; Stanley Dodge, National City; and Howard Taylor, San Diego—all of whom have pledged their support to this unusual racing project. ●

HIGHER HORSEPOWER, LIGHTER BODIES AND WAR IS DECLARED!

It was the year that the wedge grew to 426 cubes and Mopar became a synonym for winning

Author Martyn L. Schorr doing some street testing of new Ramcharger Dodge in 1963. License plates indicate car came from Dodge News Bureau in NYC!

CAPSULE COMMENTS

FOR 1963 Dodge-Plymouth presents three new engine options which offer substantial increases in power and torque in the speed ranges more frequently used by drivers.

A 383-cubic-inch V-8 with two-barrel carburetor is the standard power-plant for Polara 500 models and is optional on other 119-inch-wheelbase models. It provides an appreciable increase in power output, particularly at highway driving speeds. Direct gear acceleration from 30 to 60 mph, for instance, is 24 percent greater than the 318-cubic-inch engine with four-barrel carburetor which was the powerpack option on Dart models last year.

An optional, high-performance, 383-cubic-inch V-8 with four-barrel carburetor, dual exhausts, high-performance camshaft, dual-point distributor and other special features is also available on 1963 Dodge models. Increased displacement, compared with the 361-cubic-inch, four-barrel carburetor version offered in 1962, provides higher output

through the whole speed range. Through-gear acceleration from 0 to 60 miles per hour is improved by approximately 13 percent over the 361. This engine is available for police models.

A maximum performance, 426-cubic-inch V-8 with ram induction and twin 4-barrel carburetors, which was introduced as a 413 in the spring of 1962, will be available, in limited quantities, in 1963 models.

Standard equipment with this engine includes: two four-barrel carburetors with high-capacity air cleaners; new cylinder heads with larger ports, streamlined intake valves and larger exhaust valves; a high-lift, long-duration camshaft which is designed for high output at high engine speeds; dual, high-load valve springs and extra heavy-duty retainers; exhaust headers with three-inch diameter exhaust pipes and factory-installed lake pipe caps; and other high-performance and heavy-duty parts such as special belt pulleys, tri-metal bearings, hardened crankshaft, forged pistons and magna-fluxed connecting rods. The compression ratio is 11-to-1. A 13.5-to-1 ratio is optional.

The engine has a one-piece, aluminum intake manifold which has a short, 15-inch ram tube designed to provide maximum tuned output in the high-rpm range.

The 426-cubic-inch package also includes special heavy-duty suspension and drive train components. The Borg-Warner T-85, three-speed manual transmission is standard and is combined with a cast steel clutch housing, lightweight flywheel and heavy-duty clutch. It has a floor-mounted shift lever and linkage. The three-speed TorqueFlite automatic transmission is available as optional equipment and is equipped with a high-speed governor.

Midyear changes in the 426-cubic-inch Ramcharger engine improve its performance by increasing the air-handling capacity of the induction system. Changes include new carburetors, camshaft, fan and air cleaners as well as machined refinements in the intake manifold and cylinder head. Earlier 426 engines can be converted by machining the intake manifold and adding the new parts. ●

Factory production 426 Ramcharger installation

"Big Daddy" Don Garlits campaigned Dodge fuel rails and Super/Stock Ramcharger sedan.

1963 HIGH-PERFORMANCE ENGINES

CUBIC INCHES	BORE	STROKE	HORSEPOWER	TORQUE	COMPRESSION	INDUCTION
383	4.250	3.380	305 @ 4600	410 @ 2400	10.00	TWO-BARREL
383	4.250	3.380	330 @ 4600	425 @ 2800	10.00	FOUR-BARREL
383	4.250	3.380	360 @ 4800	470 @ 3200	10.10	FOUR-BARREL
383	4.250	3.380	390 @ 4800	485 @ 3600	9.60	DUAL-QUAD
413	4.190	3.750	340 @ 4600	470 @ 2800	10.00	FOUR-BARREL
426	4.250	3.750	415 @ 5600	470 @ 4400	11.00	DUAL-QUAD
426	4.250	3.750	425 @ 5600	480 @ 4400	13.50	DUAL-QUAD

Factory-built lightweight 426 Dodge race car

Shots show in-factory construction of new alloy-paneled car.

DIET DELIGHT

SPECIAL aluminum body parts are now available for 1963 drag-racing cars powered by the new 426 Ramcharger & Super/Stock engines. The aluminum body parts include two front fenders, hood with functional air scoop, stone and splash shields and carburetor air intake scoops. Also available are an aluminum bumper and special trim parts. This package, available factory-installed, reduces the weight of a '63 Dodge Ramcharger by almost 150 pounds.

NICE GUYS FINISH FIRST!

Trophy presentation was at Cecil County Drag-O-Way after Faubel beat Tasca Ford Thunderbolt at CARS Magazine Match Race. Looking on while Martyn L. Schorr makes presentation is Bill "Grumpy" Jenkins, Faubel's wrench. Times have changed!

ONE-and-a-half trophies-per-month for the past ten years is the average posted by drag racing champ, Bud Faubel of Chambersburg, Pa. Owner of Shively Motors, Faubel campaigns a 426 Dodge Ramcharger and has won more than 180 trophies over the past ten years. When these photos were taken, Faubel had just set a record of 124.30 mph in 11.39 seconds in his "Grumpy" Jenkins-tuned Dodge at the special CARS Magazine Match Race held at Cecil County (Md.) Drag-O-Way. Presenting the award to Faubel and Jenkins is Martyn L. Schorr, Editor of CARS Magazine. ●

STREET WEDGES
AND THE
HEMI REVOLUTION

The Chrysler Crew adds a 396-inch NASCAR Wedge,
mid-year 426 Hemi, blown exhibition cars,
rally machines and even a wheelstanding truck to its product mix!

Sonny Falcone in Plymouth Super/Stock stages with Golden Commandos entry at 1964 NHRA Indy Nationals.
It was a big year for Plymouth thanks to new Barracuda entry in the Mustang youth/sports marketplace.

Dick Landy and '64 Dodge Ramcharger S/S. When photo was taken he held the A/FX track record at Pomona with his tricked-out Dodge.

First Dodge alloy-paneled Ramcharger to come off the assembly line in Hamtramck, Michigan. Final check is being made by Simon Lupin, left, and Marty Jordan. Factory actually built race cars! New Street Wedge with 426 cubes and single-four-barrel pumped out 365 hp. It was a fantastic street performer.

1964 HIGH-PERFORMANCE ENGINES

CUBIC INCHES	BORE	STROKE	HORSEPOWER	TORQUE	COMPRESSION	INDUCTION
383	4.250	3.380	305 @ 4600	410 @ 2400	10.00	TWO-BARREL
383	4.250	3.380	330 @ 4600	425 @ 2800	10.00	FOUR-BARREL
413	4.190	3.750	340 @ 4600	470 @ 2800	10.10	FOUR-BARREL
413	4.190	3.750	360 @ 4800	470 @ 3200	10.10	FOUR-BARREL
413	4.190	3.750	390 @ 4800	485 @ 3600	9.6	DUAL-QUAD
426	4.250	3.750	365 @ 4800	470 @ 3200	10.30	FOUR-BARREL
426	4.250	3.750	415 @ 5600	470 @ 4400	11.00	DUAL-QUAD
426	4.250	3.750	425 @ 5600	480 @ 4400	12.50	DUAL-QUAD

1964—FIRST OF THE FASTBACKS!

Chrysler scoops Ford with the first fastback Ponycar and clearly establishes the Mayflower Division as the one to beat

The Valiant heritage is obvious, but the details put the Barracuda in a class by itself. With optional V-8 power, a new Barracuda could go from a standing start to 60 mph in 11 seconds.

1964 Barracuda Specifications

Interior Dimensions

Headroom, Front* .... 38.3 in.
Headroom, Rear* .... 36.8 in.
Legroom, Front .... 39.9 in.
Legroom, Rear .... 30.7 in.
Hiproom, Rear .... 56.4 in.
Seat Height, Front .... 8.4 in.
Seat Height, Rear .... 10.3 in.
Kneeroom, Rear .... 1.9 in.
    Includes cushion deflection due to passenger weight according to A.M.A. standards of measurement.

Exterior Dimensions

Wheelbase .... 106.0 in.
Tread, Front .... 55.9 in.
Tread, Rear .... 55.6 in.
Length, Overall .... 188.2 in.
Width, Overall .... 70.1 in.
Height, Overall—6-cyl. .... 53.7 in.
Height, Overall—V-8 .... 53.9 in.

Brakes

Four-wheel hydraulic, internal expanding, duo-servo with self-energizing shoes. Molded asbestos lining, bonded shoes. Size: 9 x 2½ inches, 9 x 2 inches in rear. Lining area: 153.5 square inches.

Suspension

Front .... torsion bars and ball joints
Rear .... 2½-inch outboard-mounted asymmetrical leaf springs
Shock absorbers .... Oriflow type

Standard 6-cyl. Engine

Horsepower .... 101 at 4400 rpm
Torque, ft. lbs. .... 155 at 2400 rpm
Compression ratio .... 8.5 to 1
Bore, in. 3.40
Stroke, in. 3.125
Displacement, cu. in. 170

Optional 6-cyl. Engine

Horsepower .... 145 at 4000 rpm
Torque, ft. lbs. .... 215 at 2400 rpm
Compression ratio .... 8.4 to 1
Bore, in. 3.40
Stroke, in. 4.125
Displacement, cu. in. 225

Optional V-8 Engine

Horsepower .... 180 at 4200 rpm
Torque, ft. lbs. .... 260 at 1600 rpm
Compression ratio .... 8.8 to 1
Bore, in. 3.63
Stroke, in. 3.31
Displacement, cu. in. 273

Electrical System

Heavy-duty, 12-volt, 38-ampere-hour battery. Chrysler Corporation alternator with high charging rate at low engine speeds.

Rear Axle

Type ..... Hotchkiss drive, hypoid rear axle.
Ratio with Standard 6-cyl. engine ... 3.23 to 1.

Tires and Wheels

Safety-Rim wheels with low-pressure tubeless tires. Wheels are 13 x 4½ inches with 6.50 x 13 tires standard.

Capacities

Fuel tank .... 18 gallons
Cooling system .... 11 quarts
Engine crankcase .... 4 quarts

The tried and true Slant-Six was standard in 170-cube trim and optional with a displacement of 225 cubic inches. Dealers were marketing factory-designed Hyper-Pak speed equipment and Offy four-barrel conversions as shown here.

26

Between April 1964 and the end of the model year, Chrysler-Plymouth dealers sold 23,443 fastback Ponycars. The die was cast.

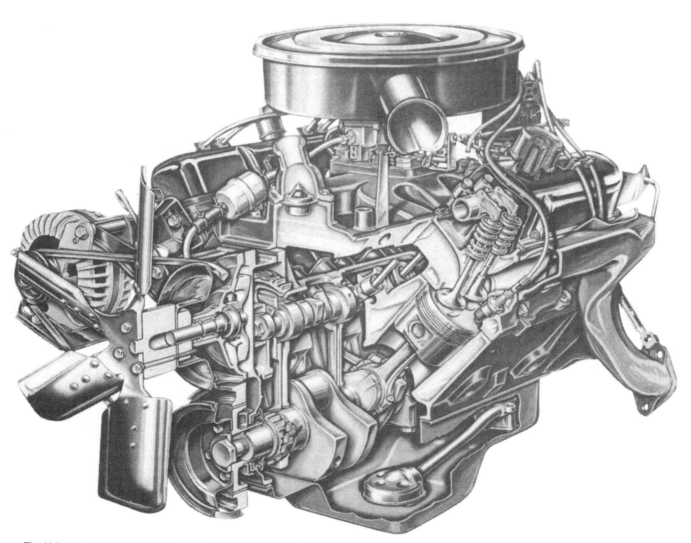

The V-8 engine was a lightweight 273-incher rated at 180 hp and fitted with a two-barrel carburetor and 8.8-to-1 pistons. Later it would be available with four-barrel and the kind of goodies needed for heads-up competition against the Mustang.

1964—THE YEAR OF THE MINI-WEDGE

Small in displacement, big on performance, the new Mopar compact V-8 helps Dodge & Plymouth cover all bases

By 1964 the mini 273-inch mill acquired a four-barrel, some internal goodies and even trick valve covers and air cleaner.

Dodge Darts with 273-inch engines were ideally suited for lower class racing and did quite well considering that the small-block was essentially a new and unproven engine.

Plymouth's Formula-S Barracuda, introduced in November 1964, offered straight-line performance plus handling qualities to compete with the high-performance Mustang. Exhaust note was outrageous. Photo was taken during a road test in 1964 for CARS Magazine.

DODGE started production of Dart models with a new, lightweight, 273-cubic-inch V-8 engine on December 9, 1963. This marked the first time an eight-cylinder powerplant has been available for the popular Dart.

"This engine was specifically designed for those customers who wish to combine the increased performance of a V-8 with the maneuverability of a compact car," Dodge General Manager Byron J. Nichols explained.

"Known as the Charger 273, this engine is the smallest and lightest V-8 built by Dodge yet will offer a performance potential equal to that of the 318-cubic-inch engine in standard-size Dodge V-8 models."

The horsepower rating—180 hp at 4,200 rpm—means that the 273 will move a Dart from zero to 60 miles-per-hour in one-fifth less time than will the optional 225-cubic-inch Slant Six engine, Dodge Chief Engineer George Gibson reported. The torque output of 260 foot pounds at 1,600 rpm is the result of studied efforts by engineers to match the 273 to the Dart powertrain components.

The 273 cylinder block is of tin-alloyed, grey cast-iron and weighs approximately 149 pounds after being machined and fitted with main bearing caps and bolts. The short 3.31-inch stroke is combined with a smaller bore size of 3.625 inches to arrive at the 273.5-cubic-inch displacement goal.

The 25-inch-long crankshaft is of forged-steel for extra durability. Main journals are 2.5 inches in diameter, supported by five babbitt-on-steel main bearings, and rod journals are 2.125 inches in diameter. Crankshaft journal overlap is .66 inches. Thrust is taken on the Number 3 bearing.

The short connecting rods are designed on 6.123-inch centers and forged to a tapered I-beam section that combines maximum strength with minimum weight.

Rods are conventional, with bushings at the ends into which the piston pins are fitted. The pins are full-floating and retained in the piston by spring steel lock rings. Piston pin bores are offset by .06 inches from the piston centerlines to prevent piston slap.

The 273 cylinder head is a chromium-alloyed iron casting weighing only 41 pounds. Four cores are used to form each head. To provide the most accurate

Legendary Racer Brown of Racer Brown Cams designed a number of cams specifically for the 273 engine fitted with factory-experimental single and dual-quad induction systems. Dodge Division pushed the camshafts and supplied them to sponsored racers.

The author testing a pre-production Dodge Dart powered by the new Charger four-barrel engine package. Shot was taken at the Chrysler Corporation drag strip in Chelsea, Michigan.

Author Martyn L. Schorr with an early HP Dart fitted by the factory with Hands aluminum wheels, race tires, tach and other engine goodies. It was a special CARS Magazine test car used both on the strip and the street.

You could order a '65 Dodge Dart with single four-barrel carb, long-duration camshaft, 10.5-to-1 pistons and engine dress-up package.

placement of port openings, a single large core forms the intake and exhaust ports for the entire head. The roof of the water jacket is cast so that lubrication oil will have a free drain-back to the tappet chamber, eliminating the need for separate drain holes.

Combustion chambers are designed for an 8.8-to-1 compression ratio with flat-head pistons. The shape of the chambers is a modified wedge with the spark plugs situated as near to the center of volume as possible for equal flame travel and uniform combustion.

Overhead valves are set at an 18-degree angle from the bore axis and operated by the camshaft through a system of mechanical tappets, tubular push-rods, and pearlitic malleable iron rocker arms of a new design. The valve layout is such that intake and exhaust valves are situated in a straight line along the cylinder head, which simplifies the rocker arm and shaft arrangement. Valves are tulip-shaped for effective seating, and have rubber cup seals to shield both intake and exhaust valve stems from excessive oil splash. The intake valve has a head diameter of 1.78 inches and the exhaust of 1.50 inches.

As the valves are in-line, both intake and exhaust rocker arms are the same. Adjustments are made by a screw in the pushrod end. The rocker shaft seats in half-round notches that are broached in the top of each support bracket and fastened down by stamped retainers and screws. These brackets, together with the valve guides, are cast integrally with the heads.

In November 1964, Plymouth announced the production of a Barracuda equipped with the new Formula S Competition package. Engineers claimed the package will make the Barracuda the finest handling car that Chrysler Corporation has ever built.

"The Barracuda with the Formula S package was designed to be a strong contender in rallies and road races with any mass-produced car built anywhere in the world," aid P.N. Buckminster, general manager of the Chrysler-Plymouth Division.

Exclusive with the Barracuda, the Formula S Competition package has the standard Barracuda body with these added elements:

1. The Commando 273 V-8 engine with four-barrel carburetion.
2. The Rallye Suspension package which includes heavy-duty front torsion bars, rear springs, and a sway bar.
3. Special 14-inch wheels that are 5½ inches wide.
5. An all-new Chrysler-designed, Goodyear-produced 6.95 x 14 Blue Streak tire with a tread design which delivers excellent cornering and road bite.
6. A tachometer.

7. Sport-style wheel covers.

Several of the above items had formerly been available as optional equipment but it is the combination of the high-performance engine, the suspension package, shock absorbers and the new wheels and tires that makes the Formula S such a formidable competition car. Engineers claim that the new tires alone are responsible for 50 percent of the improvement in the car's handling.

The tires were designed by Chrysler engineers to be a specific part of the Barracuda Formula S and will not be offered with any other car. The car's weight, its steering characteristics and the weight distribution were among the elements considered in designing the tire.

The Blue Streak has a cord angle of 29 degrees, a design characteristic which makes it more responsive to steering touch. Most tires average about 36 degrees in cord angle. The Blue Streak's cord angle is the lowest of any original equipment tire. The tire is the only one

with the stripe made of blue rubber and the brand name of white rubber.

Optional equipment to further improve the Formula S performance include either the four-speed transmission with Hurst shifter, or the console-mounted three-speed automatic transmission. The 3.23 axle is standard, and both the 2.93 and 3.55 axles are optional. Sure Grip differential is also optional with either the 3.23 or the 2.93 ratio.

The Commando 273 engine has a four-barrel carburetor; 10.5-to-1 compression; high-lift, high-overlap cam; dome-top pistons; dual breaker points; solid-lifters; special intake system with unsilenced air cleaner; low back-pressure exhaust system with exposed resonator, and an engine dress-up package. Standard with this engine, the dress-up package consists of a chromed air cleaner with a metal decal reading "Commando 273," a chromed oil filler cap and crankcase vent cap, and black crackle paint with bright anodized

aluminum fins on the valve rocker arm covers.

Included in the Rallye Suspension package are heavy-duty front torsion bars, rear springs, and a sway bar. The firm-ride front and rear shock absorbers supplement the Rallye Suspension package.

An exterior identifying feature of the Plymouth Barracuda Formula S is a special medallion located on the front fenders ahead of the front wheels.

In November, 1965, Dodge announced that 1966 Dart buyers who want more performance in a small V-8 can gain approximately 30 percent more horsepower by ordering the Charger, a high-performance version of the Dodge 273-cubic inch powerplant.

A special performance option, the package consists of a four-barrel carburetor, modified camshaft, domed pistons and a boosted compression ratio. Other modifications on the 273 that resemble the Hemi engine are a non-silenced air

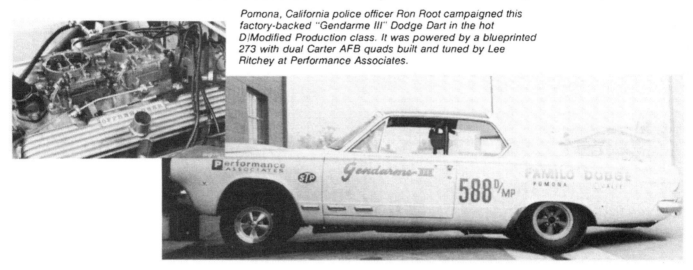

Pomona, California police officer Ron Root campaigned this factory-backed "Gendarme III" Dodge Dart in the hot D/Modified Production class. It was powered by a blueprinted 273 with dual Carter AFB quads built and tuned by Lee Ritchey at Performance Associates.

This is the car which let the drag racing world know that the Mopar 273 was a serious performance engine. Factory racer was compaigned by Plymouth's Golden Commandos and was unbeatable in its class.

cleaner and low back-pressure exhaust system.

The changes are calculated to give up to 20 percent faster acceleration. The Charger's rated horsepower is 235 at 5,200 rpm, and maximum torque is 280 at 4,000 rpm—compared to 180 hp and 260 foot pounds of torque on the standard version.

New domed pistons replace the standard 273's flat-top pistons, raising its compression ratio from 8.8-to-1 to 10.5-to-1. The higher ratio calls for premium-grade gasoline. Piston bore and stroke remain at 3.63 inches by 3.31 inches.

A longer-duration camshaft provide 248 degrees of intake and exhaust opening and 26 degrees of valve overlap versus 240 degrees duration and 16 degrees overlap on the standard 273 cam. Intake and exhaust valve lifts have been increased for better operating efficiency, and strong, higher-load valve springs improve performance at high engine speeds.

In 1966 Johnson Automotive built one of the most outrageous B/Comp cars ever to hit the strips. The Silver Bullet was powered by a direct-port fuel-injected 273 with a 318 truck crank, Isky cam, 392 Hemi valves and 12.5-to-1 pistons.

It didn't take long for the sports car racing world to learn about the 273 engine. In 1966 Bob Tullius campaigned the Group 44 Dodge Dart on the new Baby Grand sports car circuit showing a lot of high-buck imported cars the quick way to the winner's circle!

The Charger's four-barrel carburetor features air velocity-controlled secondary barrels to give maximum fuel feed on demand. At normal and low engine speeds the carburetor runs on two barrels. The non-silenced air cleaner allows a greater unrestricted flow of air into the carburetor.

For the hotter, stronger spark needed in a high-performance powerplant, the Charger has a double-breaker distributor, similar to that used in the famous Dodge Hemi and Ramcharger Wedge engines. Because one side of the distributor usually runs hotter than the other, the hot side is "ventilated" with a hole at its center. Timing is set at 10 degrees, and conventional spark plugs are used.

A straight-through muffler and re-sonator and larger exhaust and tail pipes cut down back pressure. Muffler, tail pipe and resonator are made of aluminized steel for extra corrosion protection.

The Charger's drivetrain is basically the same as that of a normal 273 engine, and the rear axle ratio remains at 3.23-to-1. But 2.93-to-1 and 3.55-to-1 ratios are available at no extra cost. An extra-cost option is a 2.93-to-1 or 3.23-to-1 Sure-Grip differential.

Also standard with the four-barrel, four-speed combination, is a 8¾-inch axle. The heftier axle is an extra-cost option with the four-barrel equipped with an automatic transmission. Three and four-speed manual transmission are also identical to those that come with the standard engine, but the automatic transmission is equipped with a high-speed governor to keep shift points compatible with the increase in maximum-power rpm.

To complete chassis changes, 5½ leaf rear springs are standard on cars with the high-performance version of the 273 engine.

Appearance items that enhance the engine's racy look are chrome-plated air cleaner, oil filler and breather cap, and the crankcase breather cap. Valve covers are painted in black crackle for sharp contrast with the bright red of the engine block, and bright anodized aluminum extrusions decorate the tops of the valve covers. Hold-down bolt heads are cadmium-plated.

STREET-DRIVING THE CANDY-MATIC

Flameouts and traffic tieups are all part of the fun and games of living with a Ramcharger on the street!

The following appears in bold capital letters on Page One of the special feature and specification booklet prepared by Dodge to supplement normal operating instructions and placed in the glove box of every Ramcharger 426-engined car:

"The 1964 Ramcharger 426 engine is designed for use in supervised acceleration trials. It is not recommended for general everyday driving because of the compromise of all-around characteristics which must be made for this type of vehicle."

Amen! (edit.)

IT ALL STARTED with a Monday morning phone call . . . just like in the movies. The honey smooth voice of Dodge Public Relations' local honcho floated through the receiver and caressed our ear:

"Say, pally," he began, "got an exclusive for you, baby. Something new we've had under wraps until now. Terrific machine . . . lots of power, *great* handling and, most important, terrific economy and driver/passenger comfort!

(We thought: he sounds just like a TV pitchman—could be a gag.)

"How'd you like to take it for a week and wring it out?"

Still suspicious, we nevertheless agreed and he told us the surprise would be waiting for us at the Chrysler West Side (of Manhattan) service center.

Ramcharger Candymatic looks right at home at pasta palace on Woodhaven Blvd. in NYC. In the Sixties Woodhaven was meca for local street racers. People could not believe their eyes—and ears!

Well, a couple of days passed before one of the CARS staff could pick the car up. In the interim we tried to figure out just what could be waiting for us.

It was late Wednesday afternoon. Managing Editor Marty Schorr had left about 40 minutes earlier to collect the "mystery". Suddenly our phone jingled.

It was Marty.

"You won't believe it . . .", he begins, "it's *got* to be a gag! Know what's sitting here for us? That Ramcharger Candy Matic that Dodge displayed at the Coliseum show . . . even has the fluorescent fixture in it that they installed to light up the interior!"

His subject is a '64 Stage III-engined, 12.5-to-1 compression sedan with Rammy valve-bodied automatic transmission, scooped aluminum hood, aluminum fenders, jacked torsion bars and small front wheels, 4.56 Sure Grip rear, cheater slicks, *no* insulation or sound deadener . . . and painted white with Candy Apple stripes and lettering so that it's an exact replica of a Ramcharger Club team car.

News Bureau. And I'll tell him to call us when it's ready."

"Beautiful," we answer. "That should fix his wagon!"

The service manager gives us a jingle Thursday morning. Tells us in some choice (edited) language:

a—The car won't start without trouble.

b—After getting it started, they find it stalls as soon as they get it in gear.

c—One brave soul finally gets the thing moving by punching the go-pedal as he pushes D1, thereupon it flames out just after rolling through the overhead door onto the street. Result: One stalled, hard to start, harder to get moving car facing west across the two northbound lanes of New York's 11th Avenue at 4:30 in the afternoon.

"Try again," we tell him. "Deadline's coming up and we have to road test the car right away!"

A second call comes from the service manager in the late afternoon, carefully expurgated quotes from it being:

a—Car is still hard to start.

b—In gear it bucks like crazy.

Needless to say, we caused a scene wherever we parked our Ramcharger dupe.

But this beast is different in one *important* respect. Having been sent from the factory to New York for the show, it hadn't been set up in Detroit for competition. Matter of fact, it hadn't been run other than to be driven on and off haulers. After the show it had been stashed at Chrysler West Side preparatory to being trucked out to the Worlds Fair for exhibit at the Hell Drivers stadium in the Fair's Transportation Section (they use Dodges).

"Our Monday morning suspicion was right," we think. This is obviously the latest in a series of good natured, *harmless* practical jokes always being played on one another by CARS people and Dodge's New York PR man.

What our "friend" figures will happen next is obvious. We'll call him and say that we don't appreciate his humor, that even if the car *was* in any kind of running condition it would still not be driveable on the street. Friendly PR man will guffaw for five minutes and spend the next few days as happy as if a departed distant relative just left him 5,000 shares of Chrysler stock.

"Hey, I have an idea!"

It's Marty, still on the other end of the line.

"Suppose I get the service manager, complain that this pig isn't useable, and tell him to get it in shape and bill Dodge

c—It can't get out of its own way.

d—It won't idle at under 1,900 rpm.

e—Won't we forget the whole damned thing and let him burn the car, drown it, abandon it . . . anything so that he can put his people back to repairing "sane" cars?

"Nope," we retort. "Keep at it. We have to have the thing running tomorrow."

The next call comes at 11 AM Friday. It's short and to the point, amounting to:

"We quit! Get it the—out of here . . . and we're billing Dodge News Bureau 49 bucks!"

WE HOLD a council of war and decide to get the Rammy over to Chrysler East Side, where the service manager likes (?) us. At least he has put up with our antics before and retained his sanity. Method of transfer: Call a limousine service. Tell them to dispatch a chauffeur to West Side so he can tool the pay cut over to East Side. And bill Dodge News Bureau.

We brief the East Side service manager on what's coming and ask that he see if he can have the boat running by late afternoon.

Rammy arrives at East Side without dings, but with one

somewhat incoherent, sweating chauffeur behind the wheel. It's taken him two hours to make the jaunt of just over a mile (at 20 dollars per hour, by the way). He staggers off.

Our friend, the PR man, jingles us at about 2 PM . . . obviously he isn't able to contain his curiosity, as he hasn't heard from us since his call Monday morning. We tell him we've been so busy we haven't had the chance to pick up his mystery vehicle. But we'll definitely do so later in the day.

"Okay" is his reply. But somehow it comes out sounding more like a question. Could it be he suspects something?

A 3 o'clock call from the East Side service manager informs us that he won't even be able to have our toy looked at until Monday morning. Just too busy.

We call Mr. PR and tell him that we'll be stuck too late to make Chrysler West Side by closing. But we'll *definitely* latch onto his set of wheels Monday. His answer is an "okay." But we can tell by the sound of it that we've just ruined his weekend.

Call from Chrysler East Side early the following Monday afternoon. Report:

a—The valves are so tight they're wondering if someone put them in water and they shrunk.

b—Timing is off by a couple of degrees . . . like *a hundred!*

c—Plugs are only two heat ranges away from what they should be.

d—The car will be running by 5 PM, but no guarantee for how long.

e—It'll run *only* if the regular grade gas is syphoned out of the tank and replaced with super premium.

We thank the friendly service manager and remind him to bill Dodge News Bureau (42 dollars this time).

Marty Schorr "volunteers" to get the car to Queens. He leaves the office late, hoping to miss the brunt of the rush hour traffic. He calls us at home later that night. Says he still hit some stop-and-go traffic and made the nine-mile trip with only seven flameouts, and at the expense of just a third of a tank of gas. Adds that the trip was good for his diet, cause driving the Rammy is a great substitute for a sauna bath with all that engine heat funneling into the non-insulated passenger compartment.

Says he's going to tool the package over to friend and

Doesn't every car have a battery in the trunk? Not visible is the gas pump in the background which shows high-test selling at 31¢ per-gallon!

"Hey man, this really is a Ramcharger." Everything is real except living with the car on the street which was unreal! It was a bear.

rodding enthusiast Dave Howell first thing Tuesday morning for some tuning.

Dave calls Tuesday after Marty delivers the car. Says he'll reset the distributor a bit and make some carburetion adjustments so the car will (he hopes) run a bit more smoothly on the street.

As soon as Marty reaches the office and opens his coffee container he picks up an extension and we call our PR "friend." We're having some trouble keeping from cracking up.

"Morning, pally," we begin. "Made it to West Side like we promised. Picked up the fancy wheels. Quite a package. Got lots of attention on the Long Island Expressway last night."

"But . . ." (from the other end)

"Anyway," we cut in, "the thing wasn't in too good shape. Had it gone over and the tab billed to you, baby doll."

(Silence on the other end)

"Have it back to you next Monday AM for sure . . . just hope we don't ding that pretty aluminum nose in all the traffic and parking it here and there. You know what hammering out aluminum costs."

(Still nothing from his end)

"Hello," we say. "You there Dad?"

(Nothing from the Pan Am Building)

"Sweetie," we continue. "You still with us, Pops?"

(Dead silence from Dodge News Bureau)

We hang up and let the laughter flow.

NOW THAT we had gone to all the trouble (and put Dodge to all the expense) of getting the Rammy running and home in one piece, we realized that we had no plans for it editorially.

"Why," asked idea-man-of-the-week Schorr, "don't we tool the dog around here and there . . . you know, play it by ear . . . and get some reaction type shots of the populous? Might make a few good spreads in the book."

That's just what we did.

Oh, yeah . . . We were saved the problem of driving Rammy back into the city by delivering it to the Hell Drivers at the Fair. It's there now should you be out there and want to take a look at it. ●

ramcharger components

CARBURETOR IMPROVEMENTS

Larger Carter AFB-3705S carburetors have been substituted to increase the breathing capacity. Primary bore has increased .25-inch. The secondary bores remain at $1\frac{11}{16}$ inches. Carburetor air horn diameter is enlarged $\frac{3}{4}$-inch.

RAM INTAKE MANIFOLD

New larger primary riser openings match the increase in the primary bore diameter of the new carburetors.

CAMSHAFT

New camshaft has a higher valve lift (.520″), and longer exhaust duration (308°).

CYLINDER HEAD

Combustion chambers have been modified to reduce shrouding of the intake valve. The intake valve port has also been changed to provide a more ideal flow of air. Stainless-steel head gaskets are extra durable.

NEW SEVEN-BLADE FAN

Complete with viscous drive unit, it provides substantial horsepower savings.

ALUMINUM FRONT-END PACKAGE*

This aluminum front-end package reduces the weight of the Ramcharger by nearly 150 pounds.

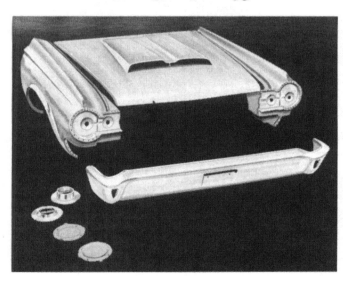

- Aluminum hood and air scoop
- Aluminum front fenders
- Aluminum front bumper and bumper supports
- Aluminum radiator air shield
- Aluminum radiator cross bar and hood lock vertical support brace
- Carburetor to hood adapter and flame arrestor assemblies
- Front and rear floor covering without jute backing
- No spray-on deadener
- No dash liners and cowl side panel silencer pads

*Std. 12.5 to 1 ratio—extra cost with 11.0 to 1 ratio.

LITTLE RED WAGON

TIME was when a new model horse-drawn surrey with a fringe on top drew the attention and admiring glances of passerby. Today, it's 425 horses pulling a "Little Red Wagon" with a bright yellow canopy that's causing "O"-shaped-lips and raised eyebrows.

The only one of its kind and the latest conversation piece in dragdom, the Little Red Wagon is no less than a super-powered, 90-inch-wheelbase Dodge compact pickup truck with a 425-horsepower Hemi-Charger engine. The yellow canopy is a help-stop-it parachute!

The unique little vehicle was introduced to the drag nation September 19 at Cecil County (Md.) Drag-O-Way by NHRA Summernational Champions Dick Branstner and Roger Lindamood, of Detroit.

Two other Detroit area men, Jim Schaeffer, co-owner of a many-trophy-winning BB/A roadster, and John Collier, drag-racing newcomer, built the first phase of the Little Red Wagon. Branstner and Lindamood combined to hone the unit to racing sharpness. They are convinced the snub-nosed pickup is capable of turning ets in the low-11s or high-10s with speeds up around the 130-mph mark.

Their Little Red Wagon is a study in engineering and innovation. ●

LITTLE RED WAGON

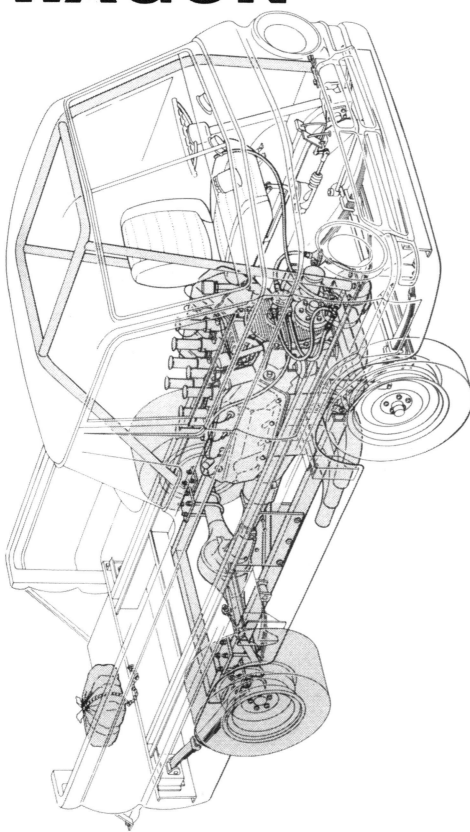

PEEKAVIEW OF THE FASTEST TRUCK IN THE WORLD -- Except for the hint supplied by the 10"-wide racing tires, there is little outwardly to reveal this Dodge A-100 compact pickup as dragracing's newest attraction, "The Little Red Wagon," driven by Bill "Maverick" Golden. Shaded areas in this phantom view show the "go" components used in the racing conversion. Alterations included: replacing the 101-hp, 6-cylinder standard engine with a 425-hp, fuel-injected Dodge Hemi-Charger V-8; installing a special 75"-long x 36"-wide welded steel tubing sub frame to give the truck's unibody construction extra muscle to withstand the weight and racing stress of the Hemi engine. Frame, which can be dropped for easy maintenance, cradles the engine, transmission and differential. Front of the frame is connected to the body by two 9/16" bolts. Three bolt holes, spaced 6" apart in either side of frame, allows floating suspension to be adapted to various drag strip conditions. Rear of the frame is suspended by the standard springs. Rear shackles were reversed to keep the LRW level. Also added were racing headers, parachute and roll bar cage.

THE ORIGINAL DODGE CHARGERS

Don Beebe of
Automotive Promotions
came up with the
blown exhibition concept
and Jim Nelson and Dode Martin
of Dragmasters turned
two Dodge sedans
into 800-hp groundshaking
tire-fryers!

Billed as the "World's Fastest S/FX Drag Cars", these unique Dodge sedans were powered by Dragmaster 480-inch Wedges running GMC 6-71 blowers. They were strictly exhibition cars designed to promote Dodge power.

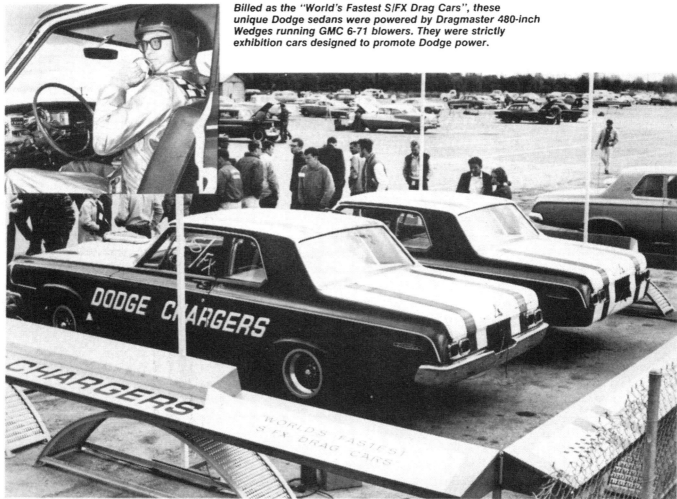

38

DODGE CHARGER SPECIFICATIONS

Dodge Two-Door sedans
Super/Stock alloy front end
480-cube wedge motors
M/T ½-inch stroker cranks
M/T aluminum rods & pistons
Ted Cyr GMC 6-71 blowers
18% overdrive ratio
Weiand magnesium manifolds
Crane cylinder heads

Schiefer 300-B roller cams
Horsepower Engineering headers
4.30/4.56 Police Car rears
Cure-Ride shocks
Dragmaster traction bars
American Racing Mags
Deist Drag Chutes
Drivers: Jim Johnson
        Jimmy Nix

Chargers ride on Goodyear-shod American mags. Note header collectors behind front wheels. Front end is streamlined via rolled pan. Headlamp openings duct cool air to engine compartment. Hilborn "bug catcher" injection mounts atop the Jimmy blower.

Dodge ramcharger

	SPEED	E.T.

WINTERNATIONALS, POMONA, CALIFORNIA
RAMCHARGERS won Top Stock Eliminator at the Winternational of NHRA, competing against the top 50 cars in the nation, with 115.08 12.44
Dodge was the first car with an automatic transmission to win this national event.

DETROIT DRAGWAY, MICH.—NHRA REGIONAL
RAMCHARGERS set new A/FX record doing 118.42 12.03
They also won Top Stock Eliminator 117.64 12.20

DRAGWAY 42, WEST SALEM, OHIO—NHRA DIVISIONAL
RAMCHARGERS took Super Stock Automatic, Stock Eliminator. 117.95 12.05
NHRA S/SA Record.
Set new track speed and E.T. record for Super-Stock Automatic.

PHENIX DRAGWAY, PHENIX CITY, ALA.
1st won by Emmitt Austin in '63 Dodge 118.21 12.09
2nd won by Billy Jacobs in '63 Dodge 117.84 12.25
4th won by Phil Carroll in '63 Dodge 115.92 12.32

MASON-DIXON DRAGWAY, HAGERSTOWN, MD.
Bud Faubel—iron ram—won Super-Stock Automatic 111.91 12.31
   and Top Stock Eliminator 112.64 12.56
Aluminum Dodge won A/FX 114.06 12.63
Faubel won Middle Eliminator against A/Gassers and altered coupes 114.79 12.41

PLEASANT GROVE DRAGWAY, SPRINGFIELD, ILL.
John Kilborn, Decatur, Ill. Dodge dealer, drove aluminum 426 Ramcharger to official AHRA Super-Stock/Automatic record of 90.00 8.07
This was American Hot Rod Assn. Record Run for 1/8-mile distance.

HOUSTON BROS. DRAG STRIP, FAIRBURN, GA.
Phil Carroll's "White Lightning" beat Nicholson's Chevrolet, driven by Hubert Platt, 2 consecutive runs 117.60 12.14
Set New Track Record.

POMONA, CALIFORNIA
Maverick won A/FX Class 115.83 11.93
Also won Street Eliminator 116.42 11.96

DAYTONA BEACH, FLA. NASCAR WINTERNATIONALS
Phil Carroll's "White Lightning" Daytona Beach NASCAR Winternationals Class Winner as follows:

	SPEED	E.T.
February 19	116.88	12.31
February 20	113.92	12.28
February 22	120.0	12.24
February 23	118.42	12.13

Bob Simmerly, of Los Angeles, in a 1963 Dodge 330, set a new Natl. Speed Record for SS/S Stick .... 115.32 —

records

	SPEED	E.T.
U.S. 31 DRAGWAY, KALAMAZOO, MICH.		
The RAMCHARGERS, in a match race with Arnie Beswick's Pontiac, won 3 out of 4. Best time and speed	121.62	12.08
DETROIT DRAGWAY		
RAMCHARGERS with Jim Thornton driving beat Frank Sanders 3 out of 3 in Detroit Dragway exhibition run	117.00	12.09
ATCO DRAGWAY, N. J.		
Bobby Harrop won Top Stock Eliminator	116.83	12.58
VINELAND, N. J. DRAGWAY		
Bobby Harrop won Top Stock Eliminator over top cars on East Coast, such as Strickler Chevy, Durham Chevy, Ramsey Pontiac, etc.	115.21	12.19
YORK, PA.		
Bud Faubel in '63 Dodge A/FX beat Malcom Durham 3 straight winning class	114.35	12.45
Faubel also won Little Eliminator	115.53	12.32
HOUSTON BROS. DRAG STRIP, FAIRBURN, GA.		
Phil Carroll's "White Lightning" beat Nicholson's Chevrolet, driven by Hubert Platt, 2 consecutive runs Set New Track Record	117.60	12.14
PHENIX CITY, ALA., DRAGWAY		
Emmitt Austin in '63 Dodge won 1st place	118.40	11.74
Phil Carroll won 2nd place	116.00	12.33
Bill Tanner won 4th place—'62 Dodge	113.64	12.52
DETROIT DRAGWAY, MICH.		
RAMCHARGERS set new A/FX record doing	118.42	12.03
They also won Top Stock Eliminator	117.64	12.20
PHENIX CITY DRAG STRIP, PHENIX CITY, ALA.		
Billy Jacobs won first place SS/S	121.00	12.30
OMAHA, ALA. DRAG STRIP		
1st place won by Atlanta Speed Shop—'63 Dodge	112.36	12.60
2nd place won by Bill Tanner	112.18	12.64
MASON-DIXON DRAGWAY		
Bud Faubel won 1st place with '63 Dodge and "Mr. Stock Eliminator". His '62 Dodge took 2nd place win	—	—
MASON-DIXON DRAGWAY		
Faubel's weekend wins also include—Stock Eliminator with '62 Dodge, Modified Stock Eliminator with '63 Dodge, A/FX, Middle Eliminator, S/SA. 76 runs and 74 wins.	—	—

...other Dodge-powered records

	SPEED	E.T.
MOORESVILLE, N. C.		
Bobby McIntyre won "A" Stock with	109.00	13.33
This car (383 Dodge) has been raced 6 times at 5 different tracks with a record of 6 wins and a track record for "A" Stock was established at every track.		
POMONA, CALIFORNIA		
New Ramcharger Truck won B/FX Class. Only other B/FX that would race him was a Les Ritchey Ford 406 with Fiberglass panels. Ramcharger truck beat him 10 lengths first run and 4 lengths second time. B/FX Chevs moved up into another class to avoid running against Ramcharger.	108.99	12.71
FONTANA, CALIFORNIA		
A/FX Golden Lancer won Street Eliminator and Monthly Street Eliminator, turning	115.83	12.39
SAN GABRIEL, CALIFORNIA		
Tony Nancy in Dodge-powered A-modified Roadster set a new strip record in class with	N/A	8.73
Tony Nancy, of Van Nuys, Calif., in Dodge-powered modified Roadster Class AA, won Competition Eliminator	152.68	9.62
Also won Class AA/Competition	164.83	8.97
LONG BEACH, CALIFORNIA		
Golden Lancer won A/FX. Beat Hayden Proffitt in A/FX Chev. 3 times running	115.83	12.23
Don Garlits, of Tampa, Fla., in Swamp Rat V, won Top Fuel Eliminator, AA Fuel Dragster Class	186.32	8.26
Set new National Fuel Class Record with	186.70	8.24
BLANEY DRAG STRIP, BLANEY, S. C.		
Bob McIntyre in 383 Dodge set a new "A" Stock Record running against several 427 Fords and 409 Chevrolets	108.56	13.30
BAKERSFIELD, CALIFORNIA		
The Dragmaster Dart won AHRA Top Eliminator Gas. Also Top Speed Low E.T. and new Natl. Record in the Stock classes.	186.00	8.49
BLANEY DRAG STRIP, BLANEY, S. C.		
Bob McIntyre won "A" Stock with 383 Dodge and broke his old "A" Stock record at this track by turning	109.75	13.13
SPORTSMAN PARK, FARMINGTON, N. C.		
Bob McIntyre in 383 "B" Stock Dodge won "A" Stock against 427 Ford, 421 Pontiac and 409 Chevy breaking his old "A" Stock record, then went on to win Stock Eliminator	108.23	13.28
SPORTSMAN PARK, FARMINGTON, N. C.		
McIntyre won "A" Stock and Stock Eliminator with 383 Dodge running against 421 Pontiac, 427 Ford and 409 Chevy. McIntyre's car is classified "B" Stock but moved up to "A" Stock in order to challenge Pontiac. McIntyre set new "A" Stock record	109.09	13.20

NEW 426 ramcharger V-8

high-performance features

Heavy-duty rear springs
A stiffer rear spring rate helps absorb the extremely high torque developed by the engine. Right rear-spring installation and heavy-duty shock absorbers are available as optional equipment for maximum traction and wheel control.

Specially designed valve gear
Mechanical valve lifters avoid pump-up at high engine speeds. High-strength valve spring retainers and high-load valve springs prevent valve "float" at high r.p.m. Easier, more precise rocker arm adjustment with locknut on the lash adjusting screw. Valve gear is rated stable up to 6,500 r.p.m. on the standard test fixture.

Deep-groove pulleys
Belt pulleys are deep-grooved to assure belt retention at high speed.

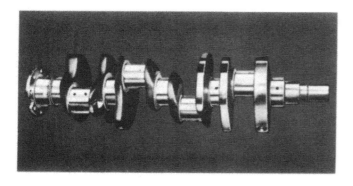

Crankshaft
Hardened journals and tri-metal bearings provide extra bearing-load capacity needed to withstand high-torque output strains.

Camshaft
Higher-lift camshaft has a 300-degree intake and 308-degree exhaust duration with a 74-degree overlap. The .520-inch lift is the highest contained in a mass-produced passenger car.

TorqueFlite automatic transmission
Heavy-duty, three-speed TorqueFlite transmission has push-button controls. It is set to upshift at engine speeds of up to 5,600 r.p.m. Maximum torque-converter ratio is 2.2 to 1. Planetary-gear ratios are 2.45, 1.45 and 1 to 1. Maximum overall breakaway ratio of 5.39 to 1 and overall efficiency are highest of any stock automatic transmission.

Fuel pump
Three valves for extra pumping capacity. High spring load provides higher fuel pressure.

Extra-large valves
Intake valves (2.08-inch diameter) are streamlined to increase air flow. Exhaust valves are ¼-inch larger than standard, providing greatly increased exhaust flow. Both are made of special, high heat-resistant alloy.

High-capacity carburetion
Hand-choked, two four-barrel Carter carburetors. No experimenting needed—each carburetor has been factory-set for maximum power and optimum fuel-air ratio.

Exhaust system
New Tri-Y manifolds and "Y" pipe has tuned 21-inch lengths between primary and secondary "Y" joints and connections. Adjacent firing cylinders No. 5 and 7 have been separated by pairing exhaust events between cylinders 1 and 5 and 3 and 7. This improves engine breathing by reducing back pressure.

Connecting rods
Beefed-up connecting rods assure maximum dependability under extreme stress.

Short-ram intake manifold

To increase power output in high-performance ranges above 4,000 r.p.m., a specially designed ram-induction intake manifold is used. Tappets may be adjusted with manifold installed.

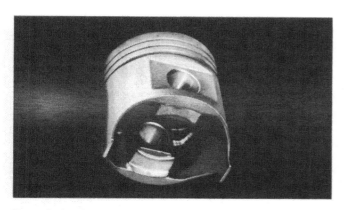

Forged aluminum pistons

Forging provides more strength than is possible with the usual casting process.

Piston rings

Top compression ring is chrome-plated, high-strength iron to resist scuffing. Number two ring is of standard design. Number three ring is of two-piece design, specially adapted for best lubrication requirements.

Drive shaft

Specially balanced for extra-fast acceleration and high running speeds. Vibration is minimized, thus prolonging service life.

"Sure-Grip" rear axle

Greater traction at both rear wheels. It prevents wheel spin on loose gravel, snow or ice. Standard axle ratio is 3.91 on 11 to 1 and 4.56 to 1 on 12.5 to 1 manual and automatic transmissions. Other ratios (2.93, 3.23, 3.55, 4.10, 4.30, 4.56 and 4.89 to 1) are optional for special driving requirements. Ring-and-pinion sets are available through your Dodge dealer.

Wheels and tires

Standard tires are 7.50 x 14″ "tubeless" Tyrex cord, front and rear. 6½K (rim-width size) rear wheels and 9.00 x 14″ rear tires are recommended for competitive events.

Ignition features

A special distributor, of full-centrifugal-advance design, has dual-breaker points. High spring load on points prevent "point bounce." Dual-breaker points produce higher plug voltage at high speeds. Special low-resistance cables and cold-running spark plugs are designed for high engine power output.

Engine oiling system improved

Opened-up oil galleries carry a larger volume of oil. The oil intake tube from the screen has also been enlarged. Larger main bearing oil grooves give better lubrication to these parts.

Special 3-speed manual transmission

Specially engineered three-speed, floor-shift gearbox for maximum-performance work. It has a (Hurst-Campbell) shifting mechanism which is spring-loaded for straight through shift action. Shafts, shot-peened gears and extensions provide added strength. Closely spaced gear ratios of 2.10, 1.44 and 1 to 1. Other heavy-duty features include 10½-inch clutch, pearlitic malleable-iron pressure plate, extra-heavy-duty torque shaft and special disc.

4-speed manual transmission (optional)

New 4-speed manual, all synchromesh, is designed for heavy-duty service. Low gear ratio is 2.66.

426
ramcharger
V-8

general specifications

Engine

Piston displacement, cubic inches..........426
Bore and stroke, inches............4.25 x 3.75
Compression ratio..........11 to 1—12.5 to 1
Horsepower........................415-425
Torque, lb.-ft.....................470-480
Carburetor....................Two 4-barrel
Cooling system............17 qts. with heater
Crankcase oil capacity........6 qts., plus 1 qt.
for filter when it
is changed

Transmissions

Standard 3-speed, heavy-duty manual, floor shift. Ratios: 2.10, 1.44, 1 to 1
Optional 3-speed automatic, heavy-duty Torque-Flite. Water cooled. Ratios: 2.45, 1.45, 1 to 1
Optional 4-speed
Ratios: 2.66, 1.91, 1.39, 1 to 1

Exhaust

3-inch dual; aluminized mufflers and tail pipes

Rear axle ratios

(Sure-Grip differential standard)
Standard—3.91 to 1 (with 11 to 1) 4.56 with 12.5 to 1
Optional—2.93, 3.23, 3.55, 4.10, 4.30, 4.56, 4.89 to 1

Compression ratio

Compression chamber volume:
  Minimum, 89 cc.
  Maximum, 93 cc.
(To reduce the volume of the combustion chamber 1 cc., .005" must be milled from the head surface. The cylinder head surface finish should be 100—120 micro-inches. For each .010" removed from the cylinder head, .012" must be removed from each intake port side of the intake manifold and .017" from the bottom of the intake manifold)
Distance from the top of the lower flat of the piston to the block deck:

	11:1c.r.	12.5:1c.r.
Minimum	.0155"	.018"
Maximum	.0455"	.043"

Bolt and nut torques

Cylinder-head bolts, 70 lb.-ft.
Main bearing bolts, 85 lb.-ft.
Connecting-rod nuts, 50 lb.-ft.
Intake manifold bolts, 30 lb.-ft.

Clutch free-play adjustment

Minimum, ½"
Maximum, ¾"

Axle-shaft end play

Minimum, .013"
Maximum, .023"

Oil

Any name-brand oil for "Service MS" may be used. SAE 30 viscosity is recommended for acceleration trials.

Fuel-pump pressure

6-8 p.s.i. at 1500 r.p.m. engine idle

Engine idle

Speed—1000 r.p.m.
Vacuum—10 inches of mercury

Automatic transmission line pressure

105 p.s.i.

Valve lash

	Intake cold	Exhaust cold
Normal driving	.028"	.032"
Acceleration trials	.028"	.032"

Ignition

Spark plugs:
  Electrode gap......................... .035"
  Type—J9Y
Ignition point gap—.014" to .019".
Dwell angle—34° to 40°, both point sets; 27° to 32°; single point sets.
10° at 800 r.p.m.

Electrical

Alternator: 35-ampere, 6-diode
Battery: 12-volt, 90-ampere-hour—trunk located

Suspension

Torsion bar, front
Leaf, rear (heavy-duty), 56" x 2½"—6-leaf
Shock absorbers—Oriflow, hydraulic-type, double-acting, telescopic.

Brakes

Lining area—195.2 sq. in.
Internal-expanding, duo-servo type, self-energizing, self-adjusting.

Tires

Standard—7.50 x 14" Tyrex cord

Fuel tank capacity

19 gallons

Wheelbase

118 inches

Piston clearances

	Comp. Ratio 11:1	Comp. Ratio 12.5:1
Normal driving	.0035"-.0045"	—
Acceleration trials	.0035"-.0045"	.009"-.010"

Piston ring end gap

.013"-.050"

Valve spring heights

Minimum........................... 1.83"
Maximum........................... 1.86"

Bearing clearances

Main bearings, .0015"-.0040"
Connecting-rod bearings, .002"-.0045"

426
high performance
V-8

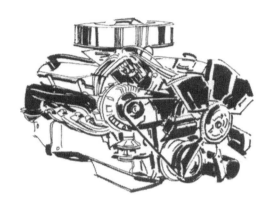

Leads Two Lives—It's suitable for everyday driving. The 426 High-Performance V-8 Engine throttles smoothly and is dependable as a standard power plant. It likes to show off on the highway. The 426 High-Performance V-8 Engine is the ultimate in "get-up" power. It's waiting to be unleashed—when you want it, when you need it. This version has a special block, crankshaft, pistons, and lubrication system. Chrome-plated cylinder head covers, oil filler cap, crankcase vent valve cap and air cleaner.

Other special or modified equipment included:

- Special, unsilenced, police-type air cleaner
- Special oversize radiator and hoses
- Seven-blade fan with viscous drive
- Hydraulic valve tappets
- Single four-barrel carburetion
- Special, modified throttle linkage
- Police-type, dual exhaust system
- 70-amp.-hr. battery
- Dual-breaker distributor
- 4-speed manual transmission (Floor-mounted shift selector)
- Heavy-duty clutch, 10½" x 6½"
- Heavy-duty prop shaft
- Heavy-duty, high-rate rear springs
- 7.50 x 14" tires on 14 x 5½" K wheels
- Sway bar
- Heavy-duty, oversize, police-type brakes

SPECIFICATIONS

Engine Type..............................OHV V-8

Piston Displacement.....................426 cu. in.

Bore and Stroke.........................4.25" x 3.75"

Compression Ratio.......................10.3 to 1

Horsepower.............................365

Torque, lb.-ft............................470

Fuel Recommended.....................Premium grade

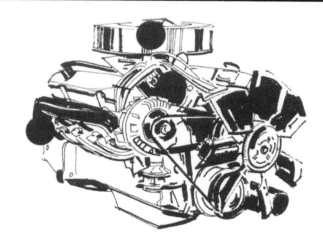

THE ULTIMATE PERFORMANCE ENGINE

Chrysler, Dodge & Plymouth bring back the Hemi
to insure domination on the drag strip,
roundy-round track and even on the water.
The beat goes on!

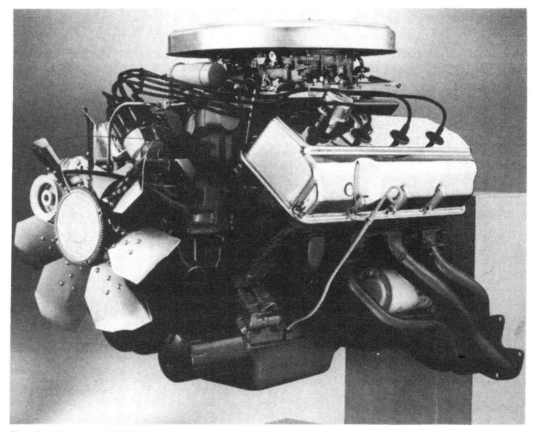

Chrysler started in 1962-'63 to work on new Hemi engine and the King Kong was ready for the competition wars in 1964.

IN DECEMBER 1962 a request was made of Chrysler's engineering staff to develop an engine and vehicle combination capable of winning stock car competitive closed circuit track events throughout the country. It was further requested that a version of the engine suitable for use in supervised timed vehicle acceleration drag events also be made part of the engine portion of this program.

Both of these applications were to share the same basic engine design and development; thus a decision on the basic engine itself was one that required careful consideration.

However, the decision for Chrysler was obvious. The Hemi engine had been a production engine from 1950 until it was discontinued in 1958. The background of development that preceeded the production version of the engine was available, as was experience in converting the en-

gine for competition use. Chrysler Hemi engines had been used previously in track events, and were still in use in many drag events. Engineering staff had also previously prepared a 271-inch fuel-injected, ram-tuned version of the original Hemi for use at the Indianapolis Speedway.

The design of the new Hemi engine began in January 1963 with the February

Continued

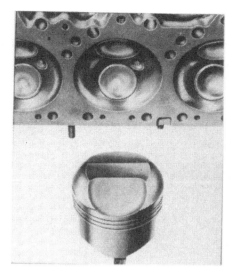

Photo shows design of new Hemi piston and matching hemispherical-design combustion chamber—one of the most effective designs in engine history.

This is the 1964 Circuit-Racing (NASCAR-USAC) 426 Hemi with single four-barrel carb, tubular headers and fresh air induction air cleaner which ducted cool high-pressure air (from the base of the windshield) to the carb.

Early factory A/FX Dodges and Plymouths ran 426 Hemi engines with tall Hilborn direct-port fuel injectors. These cars ruled the FX classes.

Hemi engines in both Dodge and Plymouth cars dominated the stock car scene until the engine was "eliminated" from competition.

23, 1964 Daytona Beach race set as the first target date.

A number of engine design avenues were initially explored in order to gain as many performance and durability features as possible while still retaining as much of the existing cylinder block tooling as practical.

The final design selected was deemed to have the potential necessary to win and the program was launched. The engine requirements were to include a single four barrel carburetor 426-inch track engine, a single four barrel carburetor 396-inch track engine and a two four barrel carburetor 426-inch drag engine. Immediately following the initial introduction of the engine, a production run of several hundred drag engines and cars were planned to be built. This would serve to give widespread usage of the Hemi on the drag strips throughout the country and also serve as production backup to the track engine.

Experimental procurement of the 426-inch Hemi engine was started in July 1963 and was completed by the end of November. The first engine ran under its own power on December 6, 1963. This engine was built as a track engine; the drag engine version was built later the same month. The 396-inch track engine had subsequently been removed from the rules and the engine was never built.

This 426-inch track engine was used extensively throughout the 1964 season. The production of the several hundred drag engines was completed by the end of the 1964 model year. Another produc-

Supercharged '65 Dodge Coronet driven by Lee Roy Yarbrough circled the 2½-mile Daytona track at a one-lap average of 181.818 mph to smash the previous record which had been set by a Mopar in 1961.

tion run of several hundred drag engines was made for the 1965 model year automobiles. with a considerable weight decrease for the engines obtained by use of aluminum and magnesium components.

The 1965 track engine usage was restricted due to a change in eligibility rules which limited the scheduled race events in which the Hemi engine was allowed to compete.

A detuned high volume street version of the 426 Hemi was designed, developed, released, and tooled as part of the 1966 model offering. With this release, full eligibility of the engine for 1966 track use was again established. A 404-inch version of the Hemi engine for use on certain tracks was also prepared for the 1966 season in compliance with the revised racing rules.

CYLINDER BLOCK

The cylinder block for the Hemi engine shares basic machining dimensions with the Wedge chamber engine cylinder block. Bore centers are 4.8 inch. Height along the bore axis is 10.725. Vertical height from the crankshaft center of 10.875, and overall block length is 23.46. The front of the block has provision for mounting the distributor and the oil pump. The Hemi engine requires an oil drain back hole in each corner of the cylinder block. Bosses extending into the tappet chamber for the cylinder head studs can be seen. The lower surfaces of these stud bosses are machined in order to provide a square seat for the stud nuts and to insure wrench clearance.

DESIGN CONCEPTS

The 1950-'58 Chrysler Hemi engine had used an included valve angle of 58.5 degrees. This feature had had enough development that a decision was made to

Closeup of the rocker arm and valve train layout of a 426 drag-racing Hemi.

Unique twin-turbocharged and GMC blown 426 Hemi powered this back-motored digger sponsored by Crane Cams to many honors on the quarter-mile during the mid-to-late Seventies.

Continued

48

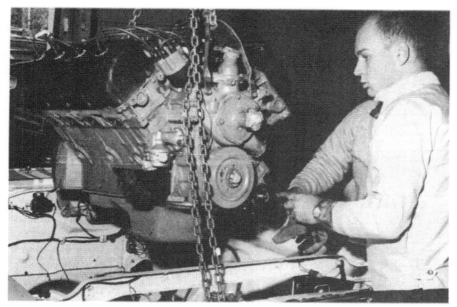

Factory engineers in the process of planting a modified 426 Street-Hemi into a Plymouth for some serious R&D work!

retain this angle for the new hemi (rounded off to 58 degrees). Any sacrifice to the intake port was not to be considered, thus the best configuration known of bringing the port straight toward the bore from the intake manifold was used. On the previous Hemi this had been no problem, since a four-bolt head pattern was used. However, with the five-bolt head pattern of the production cylinder block the inside bolt was directly in the way. This problem was solved by adding bosses in the tappet chamber of the cylinder block and providing a socket-head screw that threaded into the floor of the intake port. This screw was later changed to a stud and nut but its location remained the same.

The 426 Hemi series race engine debuted in 1964 with cast iron heads. 12.5-to-1 pistons and two induction setups: a single four-barrel Holley for NASCAR competition, or an aluminum short ram intake manifold mounting dual four-barrel Holley carburetors for drag racing. In 1965 the heads were recast in aluminum and the ram intake manifold in magnesium to reduce weight for S/S drag classes. A new cast iron head was introduced in 1966, for street production, and in 1973 a new twin-plug aluminum head was released with increased strength for supercharged fuel racing. These are about the only basic changes the race Hemi has undergone since its introduction.

1966-71 "STREET" HEMI

The Street Hemi is basically a detuned version of the full-race engine, and has many common components. Differences include 10.5-to-1 pistons, cast-iron heads, duel AFB four-barrel carburetors on an aluminum in-line manifold, and exhaust headers of cast iron (for quieter operation) instead of tubular steel. The 1966-'67 (Stage 1) engine used a mild, mechanical cam, compared to the 1968-'69 (Stage 2) version with more duration and lift. The 1970-'71 Street Hemi featured a hydraulic cam with timing events identical to the 1968-'69 stick.

When it came to the Pro Stock ranks in the mid-to- late-Seventies, 426 Hemi cars were THE machines to beat. Hemis literally owned the class.

Hemi engines revolutionized racing both on land and on the water. New Hemis replaced the old standy engines in drag racing boats and gave the airplane-engined Unlimited Hydros something to worry about.

By the mid-Seventies, 426 Hemi engines dominated
the Top Fuel ranks as well as the Funny Car scene.

In 1973 Chrysler released its new alloy twin-plug head
which gave the big Hemi even more of an edge on the
competition. Engine photo is Pro Stock 426 Hemi
taken at Sox & Martin shop.

One of the most awesome street ponycars ever sold
over the counter — the '70 Plymouth Hemi-Cuda. With
Street-Hemi engine it was unbeatable at the stoplight
or the Christmas Tree!

The Ramchargers progressed into the Funny Car business but never achieved the kind of
success they enjoyed with the original Super/Stock and A/FX Dodges.

COMPARATIVE ENGINE SPECIFICATIONS

	1964-1965 Track	1966 Track	1964 Drag	1965 Drag	1966 Street
Displacement	426	426-404	426	426	426
Bore	4.25	4.25	4.25	4.25	4.25
Stroke	3.75	3.75-3.558	3.75	3.75	3.75
Comp. ratio	12.5	12.5-12.0	12.5	12.5	10.25
Cylinder block	Cast iron stress relieved	Cast iron stress relieved	Cast iron stress relieved	Cast iron stress relieved	Cast iron stress relieved
Bearing caps	Mall. iron tie bolted	Mall. iron tie bolted	Mall. iron tie bolted	Mall. iron tie bolted	Cast iron tie bolted
Crankshaft	Forged steel shot peened and nitride hardened 15 Mu in. journals	Forged steel shot peened and nitride hardened 5 Mu in. journals	Forged steel shot peened and nitride hardened 15 Mu in. journals	Forged steel shot peened and nitride hardened 15 Mu in. journals	Forged steel shot peened and nitride hardened 15 Mu in. journals
Main bearings	Trimetal	Trimetal	Trimetal	Trimetal	Trimetal
Main journal dia.	2.75	2.75	2.75	2.75	2.75
Crankpin dia.	2.375	2.375	2.375	2.375	2.375
Piston	Impact extruded aluminum	Impact extruded aluminum	Impact extruded aluminum	Impact extruded aluminum	Impact extruded aluminum
Weight, gm	852	813	852	848	843
Top of skirt to bore clearance		0.008			0.003
Piston pin offset	0.060 toward minor thrust side	0.000	0.060 toward minor thrust side	0.06 toward minor thrust side	0.06 toward major thrust side
Piston pin OD	1.0936	1.0936	1.0936	1.0936	1.0311
ID	0.751	0.75 0.86 taper	0.751	0.751	0.685
Type	Pressed	Floating	Pressed	Pressed	Floating
Connecting rod	Forged steel	Forged steel	Forged steel	Forged steel	Forged steel
Centers	6.861	7.061-426 7.174-404	6.861	6.861	6.861
Intake valve	Silchrome XB	Silchrome XB	Silchrome XB	Silchrome XB	Silchrome XB
Head diameter	2.25	2.25	2.25	2.23	2.25
Stem diameter	0.309 solid	0.309 solid	0.309 solid	0.309 solid	0.309 solid
Stem finish	Chrome	Chrome	Chrome	Chrome	Chrome

(con't)

	1964-1965 Track	1966 Track	1964 Drag	1965 Drag	1966 Street
Exhaust valve	21-4N	21-4N	21-4N	21-4N	21-4N
Head diameter	1.94	1.94	1.94	1.94	1.94
Stem diameter	0.308 solid	0.308 solid	0.308 solid	0.308 solid	0.308 solid
Stem finish	Chrome	Chrome	Chrome	Chrome	Chrome
Valve springs installed height					
Outer	1.86	1.86	1.86	1.86	1.86
Inner	1.64	1.64	1.64	1.64	1.64
Valve closed load					
Outer	85	85	85	85	105
Inner	40.5	40.5	40.5	40.5	50
Valve open load					
Outer	280	288	272	280	184
Inner	94	96	92	94	91
Wire size - Outer	0.216	0.216	0.216	0.216	0.187
Inner	0.128	0.128	0.128	0.128	0.128
Water pump body	Cast iron	Cast iron	Cast iron	Cast iron	Cast iron
Impeller dia.	3.32	3.32	3.67	3.67	3.67
Water pump housing	Cast iron	Cast iron	Cast iron	Aluminum	Cast iron
Oil pump body	Cast iron	Cast iron	Cast iron	Aluminum	Cast iron
Oil pump cover	Cast iron with cooler tubes	Cast iron with cooler tubes	Cast iron	Aluminum	Cast iron
Oil suction pipe	Dual-fixed and swinging	Dual-fixed and swinging	Single	Single	Single
Intake manifold type	Aluminum conventional single 4 bbl	Aluminum plenum-ram single 4 bbl	Aluminum plenum-ram dual 4 bbl	Magnesium plenum-ram dual 4 bbl	Aluminum two level tandem 4 bbl
Manifold heat	None	None	None	None	Exhaust gas
Exhaust headers	Steel casting and tubes	Plate and tubes	Steel casting and tubes	Plate and tubes	Cast iron manifolds
Carburetors	Single Holley	Single Holley	Dual Carter	Dual Holley	Dual Carter
Choke			Manual	Manual	Automatic hot air
Rod bolts	7/16-20	1/2-20	7/16-20	7/16-20	7/16-20
Bolt load	0.008/0.0085 stretch	0.0095/0.010 stretch	75 ft lb	75 ft lb	75 ft lb
Cylinder head	Cast iron machined hemisphere	Cast iron machined hemisphere	Cast iron machined hemisphere	Aluminum machined hemisphere	Cast iron machined hemisphere
Chamber radius	2.42	2.42	2.42	2.42	2.42
Chamber depth	1.34	1.34	1.34	1.34	1.34
Chamber volume	172.7	172.7	172.7	170.4	172.7
Camshaft	Hardenable cast iron	Hardenable cast iron	Hardenable cast iron	Hardenable cast iron	Hardenable cast iron

(con't)

	1964-1965 Track	1966 Track	1964 Drag	1965 Drag	1966 Street
Cam sprocket attachment	Single 7/16-14	Three 3/8-16	Single 7/16-14	Single 7/16-14	Three 3/8-16
Timing chain	Double roller	Double roller	Silent	Double roller	Double roller
Valve Events (crankshaft degrees)					
Intake duration	312	328	300	312	276
Intake max open	112 atdc	106.5 atdc	114 atdc	112 atdc	106 atdc
Exhaust duration	312	328	300	312	276
Exhaust max open	112 btdc	109.5 btdc	110 btdc	112 btdc	114 btdc
Overlap	88	112	76	88	52
Intake valve lift	0.54	0.565	0.52	0.54	0.48
Exhaust valve lift	0.54	0.565	0.52	0.54	0.46
Rocker ratio					
Intake	1.57	1.57	1.57	1.57	1.57
Exhaust	1.52	1.52	1.52	1.52	1.52

A.J. & THE
HEMI HUSSEIN!

A.J. Foyt and John Mecom Jr. introduce
the Hemi engine to sports car racing
and blow a lot of minds

DRAG racing and sports car racing have traditionally been "East is East and West is West" type of situation. However, on the somewhat neutral ground of Nassau in 1964, the "twain" met!

It met during Nassau Speed Weeks, with A.J. Foyt piloting a Dodge drag engine around the road course.

The 426-cubic-inch Hemi-Charger engine found itself in the Hussein I, a sports car owned by Texas oil man John Mecom, Jr., and named after a friend of his—King Hussein of Jordan. The installation of the famed Dodge drag racing mill in a sports car proved to be a real eyebrow lifter at the Bahama event.

The theory, however, was quite sound and the end result proved to be somewhat of a vindication of the eleventh hour decision by Mecom.

The Oakes Field course consists of a series of sharp turns and short straightaways, not completely unlike several drag strips in a continuous pattern.

The acceleration power of the twin-four-barrel Dodge Hemi, as proved by its drag strip reputation, appeared to have potential in this type of racing. The installation of the big Hemi in a sports car in the first place proved to be quite a departure from the common-place small engine vehicle used in sports car club events.

Mecom brought the Hussein to Nassau outfitted with eight Webers—in two lines of fours—over a specially designed manifold.

In the Governor's Trophy Race, a 100-mile event, the Dodge with Weber carbs finished Second. But A.J. means No. 1, so the possibilities of a Second-place finish wasn't good enough!

Besides, he said, the engine was starving for gasoline. So overnight a new Hemi-Charger was stuffed in the back of the sports car and twin Holleys were bolted on. The operation was completed about forty-five minutes before the 250-mile Nassau Trophy Race!

After the Le Mans start, A.J. came past

the tower in Sixth place, behind a Ferrari and some Olds and Chevy-powered machinery. By the Ninth lap he was leading and pulling away from the field, coming out of the corners as if he were in a Super/Stock round robin at the Summernationals!

On the next lap he spun out on the first turn. When he got out in the weeds his race car ended up lodged on top of a rock. It took him two laps to get the Hussein-Dodge back on the course. By this time he was in the Eleventh lap and in Twenty-Seventh place.

Foyt turned it on. He was picking up three-seconds-per-lap on the entire field. By the Twenty-Second lap he was in Eleventh place. The possibility of being No. 1 was still there by a whisker. Then in quick succession he lost a throttle spring, his brakes started to go, and an ignition wire fell off.

Cheap adjustments at the cost of very expensive pit time. He finished the race on seven cylinders and in Eighteenth place.

Roger Penske won it in a Chaparral Chevy, followed by Bruce McLaren in an Olds-powered sports car and Pedro Rodriguez in a Ferrari.

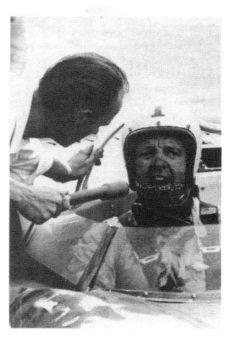

engines, the Seventh Annual provided a big surge in the domestic power plant, plus some heretofore unproved

maximum potential, was the big question mark. The car, a Cooper chassis, was resplendent in an aluminum body designed and built by Jack Lane. Even before the 500-horsepower-plus Dodge was fired, rail birds had awarded it the Best-Looking Award. The same rail birds were also predicting a limited future for the big car in view of its 1,800 pounds.

A.J., by virtue of the late arrival and not participating in the first qualifying race, was dead last and in position number 34 on the grid for the twenty-lap event.

Despite the heavy traffic and alleged handicap by weight, the Hussein-Dodge burned up the track. At the conclusion of the 50-plus miles, Foyt had passed the pack and finished number Six, earning that position on the starting grid for the big race.

In the first ten positions were included Bruce McLaren with an Oldsmobile powerplant in number One; Walter Hansgen with a Chevrolet; Jim Clark with a Ford; Roger Penske, Chevrolet; Parnelli Jones, Ford; Foyt in the Dodge; Richie Ginther, Ford; and Ron Bucknam, Ford.

The Hemi-powered Hussein made its debut at the Seventh Annual Times Grand Prix.

Tracing the Southern California classic since its start in 1958, the first few fields consisted primarily of 4.9-liter Ferraris, Aston-Martins, Maseratis, and Coopers. A few of the pioneers were there with Buicks, Chevs, or Pontiacs, but most often were among the also-rans.

In 1963 came a breakthrough when Dave MacDonald drove a brilliant race to win before a crowd of 82,000 in a Carroll Shelby Cooper-Ford.

Whereas the first six Riverside Grand Prix offered a steady transition from the foreign engine to American

innovations.

When the 1964 2000-mile race had the checkered flag, the top ten finishers read like Who's Who from Detroit.

Biggest surprise and of top interest to the pit fan and the Saturday crowd was of course the John Mecom entry, Hussein I, to be driven by A.J. Foyt and powered by the Dodge Hemi-Charger engine.

Late in arriving at Riverside, and matters complicated by a misdirected shipment of air-freighted parts, the Hussein-Dodge didn't see the 2.6-mile Riverside course for even a lap until the twenty-lap qualifying race on Saturday. Foyt, who drives a vehicle to its

The results on the Seventh Annual L.A. Times Grand Prix are now history, but worth a recap. Foyt in the Hussein-Dodge was in Second place by the Fifth lap, behind Parnelli Jones. By the Thirty-First lap it was a three-way duel between Foyt, Jones, and Penske. Lap Thirty-One proved the undoing of the gallant Texan when his fuel tank developed a leak and the Hussein pitted.

From that point on it was a close race between Jones and Penske, but Parnelli's all the way. However, Penske's Second-place ride in the Chaparral Chevy had another American innovation, his car was equipped with an automatic transmission and it did the job.

HEMI-POWER RULES!

Sox & Martin wins
74 percent of their races,
the factory goes the
'whole nine yards' with
altered-wheelbase stockers
and the street scene
gets even wilder

*During the summer of 1964, author Martyn L. Schorr
conducted extensive testing of new Street Wedge
Dodges and Hemi honkers. The good old days!*

1965 HIGH-PERFORMANCE ENGINES

CUBIC INCHES	BORE	STROKE	HORSEPOWER	TORQUE	COMPRESSION	INDUCTION
273	3.630	3.310	235@5200	280@4000	10.50	FOUR-BARREL
383	4.250	3.380	315@4400	420@2800	10.00	FOUR-BARREL
383	4.250	3.380	330@4600	425@2800	10.00	FOUR-BARREL
413	4.190	3.750	340@4600	470@2800	10.00	FOUR-BARREL
413	4.190	3.750	360@4800	470@3200	10.00	FOUR-BARREL
426	4.250	3.750	365@4800	470@3200	10.30	FOUR-BARREL
426	4.250	3.750	425@5600	480@4400	12.50	DUAL-QUAD

1965—THE MAGIC FORMULA

Chrysler engineers
turn the Barracuda into a
highly-competitive, very
serious performance car
that excells
on the drag strip, rallye circuit
and on the street

Chrysler-Plymouth sold 64,596 Barracuda Ponycars in the 1965 model year. Racing stripes, wide rectangular exhaust tip and a very throaty exhaust were sure giveaways of the Formula S package.

The Formula S Barracuda displayed less than three degrees of roll in an 0.3-G turn thanks to larger 0.87-inch front torsion bars, HD sway bar, six-leaf rear springs (4½ standard) and Goodyear Blue Streak tires on 14x5½-inch wheels. It would go to 60 mph from a standing start in 8 seconds (3 seconds quicker than same car with base V-8 engine).

1965 Barracuda Specifications

Interior Dimensions

Headroom, Front*...................38.5 in.
Headroom, Rear*...................36.8 in.
Legroom, Front...................40.6 in.
Legroom, Rear...................31.1 in.
Hiproom, Front...................56.9 in.
Hiproom, Rear...................56.4 in.
Seat Height, Front...................7.8 in.
Seat Height, Rear...................10.3 in.
Kneeroom, Rear...................1.0 in.

Includes cushion deflection due to passenger weight according to A.M.A. standards of measurement.

Exterior Dimensions

Wheelbase.......................106.0 in.
Tread, Front......................55.9 in.
Tread, Rear......................55.6 in.
Length, Overall...................188.2 in.
Width, Overall....................70.1 in.
Height, Overall
(5-pass. load).......53.5 in. on V-8 models;
53.8 in. on 6-cyl. model

Brakes

Four-wheel hydraulic, internal expanding, duo-servo with self-energizing shoes. Molded asbestos lining, bonded shoes. Size: 9 x 2.25 front shoes, front wheel; 9 x 2.50 rear shoe, front wheel; 9 x 2.00 both shoes, rear wheel. Lining area: 153.5 square inches.

Suspension

Front............torsion bars and ball joints
Rear............2½-inch outboard-mounted asymmetrical leaf springs
Shock absorbers................Oriflow type

Standard 6-cyl. Engine

Horsepower.................145 at 4000 rpm
Torque, ft. lbs..............215 at 2400 rpm
Compression ratio..................8.4 to 1
Bore, in............................3.40
Stroke, in..........................4.125
Displacement, cu. in...................225

Standard V-8 Engine

Horsepower.................180 at 4200 rpm
Torque, ft. lbs..............260 at 1600 rpm
Compression ratio..................8.8 to 1
Bore, in...........................3.625
Stroke, in..........................3.31
Displacement, cu. in...................273

Optional Commando V-8 Engine

Horsepower.................235 at 5200 rpm
Torque, ft. lbs..............280 at 4000 rpm
Compression ratio.................10.5 to 1
Bore, in...........................3.625
Stroke, in..........................3.31
Displacement, cu. in...................273

Electrical System

48-amp.-hr. standard with all engines. Chrysler Corporation alternator with high charging rate at low engine speeds.

Rear Axle

Type . . . Hotchkiss drive, hypoid rear axle. Ratio with "6" and manual transmission . . . and with Commando V-8 (all transmissions) . . . 3.23 to 1 . . . with "6" and automatic transmission . . . and standard V-8 (all transmissions) . . . 2.93 to 1.

Tires and Wheels

Safety-Rim wheels with low-pressure tubeless tires. Wheels are 13 x 4.5 inches with 6.50 x 13 tires standard on 6-cyl. model, 7.00 x 13 on V-8s.

Capacities

Fuel tank......................18 gallons
Cooling system:
  6-cyl............................13 qts.
  V-8.............................17 qts.
Engine crankcase................. 4 qts.

Engine dress-up package gave the Formula S powerplant image status to match its real performance. Finned black crackle valve covers and chromed, unsilenced air cleaner were part of the package. Hotter engine could be had with air conditioning.

Goodyear developed the Blue Streak for the Formula S Barracuda using race tire technology. Similar tire packaging was available on special Highway Patrol models of the full-size Plymouths and Dodges.

FACTORY-BUILT RACE CAR

Dodge & Plymouth pull out all the stops as they convert an assembly line into a highly-sophisticated race car shop!

Production worker at Lynch Road assembly plant lowers body onto Hemi-Charged '65 Dodge Coronet chassis. Highlight of front end of 110-inch altered wheelbase A/FX and Ultra/Stock Hemi-Dodge is 18-pound K-member which results in 25-pound front end savings.

DODGE will defend its Super/Stock drag racing titles during the 1965 season with a beefed-up and lightened Hemi-Charger engine, a new nameplate on a car with a shorter wheelbase and better weight transfer and some lightweight fender and body panel goodies thrown in for those who are inclined toward the Factory Experimental class.

The Coronet, Dodge's entry in the intermediate class of the automotive marketplace, will house the new Hemi-Charger and carry the full racing burden for the Dodge Division of Chrysler Corporation.

The Coronet drag machine will have its work cut out for it when running against the record of its 1964 counterpart. At the recent Summer Nationals, Dodge drag cars copped A/FX, S/SA, B/FX, A/MP and a Dodge Hemi powered rail—under the guidance of Don Garlits—took AA/FD.

The two major changes effecting the Super/Stock drag racing machinery for 1965 as outlined by the National Hot Rod Association are all steel bodies only and a minimum weight of 3,400 pounds.

The Coronet which carries a regular wheelbase of 117 inches has been shortened to 115 inches for drag racing purposes. The rear wheels have been moved forward to make up the drag wheelbase and add better weight transfer.

In spite of the sheet metal order, Dodge engineers have come up with a static weight distribution of 50/50 (which is slightly better than the '64 Dodge drag machine with aluminum front end pieces).

The fact that the engine is fitted with aluminum and magnesium goodies helps considerably in the weight distribution department. The lightweight engine parts make the massive Hemi mill some 80 to 90 pounds lighter than its predecessor.

A new 312-degree long duration and higher overlap camshaft improves the overall performance of the engine while allowing a greater rpm windup.

Starting from the top, the '65 Dodge Hemi-Charger sports a new magnesium intake manifold and new cast aluminum heads outfitted with replaceable valve guides and seats. Other weight reduction modifications include a cast iron or

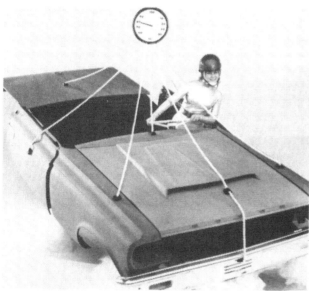

Lightweight fiberglass parts for 115 and 110-inch wheelbase Dodge Hemi Coronets. Total package from Plaza Fiberglass, less Shirley Gonda weighs 80 pounds! Complete set cost $410 in 1965.

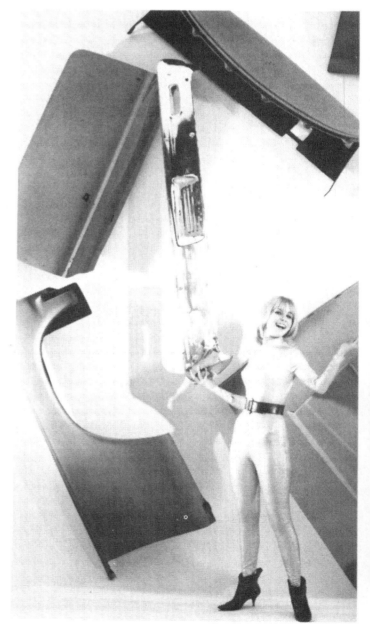

steel switch to aluminum for the engine oil pump cover, water pump housing and outlet elbow and alternator mounting bracket.

Chrome-plated valve stems add durability, give better valve guide wear and complement the high rpm camshaft by reducing valve float. An improved roller-type timing chain minimizes stretch, adds durability and maintains better and more constant valve timing. Piston tops are notched to get more valve clearance and to allow greater freedom in valve timing without the danger of a valve hitting a piston.

In the area of transmissions, Dodge engineers have fitted out the sticks with new aluminum cases and extensions. A larger drive pinion and coarser-pitch input and third speed gearset improve the durability of the four-speed stick over 1964 models. The clutch disc now contains damper springs to help soften shock loadings on the driveline.

Further concessions to weight are made in the interior of the Coronet with trim and seats of lightweight design.

The Dodge Coronet drag car is offered in a single model. A

Coronet two-door sedan. There is a choice of the famous or infamous (depending on whose side you're on) three-speed automatic transmission or the improved four-speed manual trans. The only other option is color . . . you have your choice.

The new higher lift camshaft (valve lift increase .020-inch and duration by 12 degrees) coupled with better-breathing carburetors provide a performance increase over the 1964 Hemi. Two four-barrel Holleys (R-3116) are used on the 1965 model. Although the venturi diameter remains the same (1-11/16-inch), the low-restriction design of the new carbs permits a greater air flow with better breathing qualities.

The days of the "typewriter" are gone with the switch by Dodge to the column-mounted shift. Engineers found a quick way around the difficulty, by switching the order of shift on the performance cars to a P-R-N-1-2-D pattern allowing the driver to pull the lever completely downward from Neutral and select progressively lower numerical ranges as he accelerates.

Some other areas of engine improvement on the '65 Dodge Drag Coronet include cross-bolted main bearing caps, shot-peened and hardened crankshaft, tri-metal, heavy duty main and con rod bearings, an eight-hole output flange on the crankshaft for maximum torque-transfer capacity, special, new heavy-duty outer and inner valve springs and push rods and valve tappets of hollow construction to lighten the valve train.

For those inclined toward the higher-competitive Factory/Experimental class, which from early reports will become even more highly competitive during the 1965 season, Dodge is offering lightweight front end pieces and a rear deck lid.

They have even gone to the extent of anticipating the needs of the more exotic FX-ers by including in their lightweight package a set of front fenders that will accommodate those who will move their front wheels around to gain better weight distribution.

The lightweight pieces are being manufactured by Plaza Fibreglass Manufacturing Co., 24 West Lane Court, Dearborn 7, Michigan. Mr. Rod West, of Plaza, has been designated special representative for the lightweight goodies. His telephone number is: 313-561-9152.

Pieces and prices and part numbers are as follows:

PART	Chrysler Part No.	F.O.B. Price at Dearborn
Left Front Fender, Standard	2416289	$35
Right Front Fender, Standard	2416290	$35
Left Front Fender, Altered*	2416293	$35
Right Front Fender, Altered*	2416294	$35
Hood with Air Scoop	2416286	$50
Front Bumper	2416739	$25
Left Front Door	2416295	$75
Right Front Door	2416296	$75
Decklid	2416298	$38

*Altered location of front wheel opening for use on cars where the wheelbase has been shifted to provide improved weight distribution for competitive purposes.

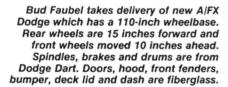
Bud Faubel takes delivery of new A/FX Dodge which has a 110-inch wheelbase. Rear wheels are 15 inches forward and front wheels moved 10 inches ahead. Spindles, brakes and drums are from Dodge Dart. Doors, hood, front fenders, bumper, deck lid and dash are fiberglass.

SMALLER IS BIGGER

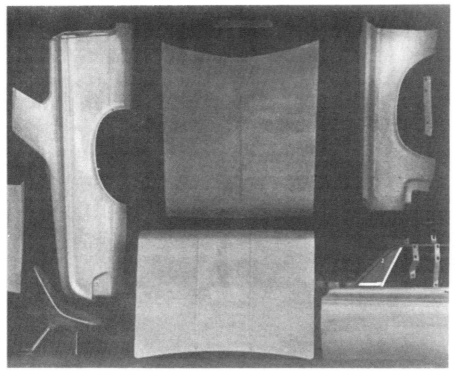

In contrast to the Hemi-program, the mini-car effort may look like small stuff but it's really the big time. Plymouth got into a very serious small-block drag racing program, Dodge pushed lightweight body parts and both passed on some very impressive 273-inch four-barrel V-8 goodies to the public.

Golden Commandos successfully campaigned a Barracuda powered by the new four-barrel 273 mini-motor. Martyn L. Schorr checks front end sheetmetal to see if new Fibercraft fiberglass body panels were installed. They weren't. New Dart fiberglass parts weigh just 103 pounds, replace 500 pounds of steel parts on 1964-'65 Darts. It's for serious racing.

HEMI UPDATE

Mopar engineers take some weight out of its King Kong groundshaker to be even more competitive in Super/Stock competition

Jack Werst (Mr. 5 and 50), ran Jenkins-prepared and factory-backed Super/Stock Automatic Plymouth. Thanks to Super Commando Hemi engine, he held NHRA record.

1965 PLYMOUTH SUPER COMANDO ENGINE

THE PLYMOUTH Belvedere Super/Stock incorporates an improved-edition of the record-breaking Plymouth Super Commando hemispherical head, high-performance engine that was introduced for drag racing in 1964, and has been setting new records ever since. This 115-inch wheelbase Plymouth has been designed to meet the 1965 specifications of the major sanctioning drag strip competition organizations.

The refined Plymouth Super Commando 426-cubic-inch Hemi engine has a host of improvements for increased performance:

• The intake manifold has been lightened by casting it in magnesium.
• Also lighter are the cast-aluminum cylinder heads. These heads have a new configuration for the intake ports which

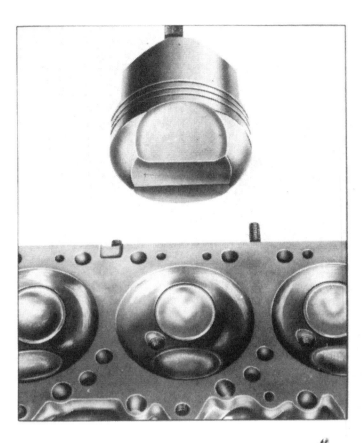

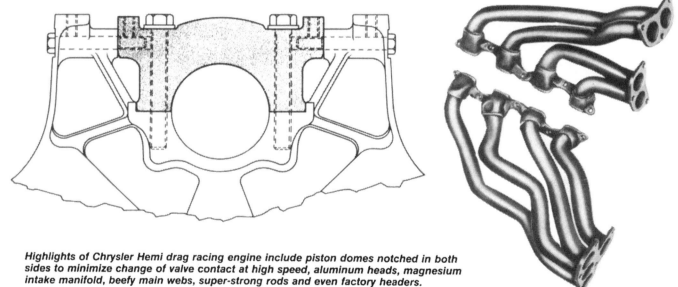

Highlights of Chrysler Hemi drag racing engine include piston domes notched in both sides to minimize change of valve contact at high speed, aluminum heads, magnesium intake manifold, beefy main webs, super-strong rods and even factory headers.

improves breathing characteristics.
• All valve stems have increased chrome plating to reduce valve guide wear.
• A new camshaft utilizes a longer duration period.
• The valve springs are stronger and considerably improve valve dynamics.
• The use of aluminum is extended to the oil pump body and its cover to reduce the weight of these components.
• Piston domes are notched on both sides to minimize the chance of their being hit by a valve head at high engine speeds.
• Timing chain is of the roller-type to minimize the tendency to stretch under acceleration run type performance. This will increase the durability of the engine.

All 1965 Plymouth Super Commando drag racing engines are being built by hand by specially-selected engine techni-cians. They are bench-assembled and carry the technician's name stamped on the finished engine.

Other components in the Super/Stock Belvedere package are essentially the same as the offering it supersedes including lightweight interior trim and seats.

With the original Super Commando, Plymouth claimed two major drag racing titles in 1964. At Pomona, California, in the NHRA Winternationals, Tom Grove's "Melrose Missile" won the Stock Eliminator title, while Hayden Proffitt drove his Super/Stock Plymouth to the Mr. Stock Eliminator prize in the AHRA Winternationals at Phoenix, Arizona.

This remarkable start of the 1964 season took up where Plymouth drivers left off when the 1963 season ended: Plymouths won five championships at the NHRA World Championships at Indianapolis, and a Plymouth had the fas-test time of any stock car at the meet.   ●

426/383/340 QUICK SPEC'S

426 Hemi Quick Spec's

Engine Type	Min.* Head Volume	Max.* Deck Height	Head Milling Specs	Brg. Clearance Rods & Mains	Conn. Rod Side Clearance	Piston-To-Wall Clearance	Ring End Gap
Street Hemi	167.7 cc	+ .536"	To reduce the chamber volume, remove .0041" from the head surface per 1 cc of chamber volume. For each .010" removed from the head, .0085" must be removed from each intake port side of the intake manifold and .0116" from the front and rear rail.	.0025/.0035	.009/.017	.003/.004 Stock Pistons	.016/.020
Super Stock Hemi	167.7 cc	+ .767"		.0025/.0035	.009/.017	.008/.010 Forged Pistons	.016/.020

*For NHRA legal engines

383/440 Quick Spec's

Engine Type	Min.* Head Volume	Max.* Deck Height	Head Milling Spec's	Brg. Clearance Rod & Mains	Conn. Rod Side Clearance	Piston-To-Wall Clearance	Ring End Gap
440 (1966-7)	73.5 cc	— .059	For the 73.5 cc chamber heads, remove .0062" from the head surface per 1 cc of chamber volume. For the 79.5 cc chamber heads, remove .0042" from the head surface per 1 cc of chamber volume. For each .010" removed from the head, .0123" must be removed from the intake face of the head.	.0025/.003	.009/.017	.0015/.002	.016/.020
(1968-70)	79.5 cc	— .027		.0025/.003	.009/.017	.0015/.002	.016/.020
440-6 bbl. (1969)	79.5 cc	— .027		.0025/.003	.009/.017	.0015/.002	.016/.020
440-6 bbl. (1970)	79.5 cc	— .001		.0025/.003	.009/.017	.0015/.002	.016/.020
426 (Street)	73.5 cc	— .042		.0025/.003	.009/.017	.0015/.002	.016/.020
413	73.5 cc	— .038		.0025/.003	.009/.017	.0015/.002	.016/.020
383 (1967 & prior)	73.5 cc	— .014		.0025/.003	.009/.017	.0015/.002	.016/.020
(1968-9)	79.5 cc	+ .0205		.0025/.003	.009/.017	.0015/.002	.016/.020
361	73.5 cc	— .038		.0025/.003	.009/.017	.0015/.002	.016/.020

*For NHRA legal engines.

273, 318, 340 V-8 Quick Spec's

Engine Type	Min.* Head Volume	Max.* Deck Height	Head Milling Spec's	Brg. Clearance Rods & Mains	Conn. Rod Side Clearance	Piston-To-Wall Clearance	Ring End Gap
340	63.3 cc	+ .045"	To reduce the chamber volume, remove .0048" from the head surface per 1 cc of chamber volume. For each .010" removed from the head .012" must be removed from the intake face of the head.	.0025/.0030"	.009/.017"	.0015/.0020"	.010/.012"
318 (1967)	57.3 cc	— .049"	To reduce the chamber volume, remove .0053" from the head surface per 1 cc of chamber volume. For each .010" removed from the head .012" must be removed from the intake face of the head.	.0025/.0030"	.009/.017"	.0015/.0020"	.010/.012"
(1968-1970)	60.6 cc	— .029"		.0025/.0030"	.009/.017"	.0015/.0020"	.010/.012"
273 (1967 & prior) 180 hp	57.3 cc	— .011"					
235 hp	57.3 cc	+ .129"		.0025/.0030"	.009/.017"	.0015/.0020"	.010/.012"
273 (1968-1969)	60.6 cc	+ .022"		.0025/.0030"	.009/.017"	.0015/.0020"	.010/.012"

*For NHRA legal engines

The club was organized by an eight-man group of Chrysler engineers in the Fall of 1962. They had the fastest Plymouths at National meets during the early-Sixties. Forest Pitcock twisted the wrenches and Al Eckstrand handled the driving of the club's altered wheelbase Hemi.

THE GOLDFISH THAT ATE MUSTANGS!

The factory-backed Golden Commandos campaign a
273-inch Barracuda that runs in the high-12s at well over 100 mph

Forrest Pitcock, left, explains the Plymouth Super/Stock rear suspension and 4.89-to-1 Sure-Grip rear package to the author before his trial runs. The best he could clock was 13.79 at 103 mph.

All sealers and sound deadeners were removed during the drag prep. Front end ground clearance is less-than-stock thanks to deep oil pan which holds 2½ extra quarts.

Author Martyn L. Schorr with helmet ready to take the Goldfish down the quarter-mile on the factory drag strip in Chelsea, Michigan. Prior to NHRA accepting the 8¾-inch Plymouth rear, the car was plagued with rear end durability problems. The Goldfish ran consistent mid-13s at 105-106 mph with dual-quads.

The Goldfish in action at Cecil County Dragoway in 1966. It competed under both NHRA and AHRA rules and posted a best time of 12.96 seconds, 108 mph in 1966. It was equipped for C/Modified, running dual-quads on an Edelbrock manifold, Isky 505-C cam and Racer Brown valve springs. Carter 3853-S quads were used.

The interior of the Goldfish was stock except for Sun tach. A block-off plate fills the space normally occupied by a radio.

Rear tires were M&H Racemaster Super/Stock cheater slicks pinned to Formula S Barracuda steel wheels. The 8.50x14-inch grooved slicks worked well with the Super/Stock rear fitted with 4.89-to-1 cogs.

COMPETITION CAPER

WHEELSTANDING BARRACUDA... called the "Hemi Under Glass", this fantastic hemi-engined Plymouth Barracuda makes like a flying fish with the drop of the accelerator. Hurst Performance Research has engineered the "Hemi Under Glass" . . . powered by a rear-mounted Plymouth hemi-head engine that can be seen through Barracuda's big rear window . . . to do nearly the entire quarter-mile run on its hind wheels. Bill Shrewsberry of Los Angeles, California, is the drag racing driver who puts this unusual Barracuda through its paces to make it the nation's most popular exhibition dragster. A close look at the picture shows the little car has all four wheels off the ground and is balancing on rear bumper-casters.

Another Barracuda, **"THE POLITICIAN"**, owned and driven by Ralph Costa of Birmingham, Michigan, waded through the nation's toughest competition to the F Stock Automatic class victory. Costa's winning elapsed time was 14.20 seconds at 99.00 mph.

1965 was the first year Barracudas have been entered in "Nationals" F/Stock competition.

THE GOLDFISH (shown on opposite page) . . . hot Barracuda of the Detroit drag team called the Golden Commandos . . . tripping the quarter-mile lights in a record-shattering elapsed time of 13.47 seconds at a top speed of 103.68 miles per hour to win the F/Stock stick class in the '65 N. H. R. A. "NATIONAL".

KING RICHARD AND HIS HEMI-CUDA

Richard Petty tries his hand at drag racing while NASCAR ponders some less-than-desirable rules changes!

Richard, and the late Ronny Householder, clown around together at NASCAR headquarters after the rules change allowed the Petty Blue Hemis to compete. Householder ran the Chrysler Corporation stock car racing program with an iron fist.

RANDLEMAN, North Carolina, is a small community in the central part of the state. Drive north from Randleman on Highway 220 and before long you reach an even smaller community called Level Cross. It's like thousands of other small, quiet rural communities throughout the country—except during the summer. That's when you're likely to see large car haulers and various closed vans skittering in and out of Level Cross, which just happens to be the home base of the Petty Engineering Company.

Headed by NASCAR's Petty family, the firm prepares and fields NASCAR race cars. In stock car racing circles, the Richard Petty legend reigns supreme. In 1965 when NASCAR rules put the Petty Plymouths on the sidelines, Richard tried his hand at drag racing. Let's take a look at what happened when Petty put a Hemi in a Barracuda!

Needless to say, the 1964 season was a good one in all respects for Petty Engineering. But the NASCAR season runs from January through early-November, and the months between September and January are usually *slow* at the shop. Like all company presidents, Lee Petty had to face the problem of trying to keep skilled mechanics busy, or risk losing them to a competitor if he couldn't provide work for them and thus keep them in weekly paychecks.

In 1965 his solution was a novel one for Petty Engineering. With skilled mechanics available as well as a great driver who just happens to have drag racing experience, Lee reasoned, why not build a drag car as an engineering exercise and then, if the car proved potent enough, go out and pick up some of the big prizes being offered by drag strip promoters to top crowd pleasers? The more thought he gave to the idea, the better he liked it.

Since the company's five-year-old working arrangement with Chrysler-Plymouth Division of Chrysler Corporation had been mutually beneficial, Petty Engineering naturally decided to use a Plymouth car. And since Plymouth's Barracuda was a short wheelbase product with good aerodynamic properties and an engine compartment large enough to accept a Hemi—and had not been used on a drag strip with Hemi power—it was the immediate choice. (And with Ford going the overhead cam Mustang route, it's possible the Chrysler-Plymouth people were interested in the feasibility of producing Hemi Barracudas in the future.)

Thus, on October 6th a spanking new '65 Barracuda rolled into the Petty shop and went under close scrutiny. By the evening of the next day, major modifications had been decided upon and the car had been stripped of every removable part. On October 8th it was moved from the main shop to the wash pit, turned on its side, and relieved of all undercoating and body filler.

Back it went to the shop, out came cutting torches and air chisels, and there

The first family of stock car racing—the Pettys—photographed in 1968. The grandmaster himself, Lee Petty, is shown at the left with sons Maurice, center, and Richard.

First time out in the Petty-built Hemi-Cuda, Richard clocked a 10.40-second et. At its first official showing, Richard ran 141 mph in 10.40 seconds. Car sported many leftover NASCAR parts and pieces.

Makeshift aluminum scoops at the rear of the hood duct fresh air to the Holley quads mounted atop the blueprinted 426 Hemi. Engine setback is obvious.

began a number of days of revamping, especially in the area of the engine compartment. Installation of one of the 20 or so 426 Hemis lying in the shop followed the making of new motor mounts. This was an "old" all-steel 426 modified from NASCAR to twin four-barrel operation and mated to a competition-valved Torqueflite.

By the time the front end was completed, only spindles and the lower ball joints were left on the stock Barracuda parts. Steering linkage and upper and lower A-frames were custom made. The steering box had come off an old Fiat that had been sitting behind the shop building and was hooked to the wheel with heavy duty U-joint sockets. Front brakes are stock, but their drums came off a '60 Valiant racer and are Kelsey-Hayes units. 5.50 X 13 Firestone racing tires ride on mag rims.

The Petty crew decided to use a rear end out of one of their NASCAR Plymouths complete with floating hubs and axles. Brakes are 11 X 3 inches using Kelsey-Hayes finned aluminum drums. Shocks are stock '64 Plymouth at the front and race-car-type units at the rear. Rear springing was left stock but fitted with extra leaves. Of course, the Barracuda rear wheel wells were cut out to accept big slicks.

After a competition model '64 Plymouth driveshaft was cut down and mated to the transmission tailshaft and rear end center section, and after exhaust headers had been fabricated and given preliminary tests, the interior became a center of interest. Because the firewall had been moved backward to permit installation of Hemi, it was decided to locate the master cylinder on the floorboard inside the cockpit. One fiberglass bucket seat was installed and the previously gutted interior was fitted with black carpeting that runs right up the sides to the window openings. Final touch-ups included painting the underside of the car light blue and the exterior "Petty Blue" and making final tuneups.

The car was given its maiden runs in mid-November and, with Richard behind the wheel, clocked a best et of 10.40 seconds. At its first official appearance on the Piedmont Strip in Greensboro, November 22nd, the Barracuda clocked a 141 mph, 10.40-second best time trial run and a top time of 138 mph in 11.40 seconds during actual runoffs. Shortly after, King Richard returned to the world of roundy-round racing and continued his winning ways.

FOR THE RECORD!

The Summers Brothers took two cars to the Bonneville Salt Flats and by November 1965 owned new World Unlimited Class and International Class A records of 409.695 mph for the Flying Kilometer and 409.277 mph for the Flying Mile. Plus, a new American B/Production Stock Car record of 156.35 in a 1966 Street Hemi Satellite

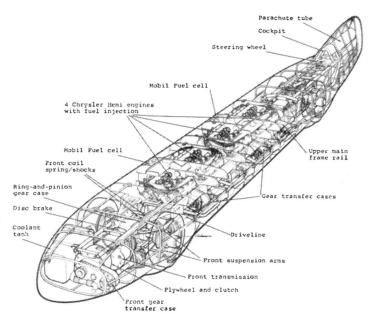

THE GOLDENROD isn't the first four-engined automobile ever built, but if its builders, Bob and Bill Summers, have anything to do with it, it will be the fastest.

The two youthful (28 and 29) Ontario, California hot rodders feel confident that when Bob climbs behind the wheel late this summer and points the machine along Utah's Bonneville Salt Flats, records will fall.

Bob and Bill Summers call the Goldenrod "an engineering exercise designed to do the ultimate in this type of car."

The type to which they refer is long and lean . . . 32 feet overall, 48 inches wide at the front wheels, and only 28 inches above the ground at the hood. The highest point is 42

inches at the tail fin.

Wind tunnel tests with a six-foot-long scale model have given the pair good reason for confidence. Stability should be excellent, better in fact than the single-engine streamliner that Bob drove 323 mph in 1962. Although it is doubtful that Bob will try it, calculations indicate the car is so stable that it would be safe for him to remove his hands from the steering wheel at 500 mph!

And the 2400-horsepower total from the four stock Chrysler Hemi engines should be sufficient to bring the record back to the USA.

Bob Summers has designed and engineered the car, utiliz-

ing a unique drive system. He has arranged the engines in pairs, the front two driving front wheels, the rear pair operating the rear wheels. A common driveline along the left side of the car keeps all four engines turning at the same speed. Both he and his brother are collaborating in the car's construction.

How does a team of talented but hardly wealthy hot rodders put together a car valued at a quarter-million dollars?

It was a difficult road, but determination paid off, and Bob interested four major sponsors in furnishing essential equipment and necessary cash.

Chrysler Corporation is supplying the Hemi engines, care-fully assembled to stock specifications, except for fuel injection and dry sump lubrication, required because of the car's extra-low profile.

Firestone Tire and Rubber Co. is building special 600-mph Nylon tubeless tires, vital to the Goldenrod's success.

Hurst Performance Products has designed a special shift mechanism that will operate the two transmissions simultaneously. In addition, the custom-forged aluminum wheels carry the Hurst name.

And the Mobil Oil Co. is compounding special lubricants to withstand gear heat and pressure, and preparing the super premium racing gasoline. •

73

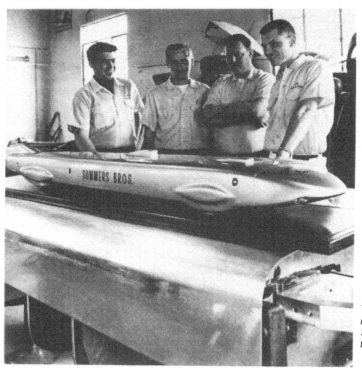

THE ULTIMATE SALT SHAKER!

A close look at the longest, narrowest, lowest package of piston-power horsepower in the history of the land speed record

The crew poses proudly with the completed scale model Goldenrod mounted on the jigged-up chassis. On November 12, 1965, Bob Summers hit 409 695 mph for the Flying-Kilometer and 409.277 mph for the Flying-Mile at Bonneville.

George Hurst and the Summers Brothers check out some of the gear and drive components used in the transmissions and locked rear ends.

Bob Summers examines one of the differential units for his streamliner during the early stages of construction. He engineered the car and handled much of the construction and driving.

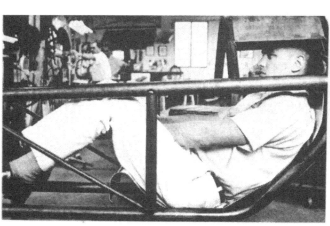

Bob assumes the semi-reclining driving position, surrounded by chassis members. From his position he has 32 feet of "hood" ahead of him!

GOLDENROD SPECIFICATIONS

CHASSIS AND BODY

Length overall—32 feet (384 inches)
Wheelbase—207 inches
Tread, front and rear—36 and 24 inches
Overall height—(to hop of tailfin) 42 inches; (to top of engine hood) 28 inches.
Overall width—48 inches
Ground clearance—5 inches
Frame—Mild steel. Lower rails: 2-inch diameter x ⅛-inch wall. Upper rails: 2 x 6-inch
        rectangular tubes. 3/16-inch wall, tubes mounted vertically for
        maximum rigidity.
Body material—Harvey aluminum; alloy 3003, .064-inch thick.
Wheels—Aluminum. Hurst-designed, forged by Harvey Aluminum. 16-inch diameter x
        6½-inch rim width. Demountable rim.
Tires—6.50 x 16 Firestone tubeless Nylons; special low-profile treadless design.
        Width of treat contact area: 4 inches. Static dia: 23 inches. Inflation:
        150 psi. Design speed: 600 mph.
Braking systems—Airheart triple spots mounted on front and rear pinion gear coupler
        flanges for use at 100 mph and below. Deist parachutes for high
        speeds: pilot chute; 8-foot diameter first stage for maximum
        speeds; 24-foot final chute for 250 mph and below; plus emergency
        8-foot chute. Automatic systems with manual override.

ENGINES AND DRIVE TRAIN

Engines: four Chrysler Hemi V-8s, mounted in-line and coupled in pairs back-to-back,
        front pair driving front wheels, rear pair driving rear wheels. Engine
        rpm synchronized between pairs by mechanical coupling. Except
        for dry-sump, lubrication and fuel-injection (required for low overall
        height) engines are to stock specifications throughout.
Bore and stroke—4.25 x 3.75 inch. Displacement—426 cubic inches each engine.
Estimated horsepower—600 @ 6,600-6,800 rpm, each engine.
Fuel—Racing gasoline, 105 research octane, supplied by Mobil Oil Co.
Lubricants—Mobil Oil Co. products.
Fuel supply—five gallons-per-engine in four tanks.
Transmissions—two, five-speed Spicer units, utilizing top four gears.
        Ratios—second 2.6-to-1
                third 1.5-to-1
                fourth 1.19-to-1
                fifth 1-to-1
        Simultaneous synchronized shifting via special Hurst Shifter.
Clutches—two Schiefer double-disc, hydraulically-actuated.
Ring-and-pinion ratios—1-to-1, locked rear ends.
Final drive ratios—May be varied. Anticipated: .95-to-1 to 1.05-to-1.
Steering—Chrysler, hydraulically-actuated, 10 degrees limit.
Suspension—Fully-independent, all four wheels via upper and lower A-arms. Upper
        arms pivot on frame, act on four special Monroe coil spring/shock
        units mounted inboard.

PERFORMANCE DATA

Frontal area—nine square feet. Coefficient of drag—.117
Total Weight—5,500-6,000 pounds (estimated).
Target speed: 450-500 mph.

*Firestone development engineer
Bob Martin shows Bob Summers the latest
in treadless land speed record tires.
Before tires were supplied for the Goldenrod,
they were tested at Firestone's Akron,
Ohio, plant at speeds to 600 mph!*

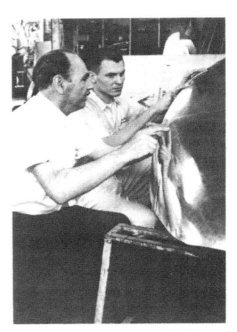

*Master "panel beater" and body builder
Jack Sutton checks out some panels along
with Bob Summers. Sutton built the entire
body in his small specialty shop
in Los Angeles.*

HOT 'CUDA HITS 142 MPH AT BONNEVILLE!

In a letter to this magazine, Wilford Day of Cedar City, Utah tells an amazing story of running the Bonneville Speed Trials for three years with his 1964 Barracuda. His car is powered by a 225 cubic-inch aluminum Slant Six with a modified head, special pistons that raise compression ratio to 11 to 1, a modified crankshaft, one Plymouth Super Stock AFB carburetor on a Weiand manifold and the old factory Hyper-Pak cast iron headers. It also has a four-speed manual transmission and a 2.93 rear axle. He used the original 7.00 x 13" Goodyear Custom tires.

Now for the great results . . . it turned 142 miles per hour! This is probably the world's fastest six-cylinder sedan. The car can be, and is, driven on the street . . . and even has factory air conditioning! (He explains that he has two engine short blocks that he swaps back and forth, saving the hot one for Bonneville.)

However, the mild one is hopped up too, and is putting out about 220 horsepower. The hot one develops about 275 "Detroit" horses.

Mr. Day's Barracuda has been featured in at least eight national magazines, in TV commercials for gasoline, on the 1965 Bonneville poster, in the 1965 Winternationals Car Show Program and on the cover of the 1965 Bonneville Nationals Program. He took the car to the 1965 Winternationals Car Show and was also invited to the Motorama in Los Angeles in December of 1966.

This Barracuda set a speed record for its class at Bonneville in 1965 by doing 126.49 mph . . . but the engine had two burned pistons and wasn't running right. When he arrived at Bonneville in 1966, Ak Miller (Ford's "Performance Advisor"), had the record up to 139.06 mph with his 221 cubic-inch V-8 Mustang.

His '63 Fairlane V-8 engine had all the good stuff that Shelby puts on his Cobras: 2 four-barrel carburetors, headers, hot cam, magneto, reworked 289 heads . . . everything! *Sixes and V-8's run together in the same class, the only limit being 229 cubic inches and a near stock body.*

Mr. Day went out and turned 139.75 . . . then 142.40! Then Ak's Ford crew started tearing down the Mustang. They came up with some Hilborn fuel injection equipment from another car in their stable, installed it in the Mustang and went out to raise the record to 143.23 . . . but they had to come up with that fuel-injected V-8 to beat the Barracuda six. Mr. Day says, "I guess a hobbyist like myself, on a budget, with a six cylinder engine, a single carburetor and a street equipped family sedan with a wife and son for a crew, isn't supposed to beat a factory entered V-8 with everything available. That Mustang was equipped with a special close-ratio transmission, Bonneville tires, hood scoop and fuel injection. We beat 'em on carbs but the fuel injection was just too much. But we sure shook 'em up and had fun doing it. And just between us, there are some slant six believers in the Ford camp!"

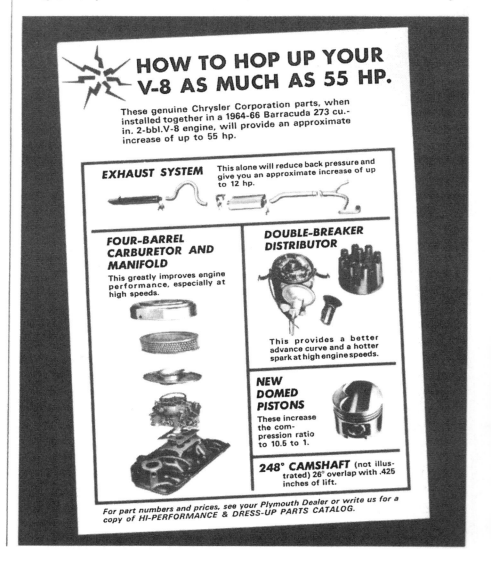

WORLD CLASS CORONET

Lee Roy Yarbrough, with some help from NASCAR great Ray Fox, sets a new World speed record for closed courses at Daytona on February 26, 1965. He circled the 2½-mile speedway at a one-lap average of 181.818 mph. Power for the Fox-prepared Dodge Coronet came from a blown and injected 426 Hemi engine.

Car builder Ray Fox, right, congratulates LeeRoy after setting Daytona closed course record. One lap average was 181.818.

Powered by a GMC 6-71-blown Dodge Hemi, Lee Roy Yarbrough's Dodge Coronet NASCAR racer broke the existing Daytona Beach closed-course record set by Art Malone in 1961 in a Dodge-powered screamer. Ray Fox Engineering constructed it.

OFF-ROAD SUPERCAR

National Rally Champion Scott Harvey joins forces with
NASCAR ace David Pearson and comes up with a Hemi-powered
Coronet that'll go anywhere!

*It may look like the driver of this Coronet Hemi Super/Stock ran off
the end of the strip and ended up in the dirt, but this is one Hemi car
that's at home in the dirt!*

*Pearson and Harvey putting their Hemi off-roader through its paces
before leaving for the Trans-Canada rally in April, 1965.*

A CAR that would make an ideal police cruiser; one that can do better than 100 mph on rough, back roads; more than 135 mph on paved stretches; take fast, tight curves with all four wheels glued to the ground; brake quickly and repeatedly without fading and still handle like any ordinary car on the highway.

That's the '65 Dodge Hemi-Coronet that David Pearson, well-known stock car racer from Spartanburg, S.c., drove in his first road rally—the Trans-Canada, 4,200-mile run from Montreal to Vancouver, April 24-30, 1965.

When the 117-inch-wheelbase car, by far the largest entry in the event, was wheeled into the garage for a "race lifting," it was just like any other ordinary Coronet. A few weeks later, it emerged as a different machine. The 426-cubic-inch, hemispherical combustion chamber powerplant was tuned to perfection; the suspension had been altered, tires changed, instruments added to the panel and a myriad of other details handled. Scott Harvey, of Dearborn, Michigan, SCCA national rally champion 1963-1964, prepared the Coronet for off-road use.

"We run on some very narrow roads in the mountains and being able to stop in a straight, predictable line is essential lest we face the possibility of running off the side of a mountain." The disc brakes are the same as those used on the Dodge Polara police car, Harvey pointed out.

Heavy-duty shocks of the type used on Dodge taxi cabs and police cars were installed and heavy-duty hubs, which are 30 percent bigger than standard, were used. A sway bar, similar to that used on stock cars in NASCAR circuit racing was welded to the K-member. Harvey said: "Higher rate, and greater arc springs, with a rating of 145 pounds-per-inch, replace the standard 110-pounds-per-inch springs. Use of these springs, adjusting the front torsion bars 1½ inches, and changing the 14-inch wheels to 15 inches, gave us the 8-inch road clearance we needed to help clear rocks and ruts.

"The heavy-duty shocks, sway bar, and special springs provide the car with a high degree of ride control and roll stiffness needed in tight cornering." The 7.35

x 14 stock tires were replaced with Dunlop SP 9.00 x 15 tires, Harvey said.

"These tires are good on gravel, and loose, wet and icy surfaces and are also very good on dry macadam. The cords are radial and run across the tire at 90 degrees. "On days when snow and mud are expected, Pearson will switch to 8.50 x 15 or 9.00 x 15 Goodyear snow tires." Another advantage of the 15-inch wheel, Harvey said, is that is provides more air circulation for cooling the brakes.

Exposed parts on the bottom of the car were streamlined to deflect or ride over rocks and other road obstructions. A ¼-inch mild steel plate was installed over the rear axle housing and steel gussets were welded to the spring hangers.

A metal cover extending from the front bumper to the rear of the oil pan was installed to protect the oil pan and to keep snow, dust and dirt from being sucked up by the radiator fan to contaminate the engine. The front half of the cover is made of aluminum and is about the width of the radiator. The rear part of the cover is made of 3/16-inch steel, just a little wider than the oil pan.

Other protective measures, Harvey pointed out, were armoring of the fuel lines with a coil-spring-type cover and routing the line through the driver compartment to reduce the possibility of damaging or crimping the line from rocks or other obstructions. Where the line passes near the muffler, an aluminum shield was inserted to lessen the possibility of vapor lock that might be caused by the heat of the muffler.

The oil pan was enlarged by adding metal "bubbles" to either side of the pan. This increased the capacity from eight quarts to ten. The pan was also baffled to keep the pickup constantly bathed in oil during tight turns or quick stops and starts.

Everything in preparing the car for the rally was done on a "if-one-part- fails-another- steps-in-to- take-its-place" basis. Even the exhaust pipe was double-braced. In the event the regular bracket failed from striking an obstacle, another located near the rear bumper prevented the pipe from dragging.

In the trunk, there are two spare tires, an auxiliary electric fuel pump and a 13-gallon spare fuel tank taken from a '60 Dodge Lancer. The battery is situated in the trunk and provides better weight distribution. The battery in the engine compartment was removed but the mounts were retained in the event of an emergency and a battery could be quickly installed.

The regulation fuel tank has a protective double-strapped aluminum cover of .060-inch thickness. A layer of one-inch-thick felt padding between the cover and the tank further protects the tank against damage.

Besides finely tuning the engine, several alterations were made to the racing powerplant to provide better low speed operation and a *more flexible* engine in driving on icy and gravel roads. Harvey explained:

"So Pearson would be able to use available fuels, the pistons were changed, reducing the compression ratio from 12.5-to-1, to 10.25-to-1.

"To give him a more flexible engine, a camshaft with less duration and overlap, a different intake manifold and four-barrel carburetor were installed.

"This caused a slight sacrifice in horsepower but it still gave us a fine engine for the quick acceleration and braking found in rally competition."

The rear axle ratio on Pearson's rally car is 4.30-to-1 compared to the standard passenger car's 2.93-to-1.

The instrument panel took on mileage counters, an oil pressure gauge, tachometer, and aircraft cockpit-type lights for the navigator. Next, a pencil beam spotlight with a ¼-mile reach was placed on the car roof and the car was then about ready for competition.

Pearson preferred the oval racing-type driver's seat to the deep bucket seat-type used by most rally drivers. Metal tubing wrapped in foam rubber and taped was attached to the seat to Pearson's liking, keeping him snugly in place in tight turns.

"It took about 300 man hours to prepare the car. It took Pearson 100 driving hours—the length of the rally—to determine the durability of man and machine."

After they finished the rally, the car was returned to Dodge Division and then shipped to New York City for delivery to Martyn L. Schorr. The author lived with the car for one month, using it for daily commuting to work. It was a bear!

The rally ran from Montreal to Vancouver, covering a distance of slightly over 4,000 miles.

Trunk of Hemi-Coronet sports dual spares, extra electric fuel pump and a spare 13-gallon fuel tank pirated from a '60 Dodge Lancer. Battery also mounts in trunk for improved weight distribution.

"ROAD RALLYING GOOD HOBBY" ... SAYS DISTAFF HALF OF CHAMPION-SHIP TEAM

When a husband-wife team wins the National Rally Championship, as Dennis and Sally Koelmel did in their 1965 Barracuda, you know that they have been spending their weekends together. You know it because road rallies are run mostly on weekends. During the rally season, which extends from March to November, the Koelmels are home for about only one weekend every month. All other weekends are spent preparing for and driving in rally competition.

"Rally driving is a good hobby, because both husband and wife can travel together through scenic, historic out-of-the-way places, experience new adventures and meet many interesting people" says Sally Koelmel. Sally and Dennis have established many friendships across the country and it's a real thrill for them to get together with these people when their paths cross at the end of some rally competition.

One appeal that is no stranger to the feminine mystique is an innate appreciation for fine clothes. This undoubtedly is one reason Sally likes road rallying. "People who participate in road rallies are very clothes-conscious" Sally observes, "they wear clothes that are in good taste . . . clothes styled with the latest fashions. You generally find rally people are better dressed than people in many other sports".

On the weekend rallies, Sally does the navigating . . . which is a pretty exacting job. Rallies are conducted throughout the countryside at posted road speeds. Numerous checkpoints are set up in advance along the route. The trick is to arrive at each checkpoint at an exact stipulated time . . . to the second, if possible . . . not too early, not too late! Rally competition has gotten so keen that even a couple of seconds one way or the other can be costly in the final tabulations.

Sally's job is to precisely compute the time they will arrive at each checkpoint. She uses a mechanical calculator to make a series of computations along the way, so Dennis can more accurately set the road speed of their Barracuda in anticipation of their next checkpoint. Sally's careful calculations complement Dennis' skill at the wheel to produce a winning rally team. The Koelmels competed against a foreign-made car in one rally that was equipped with a computer costing more than the car!

The chatter of washboard roads and the patter of flying gravel against the wheel wells are familiar sounds along rally routes. But backroads and Barracudas go together like bacon and eggs, so our "Baccaruda Team" (as the Koelmels call themselves) usually picks up points over less versatile competitors when the going gets rough.

"You've got to do a lot of defensive driving to be a successful rally driver", Dennis maintains. "You never know when a stray goat or a farmer driving a tractor will appear on the road around the next turn. We've been pretty lucky . . . over 100,000 miles on the road and so far haven't dented a fender".

Back home in Huntingdon Valley, Pennsylvania, a suburb of Philadelphia, the Koelmels begin their week days by getting up at six in the morning, eating breakfast and leaving for school by seven-thirty. Dennis is a school teacher. Sally is secretary to the school principal. Dennis has been teaching for five years, has a Masters Degree and is working on a principal's certificate. They're usually home by five in the afternoon, have dinner at six and are then ready for evening activities. This includes answering many phone calls concerning their rally activities and successes . . . and some night school for Dennis.

After washing the dinner dishes, you're apt to find Sally cleaning six or seven trophies with silver polish. The Koelmels have so many trophies from rally wins that Sally polishes a number of them almost every evening just to keep them sparkling. When asked if Dennis helps with this task, Sally smiled and said, "he doesn't even know where the polish is kept."

Sally says that many of their friends live right in their neighborhood, in fact on the same block. The Koelmels frequently attend concerts, plays and movies with these friends. Sally's girl friends are more interested in the trophies that are displayed in the Koelmel household than in the technical aspects of how they were achieved. She confided that her mother is in this same category but that her father knows what rallying is all about and likes to converse with them concerning their rally experiences.

Among the trophies that catch the ladies' eyes are a silver punch bowl set on a silver tray and an engraved silver chafing dish indicating their first-place finish in a rally.

The secret to the Koelmel's rallying success is teamwork. "It takes a system with certain duties for both driver and navigator to perform along the route", maintains Sally, "and each constantly checks on the other". The rally committee establishes the average road speeds to be maintained between checkpoints in advance, the routes to be followed and the route clues along the way . . . which incidentally requires a sharp lookout on the part of the driver. As navigator, Sally uses an odometer calibrated to hundredths of a mile, a stop watch, the mechanical calculator mentioned above, and a clipboard for recording data. Special overhead lights, a compass and a holder for the calculator are also part of the rally gear. "I find out exactly how much time it takes us to go a tenth of a mile", Sally explained. "That lets Dennis know whether we're going to be early or late at the next checkpoint. My constant checking and his fine adjustments to our road speed are what pay off at checkpoints and in final rally standings".

BARRACUDA ...AN EXCELLENT RALLY CAR!

by Scott Harvey

Car rallying can be fun for anyone who likes to drive, enjoys competition and likes to get out into the by-ways and back-roads of the countryside. Of course, many rallies are set up and run right through the heart of big cities at posted speed limits. These are the fun-type rallies that demand alertness on the part of both driver and navigator in following the somewhat obscure directions of the rally route.

Checkpoints are set up along the route beforehand—and in the more serious rallies, contestants are scored by their ability to reach these checkpoints at precise times. Being early or late loses points for the rally team—the greater the timing error, the greater the point loss. These are definitely not speed races! They are designed mostly for fun, but also to provide competition in alertness and timing of rally teams. Exceeding posted speed limits disqualifies the team.

Rallies can be set up by your local Barracuda Owners Club and can include members of several clubs as well as any of your friends who might like to participate, regardless of the make of car they are driving.

For more competitive rallies, that are run over unpaved roads and hilly terrain, Barracuda's Formula "S" package is what you might need. It is designed to convert Barracuda into a top-notch competitive rally car. The Formula "S" Package features heavy-duty front spring torsion bars and rear leaf springs, and heavy-duty shock absorbers. This combination gives Barracuda a firmer, more controlled ride that reduces the amplitude of suspension oscillations over road bumps and provides the driver with quicker response to his steering maneuvers. In addition, a front-end anti-sway bar is installed with this package to keep your Barracuda level in turns and to eliminate car swaying in rough driving situations.

The Commando 273 V-8 engine, rated at 235 horsepower, gives a Formula "S" Barracuda a real advantage in getting up to speed quickly after having been slowed because of some obstacle along the route, as frequently happens.

You also get a tachometer to check engine r.p.m's, 6.95 x 14" Special Blue Streak tires and heavy-gauge, wide-rim 14" wheels to improve roadability. And if you intend to compete for awards in the big rallies, I would recommend that you install the optional front-wheel disc brakes, for greater resistance to brake fade under repeated hard braking applications; a fast-ratio manual steering gear, for quicker steering response; a limited-slip differential (Sure-Grip), to provide better rear-end traction in turns and over loose or slippery surfaces; and either a four-speed manual transmission for a greater selectivity of driving gears for varying conditions, or a TorqueFlite automatic if you prefer the computerized shift. Incidentally, TorqueFlite provides excellent downhill engine braking in "2" or "1" drive ranges and can save your brakes in mountainous country.

Although special, accurately calibrated odometers, stop watches, calculators, slide rules and other devices are used by rally teams to help compute distances travelled, road speeds and times, it's experience that pays off in the final analysis. The more experience a rally team has with controlling the many variables, the better their chances become of winning.

If you ever get a yen to enter a highly competitive Canadian rally, which takes you over miles and miles of rough and unpaved roads, be sure to equip your car with underplating to protect the gas tank, muffler, oil pan, rear axle, rear shock absorber mounting plates and the brake and fuel lines.

Spring-like coiled steel material is available in various lengths for slipping over the brake and fuel lines.

The rugged 850-mile Canadian National Rally and the Shell 4,000-mile Rally and the like, are strictly for experienced drivers and fully equipped cars. These are endurance runs that test both man and machine and even the best many times have difficulty finishing. Road hazards, weather con-ditions and performance tests along the way take their toll and frequently less than half of the entrants actually finish the rally.

So join in on the rallying! But pick a type of rallying that you are fully equipped to participate in—and one that will give you the most enjoyment.

UNDERPLATING USED IN RUGGED CANADIAN RALLIES!

GAS TANK ARMOR   REAR AXLE SHIELD   FUEL LINE PROTECTOR

IN 1965 Scott Harvey of Dearborn, Michigan, won the U.S. Rally Driver Championship of the Sports Car Club of America for the second consecutive year.

Driving a '64 Valiant V-8 sedan, Harvey won two First places, one Second place and one Seventh place in four of the 13 national rallies sanctioned by the SCCA during the 1964 season. He finished with a better point score than any other driver at the annual convention of the SCCA in Philadelphia.

Harvey's victory came in the Club Class, open to all members of the SCCA. He took First place in the Andiamo Rally, July 31-August 1, Ohio region, and the Rolling High Rally, September 25-27, New Mexico; Second place in the On Wisconsin Rally, June 5-6, Milwaukee region, and Seventh place in a Barracuda in the Appalachian Rally, November 7-8, Philadelphia Region. Under SCCA rules,

his best three rally performances counted in his point score for the season.

Harvey also drove a Valient two-door sedan in international competition during the 1964 season. He finished Third in his class in the Monte Carlo rally in Europe, January 18-21. In the Shell 4000 Trans-Canada Rally, he was running Third on the last day only to be involved in an accident and finished 14th over-all, Third in his class.

In the 1964 SCCA road racing competition, Harvey drove a Valiant with a six-cylinder, 170-cubic inch Hyperpak engine and won the Central Division 2-to-3 Liter touring car championship. He scored victories in the sedan classes at the Mid Ohio Raceway, Mansfield, Ohio; the Waterford Hills course near Detroit; the Kent Fields course near Grant Rapids, Mich., and Indianapolis Raceway Park.

HEMI
SPORTS RACER

Bob McKee handcrafts a back-motored Mopar sportster
that's right on the money

Chassis-designer Bob McKee is one of the
country's top exotic chassis and powertrain builders.

Bob Montana poses in the Town & Country Plymouth (Phoenix,
Arizona) sleek Hemi-powered, mid-engine sports car.

Car was built in 1965 around a factory Super/Stock Hemi drag
engine blueprinted for roundy-round racing. Even the dual Holleys
were maintained.

McKee designed and built the quick-change transmission and rear
(trans-axle) for use with the Hemi engine. All components had to be
designed specifically for this unique Hemi car.

THE YEAR Of The STREET HEMI

Anything that consistently cleans house at Daytona can't be all bad on the street!

Martyn L. Schorr test driving the '66 Dodge Charger and Plymouth Barracuda. In 1966 Charger received CARS Magazine's Top Performance Car of the Year award. Test Charger is Street-Hemi-powered.

CAPSULE COMMENTS

THE new Street Hemi for Dodge and Plymouth is big news. They "de-tuned" it for the street by dropping the compression to 10.5-to-1, using a milder 276-degree solid cam, tighter piston clearances, two four-barrel carbs in line with exhaust heat, street ignition, and new cast iron exhaust headers that will fit in the various passenger car chassis without increasing the restriction too much. There's no question that this is the hottest street engine in the 1966 crop. It's just about *got* to be. It has the same valve and port sizes as the racing hemis, huge venturi area with the two big Holley carbs, a good exhaust system, a strong cam, and the solid lifters should let you go to 7,000 rpm before shifting!

Incidentally, it's interesting to note that Chrysler didn't retool the head castings for an exhaust-heat crossover passage for the new street engine. They take their exhaust heat to the intake manifold from the right exhaust manifold outlet by moving it up to the rear carb through small tubes and a special thermostatic valve. It does the job—that is, it gets enough heat under the rear carb to vaporize the fuel in cold weather—and yet it saved re-tooling the racing heads. This is

not the smoothest street engine in the industry, obviously. But it should give you 0-60-mph times in the 5's anytime you want them!

You will also note the new 440-cube engine for '66 Chryslers, Imperials and Dodges and Plymouths. This is a bored and stroked version of the 413 block. It was originally intended only for the Chrysler and Imperial luxury cars, but the Dodge boys wanted it as a highway engine for their heavy Polara models. It's rated at a conservative 350 hp with hydraulic cam, four-barrel carb and dual exhaust, but it has tremendous mid-range torque and should make a wonderful engine for the guy who wants ultimate smoothness, quiet and flexibility on street and highway. If you think the 383 engine is responsive, try this one! ●

Dodge and Plymouth continued its winning ways with dual-quad 426 Hemi. Charger offered unique fold-down split rear seats with full-length console.

Plymouth had all bases covered—from F/Stock to Super/Stock. Four-barrel mini-273 carried 235-hp rating in Barracuda. Intermediate Plymouth with Street Hemi was dynamite on the street or the strip in A/Stock.

1966 HIGH-PERFORMANCE ENGINES

CUBIC INCHES	BORE	STROKE	HORSEPOWER	TORQUE	COMPRESSION	INDUCTION
273	3.630	3.310	235 @ 5200	280 @ 4000	10.50	FOUR-BARREL
383	4.250	3.380	325 @ 4800	425 @ 2800	10.00	FOUR-BARREL
426	4.250	3.750	425 @ 5000	490 @ 4000	10.25	DUAL-QUAD
440	4.320	3.750	365 @ 4600	480 @ 3200	10.10	FOUR-BARREL

426 STREET HEMI

This race-engine-in-disguise offers more real horsepower than any other production engine ever built!

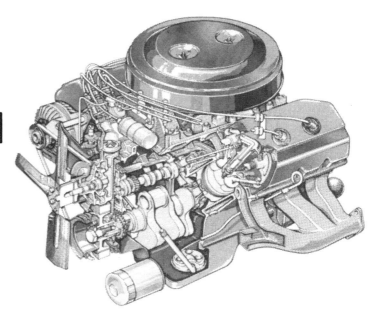

Cutaway of new Street Hemi reveals all the goodies the factory has poured into what has got to be the strongest engine ever designed for street use.

THAT'S RIGHT. The dome-shaped combustion chambers are no longer the exclusive province of the race car, and street machines will now benefit from their extensive competition experience. Comparing the street and race versions, you'll find that both are using the same heavy-duty block with cross-bolted mains. It is quite a production feat to hold the block and main bearing dimensions so that these pieces will fit.

When the Hemis first appears at Daytona, competitive engineers grumbled about their being "tool room pieces," but here they are in production. The new Hemi has a milder cam, with considerably less valve overlap, and this brings idle speeds down to an acceptable combination for street-and-strip use. The duration is reduced and the exhaust opens later, while the intake closes earlier. This is a good way to pick up some extra low-end torque while keeping the package streetable.

The new cast iron heads differ somewhat from their aluminum counterparts both in weight and in some of the accessory mounting bosses for power steering and air conditioning pumps. Valve sizes, however, remain the same, and all of the good valve train parts were retained. Racing slugs were deemed too noisy for street use, so piston clearances were tightened and expansion control slots used at the top of the skirts. These pistons are still impact extrusions rather than castings. One amusing contradiction is that the race engine is fitted with pins that are pressed into the rods, while the street machine has full-floating pins. The race pins and pistons are not interchangeable with the street units unless you are willing to do some machine work since the street pin is smaller.

Long-branch cast-iron exhaust headers are used for efficient flow. You would gain some power and save a little weight by going to tubular headers for competition, but for normal street use there would be little to be gained from the change. The heads do not have provisions for an exhaust cross over, so the exhaust is piped from the headers to the intake manifold and back across to the other header. The

Back in 1966 you could get the 426 Street Hemi with four-speed manual (shown) or excellent automatic transmission. Automatic was nicer!

external piping is light, easily disconnected and offers the additional advantage of not entailing heat rejection to the engine coolant.

Originally, the 426 Hemi was going to be available for most of the expensive lines. But by midsummer, the availability of the 426 Hemi was restricted to just two body styles: the Plymouth Satelite on a 116-inch wheelbase, and the 2-door Dodge Coronet on a 117-inch wheelbase. Some frantic name changes took place as well. Originally Plymouth was going to call their version the "Street Hemi" but some devious corporate logic prompted the change to "Hemi²" or "Hemi Squared." Dodge, with its habit of calling a spade a spade, just named it the "Hemi-Charger Maximum Performance Acceleration Engine," which isn't a bad designation, even if it is a bit long. Most people will call it the Hemi, and the

engineering designation is "A102." The main thing is that it lays down a pair of rubber streaks that disappear with the car down the horizon.

When NASCAR tried to lay down the law to Chrysler on race engines, Ron Housholder made a very simple pronouncement, the sum and substance of which was "We'll race elsewhere." Race they did with their Hemi engines, and what USAC gained, NASCAR lost, and probably more. The point is that no race organization should be able to change the rules on something as basic as the type of engine to be run unless they serve a reasonable notice, and three months is ridiculous. It takes anywhere from six months to a year to work out a chassis and engine combination to where it becomes competitive, and longer than that to work out a suitable engine. ●

Author checks out new emblems used by Dodge on Street Hemi models. Plymouth Street Hemi at speed on the New Jersey Turnpike. Car was supplied by Plymouth Public Relations in NYC (George Taylor), set up by local shops and raced by Martyn L. Schorr. Richard Petty and Ronny Householder pulled out of NASCAR when Hemi was banned. Ronny ran stock car operation for Chrysler.

1966 Barracuda Specifications

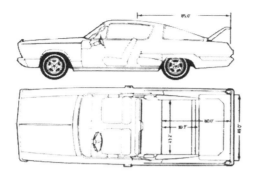

Interior Dimensions

Headroom, front * . . . . 38.3 inches
Headroom, rear * . . . . 36.8 inches
Legroom, front . . . . 40.7 inches
Legroom, rear . . . . 30.6 inches
Shoulder-room, front . . . . 54.2 inches
Shoulder-room, rear . . . . 52.6 inches
Seat height, front . . . . 8.0 inches
Seat height, rear . . . . 10.3 inches
Kneeroom, rear . . . . 1.1 inches

*Includes cushion deflection due to passenger weight, according to Automobile Mfg. Assn. standards of measurement.

Exterior Dimensions

Wheelbase . . . . 106 inches
Tread, front . . . . 55.9 inches
Tread, rear . . . . 55.6 inches
Length, overall . . . . 188.3 inches
Width, overall . . . . 70.2 inches
Full rated load . . . . 915.0 pounds
Height, full rated load,
   6-cylinder . . . . 52.9 inches

Tires and Wheels

Safety-Rim wheels with low-pressure tubeless tires. Wheels are 13 x 4.5 inches with 6.50 x 13 tires standard on 6-cyl. model, 7.00 x 13 on V-8s.

Capacities

Fuel tank . . . . 18 gallons
Cooling system:
   6-cyl. . . . . 13 qts.
   V-8 . . . . 18 qts.
Engine crankcase . . . . 4 qts.

Standard 6-cyl. Engine

Horsepower . . . . 145 at 4000 rpm
Torque, lbs.-ft. . . . . 215 at 2400 rpm
Compression ratio . . . . 8.4 to 1
Bore, in. 3.40
Stroke, in. 4.125
Displacement, cu. in. 225

Standard V-8 Engine

Horsepower . . . . 180 at 4200 rpm
Torque, lbs.-ft. . . . . 260 at 1600 rpm
Compression ratio . . . . 8.8 to 1
Bore, in 3.625
Stroke, in. 3.31
Displacement, cu. in. 273

Optional Commando V-8 Engine

Horsepower . . . . 235 at 5200 rpm
Torque, lbs.-ft. . . . . 280 at 4000 rpm
Compression ratio . . . . 10.5 to 1
Bore, in. 3.625
Stroke, in. 3.31
Displacement, cu. in. 273

Electrical System

48-amp.-hr. battery standard with all engines. Chrysler Corporation alternator with high charging rate at low engine speeds.

Suspension

Front . . . . Torsion bars and ball joints
Rear . . . . 2½-inch outboard-mounted asymmetrical leaf springs
Shock absorbers . . . . Oriflow type

Brakes

Four-wheel hydraulic, internal expanding, duo-servo with self-energizing shoes. Molded asbestos lining, bonded shoes. Size: 9 x 2.25 front shoes, front wheel; 9 x 2.50 rear shoes, front wheel; 9 x 2.00 both shoes, rear wheel. Lining area: 153.5 square inches.

Rear Axle

Type . . . Hotchkiss drive, hypoid rear axle. Ratio with all 225-cu.-in.-engines with manual transmissions . . . standard V-8 with 4-speed manual and Commando V-8 (all transmissions) . . . 3.23 to 1. With 225-cu.-in. and automatic and standard V-8, (3-speed and automatic transmissions) . . . 2.93 to 1.

The Formula S option cost $258 in 1966 and included the four-barrel 273 engine with solid-lifter cam and valve train, dual-point distributor, 10.50-to-1 pistons, Carter AFB carburetor and free-flow exhaust system. Oversize 10-inch drums and front disc brakes supplied the stopping power.

11 cars . . . all Plymouths . . . qualify for Top Stock Eliminator at NHRA Winternationals.

And speaking of fast, the Hemi (and some of its smaller-inch cousins) manages to get specially modified Plymouths from one end of a ¼ mile to the other ahead of its competition in some really hot elapsed times.

Like the last NHRA Winternationals. The only cars to qualify for Top Stock Eliminator were Plymouths. Eleven of them. And Plymouth took nine class wins at the meet.

And two of these class wins were scored by Plymouth Barracudas, relative newcomers to big-time drag racing. The Barracudas also made a big dent in the NHRA Springnationals, where Richard Petty won the B/Altered class with his Hemi-powered Barracuda. This was where the season's most unusual exhibition car made its debut. The rear-engined wheel-standing Hurst "Hemi Under Glass," a Plymouth Barracuda powered by the Plymouth 426-cubic-inch Hemi engine and driven by Bill Shrewsberry.

"Drag-on-Lady" hits 129.30.

Among the records set by Plymouths in drag races is the S/SA top speed mark of 129.30 set at Palmdale, California in August by Shirley Shahan with her Hemi-powered Plymouth "Drag-on-Lady."

Plymouth won two classes and tied another at the premier running of the SUPER STOCK Magazine Nationals at York, Pennsylvania in August.

At the CARS Magazine meet at Cecil County, Maryland, August 21, Hemi-powered Plymouths won in three classes.

Hemi-Cuda: 171.85 in 8.88.

And, before we forget the quick-quarter machines, remember that the "Hemi-Cuda" campaigned by the Southern California Plymouth Dealers has been eating up the competition. Last November it became the quickest and fastest stock-bodied, stock-wheelbase drag machine going. At Carlsbad (Calif.) it cranked off a 171.85 in 8.88 !

So, any way you count it . . . drag strip, super stock track, or the Salt Flats, you're going to find Hemi-powered Plymouths out in front. You may not need quite as much as the Hemi turns out, but whatever you're looking for in a car, Plymouth probably has more of it than anyone else.

Any time you're in doubt, remember things like torsion bars, the Hemi, the TorqueFlite transmission . . . every one of them available in Plymouths. And the standard safety equipment: padded instrument panel and sun visors, inside and outside rear-view mirrors, back-up lights, anti-windlift windshield wipers and electric washers, safety inside door-release handles. All of these safety features, combined with proving-ground safety research and the actual on-the-race-track testing are what make the '66 Plymouth synonymous with safe, dependable performance. And make the Plymouth the great road machine it is.

In addition to "the hot ones," we do make a variety of luxury cars . . . and some surprising economy models too. You can check them out at your nearest Plymouth Dealer along with the hot machines. But if your real dream is a Hemi-powered Plymouth Belvedere, check the next page.

ⓈFormula 'S'

Some like 'em hot . . . and the '66 Plymouth Barracuda with the Formula 'S' Package fills the bill. The big, husky Commando "273" for get up and go. The rallye suspension and heavy-duty shocks for improved handling and cornering. Wide-rim (14" x 5½") wheels and special Blue Streak tires for road-hugging traction. A readable tachometer that replaces the standard vacuum gauge. Wheel covers that simulate bolt-on wheels. Optional equipment includes a new center console for either the 4-speed manual or the automatic transmission. It extends from the back of the front seat up to the instrument panel, and features an ash receiver and a storage compartment. Caliper-type disc brakes on the front wheels. They are ideally suited for those who want the predictable, stable action so necessary for rallies. Highly resistant to exposure to water, dust or temperature extremes. Formula 'S', the Barracuda optional package that could change your thinking about fastback performance just as radically as Barracuda changed America's thinking about fastback versatility.

Chrysler engineer Scott Harvey was a prime force in the design and development of the Formula S package, first debuted on his '62 Valiant test car. He won the 1966 SCCA National Rallye Championship in his Team Star-Fish Barracuda. Barracuda Formula S cars took First and Seconds at the 850-mile Canadian National Rally in 1965.

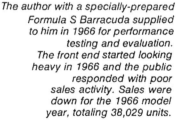

The author with a specially-prepared Formula S Barracuda supplied to him in 1966 for performance testing and evaluation. The front end started looking heavy in 1966 and the public responded with poor sales activity. Sales were down for the 1966 model year, totaling 38,029 units.

THE BLOWN & THE BAD

Bud Faubel almost revolutionized
stocker drag racing back in 1966
with his intercooled twin-turbo Hemi-Honker

Gentleman drag racer Bud Faubel takes a break during the test runs. Faubel sold Dodges and was well-connected with the factory racing engineers.

Faubel, Keller and crew push the unique twin-turbo Hemi Coronet up to the line for its maiden run. First time out top end was over 160 mph.

THE NAME Turbo-Honker derives from its hybrid make-up—the strange result of a unique combination of aircraft and automotive engineering.

Turbo comes fcom turbocharging, a form of supercharging which is used extensively by aircraft manufacturing firms to get the most out of reciprocating airplane engines.

The word Honker, however, draws its source from other, somewhat less exotic beginnings.

Stock car driving great Marvin Panch and drag racing car driving great Bud Faubel had been brought to Daytona Beach for the Pure Oil Performance Trials in 1961.

The practice for these brake, acceleration, and economy trials—which goes on for some two weeks before the main event—becomes something less than stimulating for race drivers.

So it happened that Panch and Faubel ended up side by side one day on one of the practice roads of the Daytona International Speedway, Panch with his big-engine Pontiac, Faubel with his big-engine Dodge.

The age-old challenge presented itself.

"I'll betcha my car can beat yours. Let's race."

Who issued the challenge to whom has been lost.

Faubel with his drag racing experience had the advantage over Panch.

Although the race could be colored with adjectives, the fact is that Faubel "blew Panch out of the tub."

When they pulled beside each other again Panch rolled down his window and said to Faubel: "That's a real honker you've got there."

Faubel has had a lot of "real honkers" since then and each one of his drag racing cars has been named exactly that— "The Honker."

There have been Honkers of 1962, 1963, 1964, 1965 and 1966 vintage. All winners. All record holders.

When Faubel and his Honkers became caught up in the "show biz" season of drag racing, he started looking around for an idea.

As vice-president of a Dodge dealership in Chambersburg, Pennsylvania, Faubel wanted to maintain the product image. He wanted a car that looked like what he sold.

Bob Keller, a Long Island, New York, aircraft engineer was also a performance freak.

He had been playing around with a turbocharger on his slant six-cylinder engine with excellent results at local drag strips in lower racing classes. Keller and Faubel met and the die was cast.

In simple form: Why not turbocharge a Hemi drag car and come up with a real wild stormer?

Faubel agreed to supply the car and engine, Keller the know-how and a contact with Wolf Schlegal, of the AiResearch Industrial Division, Garret Corporation, who would come up with the turbocharging goodies.

For those of less exotic backgrounds, a turbocharged Hemi looks much like a plumber's nightmare in person, but on paper it resembles a Rube Goldberg idea for boiling eggs in the trunk of your car!

It really turns it on. It takes the "advertised" 425 horsepower and ups it to somewhere in the neighborhood of 1,300 to 1,500 raw, wild horses.

In the case of the turbocharger the system uses exhaust gas energy, which would otherwise be wasted, and instead turns it into useful power by passing it through a turbine on its way out of the engine.

In short, it works much like the old water wheel method: as long as the water is going downhill they decided to put a wheel in its way and force the water to turn the wheel and provide energy.

In the case of the car, the exhaust turbine is directly shafted to an intake compressor which brings in outside air, compresses it and forces it into the combustion chamber.

An innovation in the Turbo-Honker was the addition of an intercooler system.

Applying the water-wheel principle to such things as automobiles and airplanes, engineers figured out, among other things, that air when compressed gets hot, and for every degree you cool it you gain some horsepower.

For every 100 degrees they cool the ambient air they receive in return a 15 percent increase in horsepower. So they cooled it with an intercooler system that results in additional boost.

Basically these were the two innovations added to Faubel's Turbo-Honker—a turbocharger and an intercooling system.

To accomplish this there were two 15-gallon tanks mounted in the trunk of the car—one to feed the intercoolers, the other to cool the engine—and about ten yards of pipe, surplus aircraft hose, and an assortment of couplings, valves, switches, dials, and gauges.

The car's weight was upped to 3,800 pounds from its original 3,200.

The compressin ratio of the engine was lowered to 7.5 from its original 12.5-to-1 for durability purposes with the rest of the Hemi-Charger power plant remaining exactly stock.

The car turned the quarter-mile with a terminal speed of over 160 miles per hour. The first time out.

Keller, a relatively nonexcitable engineering-type, said: "That's not bad for a starter, but we'll get it going better as we move along."

Under all that tubing, plumbing and hoses rests a blueprinted Hemi with Hilborn injection and two gigonda turbochargers.

Fuel injection manifold is Hilborn affair which has been modified to take one-turbo-per-bank of cylinders. All lines are braided-steel aircraft pieces.

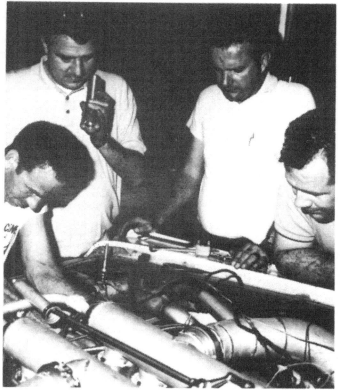

Faubel looks on whie aircraft turbocharger specialists make some final adjustments before heading to the track. The man in the background holding the flashlight is Dodge public relations honcho, Moon Mullins.

Dual 15-gallon water storage tanks in the trunk are for the intercoolers which allow the boost to be turned up without fear of detonation and potential engine destruction.

BABY GRANDS STEAL THE SHOW

It was a carryover year on the street and the factory takes a whole new look at sporty car sedan racing

Bob Tullius in the Group 44 Dodge Dart sedan racer leads the pack through the esses. Mini sedan racers were called "Baby Grands" as they were built like mini NASCAR cars. Wedge 440, left, powers CARS Magazine Dodge Coronet R/T on facing page—tuned by Motion.

PERFORMANCE-WISE, Chrysler meets buyers head-on, but the "sleeper" of this line for 1967 may well be the 440-inch wedge engine. Reputed to be competitive with the 426 Hemi in the quarter, this engine is more practical for street use and is much cheaper. Chrysler's 1967 string of two sixes and nine V-8's includes two versions of the 273, two of the 383 and two of the 440.

Beginning with the 273 there is a 180-hp @ 4200 rpm normal version with 8.8-to-1 compression ratio and a 235-hp @ 5200 high-performance package with 10.5-to-1. The vast difference between the two is rather obvious: either you want performance or you don't. Aside from the D/Dart equipment which still may be available through Chrysler's Product Planning branch, it's possible to build to almost any degree of performance desired through selection from Mopar parts.

It was a busy year for the author, then Editor of CARS Magazine. New Dodge R/T was set up for the street with 440 Wedge by Motion. Charger had Street Hemi power, like Plymouth, right.

Even the 170- and 255-inch Sixes are included in this act. For the sixes a special carburetor (#2463849), intake manifold (#E8467M) and air cleaner (#2465310) will handle carburetion increases, while a camshaft (#E7885M) and lifters (#2469501) can be selected for interior engine modification.

To present a complete list at this time would turn this story into a parts catalog, for Chrysler is well aware of the weekend demands being placed on its entire engine line. Comparable carburetion and camshaft components are available for the other Mopar engines, up to and including the 440. Special clutch components, bellhousings, manual-shift throttle bodies, and special torque converters are also included in a selection that encompasses rear-gear sets ranging from 3.23 to 3.91 in A-bodied cars and 3.73 to 4.89 in the big-car category. Most of these ring-and-pinion gear sets retail for about

$50, and many are available with Chrysler's Sure-Grip differential.

The sneaky part of the relationship between the top-end 440 and 426 Hemi is the fact that the two engines are separated in terms of torque potential by only 10 lbs-ft., thus accounting for the closeness in performance up to near 80 mph in comparable cars.

The Street Hemi, which may be viewed in afterthought as a stopgap, is just too much car for the average enthusiast, both in brute muscle and extra cost. The new 440 engine features the excellent torque characteristics of a wedge, and will keep up with the Street Hemi in factory trim. It's far and away easier to maintain, considerably cheaper, and with comparable performance, will probably put the street Hemi back into the racing-only category.

One last point: There are several suspension pieces to be considered that are almost mandatory with top-end Chrysler power. Sway bars (#1857906) for Plymouth and Dodge (excluding 880s), stiff torsion bars (#2071628 and #2071629) for Darts, Valiants and Barracudas, quicker steering units and heavy-duty shock absorbers are all vital for proper handling and in the majority of cases, money can be saved by ordering such options on the new car rather than installing them afterwards. ●

Top street option in intermediate Plymouth and Dodge models was 426-inch Street Hemi with four-speed or Torqueflite. Plymouth with Street Hemi power gets it on at the Chrysler Proving Grounds, Chelsea, Michigan.

1967 HIGH-PERFORMANCE ENGINES

CUBIC INCHES	BORE	STROKE	HORSEPOWER	TORQUE	COMPRESSION	INDUCTION
273	3.630	3.310	235 @ 5200	280 @ 4000	10.50	FOUR-BARREL
383	4.250	3.380	325 @ 4800	425 @ 2800	10.00	FOUR-BARREL
426	4.250	3.750	425 @ 5000	490 @ 4000	10.25	DUAL-QUAD
440	4.320	3.750	375 @ 4600	480 @ 3200	10.10	FOUR-BARREL

PLAYIN' A BABY GRAND!

WHEN you hear talk about "Baby Grands" these days be assured it has nothing to do with anybody's philharmonic. But the music of the tuned exhaust headers of the Sedan Class cars in the Sports Car Club of America series is providing immense interest in competitive racing circles throughout the nation.

The term Baby Grand comes from the makeup of the compact Dodge Darts, Plymouth Barracudas and Ford Mustangs competing for national honors in this newest phase of American automobile racing.

"They look like baby grand national stock car racers," somebody said . . . and the name stuck.

The cars come complete with roll cages, fifteen-inch

wheels and the throaty roar of the big four-barrel carburetors dumping gas into highly-tuned small V-8 engines and pushing exhaust into three-inch OD collectors from individually tuned 1½ inch pipes off of each cylinder.

In the sports car racing circuit where the overall sound of competition has traditionally been more like that of a swarm of angry hornets, as the small foreign cars snaked around the road courses, the brassy Baby Grands are making a big hit.

Bob Tullius and Dick Gilmartin, who had given up their respective professions to devote full time to their hobby— auto racing—were the first to take the Dodge Dart on the Baby Grand circuit.
●

1967—THIS BARRACUDA BITES WHEN CORNERED!

Fresh European styling and a wide range of powerplants
put the Barracuda in a class by itself

A new convertible is one of three models in
the Barracuda lineup for 1967. Power top
is standard along with a glass rear window,
stamped steel linkage and well-detailed
interior fabric lining.

Convertible models from the
1967-1969 era are highly-
collectible and rarely seen
on the market. The one
has non-stock mag wheels
and some dress-up mods.
Convertible production in
1967 hit 4,228 units.

Specs.

ENGINES:

	273 V-8	383 V-8
Bhp @ rpm	235 @ 5200	280 @ 4200
Torque, lbs.-ft.	280 @ 4000	400 @ 2400
Bore	3.63 in.	4.25 in.
Stroke	3.31 in.	3.38 in.
Displacement	273 cu. in.	383 cu. in.
Compression ratio		
Nominal	10.5 to 1	10.0 to 1
Maximum	11.69 to 1	10.55 to 1
Combustion chamber volume,		
min. allowable	57.3 cc.	73.5 cc.
Deck height	+.129 in. Max.	−.014 in. Min.
Carburetion	1 4-bbl. Carter	1 4-bbl. Carter
Throttle dia.	1.44 in. primary;	1.44 in. primary;
	1.56 in. secondary.	1.56 in. secondary.
Camshaft duration		
Intake	256°	264°
Exhaust	256°	268°
Overlap	34°	40°
Lift @ 0 in. lash		
Intake	0.415 in.	0.425 in.
Exhaust	0.425 in.	0.437 in.

Camshaft timing–273 V-8   Camshaft timing–383 V-8

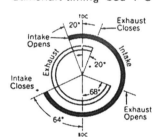

Valve diameter		
Intake	1.78 in.	2.08 in.
Exhaust	1.50 in.	1.60 in.
Tappet type	Solid	Hydraulic
Tappet Clearance		
Intake	.013 in. Hot	—
Exhaust	.021 in. Hot	—
Max. valve spring pressure		
Closed	103 lbs. @ 1.62 in.	136.5 lbs. @ 1.83 in.
Open	184 lbs. @ 1.31 in.	210 lbs. @ 1.43 in.
Crankshaft journal diameter		
Mains	2.500 in.	2.625 in.
Connection rods	2.125 in.	2.375 in.
Ignition		
Type	Double breaker	Single breaker
Point gap	.014—.019 in.	.014—.019 in.
Dwell	28°—32°	28°—32°
Timing	5° BTC (4-spd.)	12.5° BTC
	10° BTC (Auto)	
Spark plug type	Champion N-14Y	Champion J-13Y
Gap	.035 in.	.035 in.
Firing order	1-8-4-3-6-5-7-2	1-8-4-3-6-5-7-2

For additional features of these engines, see page 21.

IT'S A BIRD! It's a plane! It's a Super-fish! For the first time in its very short career the Barracuda can truly be called a Supercar. In stock form it has image written all over it, and if the right boxes are checked, you could get matching muscle under the hood.

The original compact sporty fastback, which suffered since 1964½ from *half-fast* styling (fastback body with Valiant front end) and limp merchandising, was completely restyled and repowered for 1967. The aerodynamic styling came straight from the "land of the leaning tower" and the 383-cube power option put it in contention for honors in the Supercar Sweepstakes.

For the first time members of the Supercar Set could order the Barracuda with a 383-cube four-barrel engine which had been used with great success in the middleweight Mopars. A reasonable amount of rear end cogs, choice of either the "dial-a-win" three-speed or "do-it-yourself" four-speed, disc brakes and a full complement of suspension parts backed up the new super-power option.

Although totally new, the sleek 1967 model retained the basic lines which made the previous models distinctive. The '67 Barracuda was still a two-door full fastback hardtop with a large rear window. The characteristic rear window, however, does not wrap into the body sides as on previous models. Stylists under the direction of Elwood Engel chose sculptured metal over chrome or-namentation to emphasize the new front and rear fenders, side panels and the overall flowing lines. Leading edges of the front fenders protrude beyond the grille and the tops of the fenders. They form peak lines which are carried back the full length of the car, rising gradually in the area above the rear wheels. The sleek aerodynamic lines are further enhanced by the addition of curved glass side windows.

The original weak link in the car's design, the grille area, was strengthened for 1967. Design of the grille is new, for Plymouth at least, although it is divided in the center to retain the head-on identity established by earlier models. European-style road-type parking lights are located in the continental grille. The pancaked hood is also new as are the scoop-type trim panels.

From the rear the new Barracuda also comes on like a European GT machine. The polished aluminum snap-open gas filler looks like it was pirated from a racing machine. The plano-concave rear end treatment takes on the appearance of a semi-spoiler and works well with the tailored tail blinkers.

Horsepower & Torque Curves—273 V-8

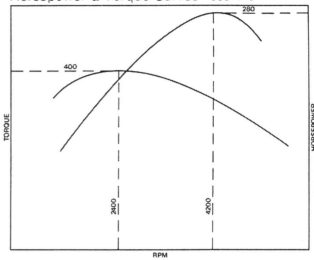

Horsepower & Torque Curves—383 V-8

POWER TRAIN COMBINATIONS:

Engine	Transmission	Standard axle		Sure-Grip		
		Axle Ratio				
		2.93	3.23	3.23	3.55	3.91
273	4-speed		std.	std.	opt.	opt.
	Automatic	opt.	std.	std.	opt.	opt.
383	4-speed		std.	std.		
	Automatic		std.	std.		

Ratios of 3.73 and 4.56 are also available on a dealer-installed basis.

AXLES AND TRANSMISSIONS:

273 4-speed: Fully synchronized, with bronze alloy shift forks. Torque-lock feature prevents gears from slipping out of mesh under deceleration or overrun. Ratios are 2.66, 1.91, 1.39 and 1.00. Axle ring gear diameter with this unit is 8.75 in.

383 4-speed: Same as above.

273 Automatic: High-upshift type; compatible with the high-rpm torque characteristics of the 273. Torque converter diameter is 10.75 in. Ratios are 2.45, 1.45 and 1.00. Manually shiftable. Standard axle ring gear diameter is 7.25 in. Diameter with Sure-Grip is 8.75 in. Maximum stall ratio is 2.2:1.

383 Automatic: Similar to that of the 273; but uses an 11.75 in. dia. torque converter. Upshift speeds are

This Formula S 383 Barracuda sports a 440-cube air cleaner, yet is stock original right down to the seldom-seen "Coke-bottle" hubcaps. Chrysler-Plymouth sold 30,110 fastback models in 1967.

The unique utility-plus feature of the Barracuda was retained and refined for 1967. Because of the design of the deck lid it's easier to get into the seven-foot-long cargo area. The folding rear seat is fitted with a floor catch which eliminated the noise-making old-style catch bar. A new bench-type front seat with a folding arm rest was standard with newly-styled buckets being optional at extra cost. The three-gauge instrument cluster was also new for 1967 and features a standard vacuum gauge and an optional tach. In-terior options include a wood-grained instrument panel and door trim accents and brightly-trimmed pedals.

The 1967 model is lower, longer and wider than its predecessor. Wheelbase checks out at 108 inches (two inches longer) and the overall length checks out at 193 inches (nearly five inches longer). Heavier-duty 14-inch wheels are standard regardless of engine-suspension choices.

Performance of the 383 Barracuda is very similar to that of a 440-cube GTX with basic equipment. The 383 engine carries a 280-hp rating and pumps out 400 foot pounds of torque at 2,400 rpm. Compression is 10.1-to-1.

Safetywise the hot Formula S Barracuda rates pretty high with its energy-absorbing steering column which telescopes at a controlled rate in the case of a collision and dual master cylinder braking system. Each system has its own master cylinder, and a warning light on the dash keeps the driver informed if there is a loss of pressure in the system.

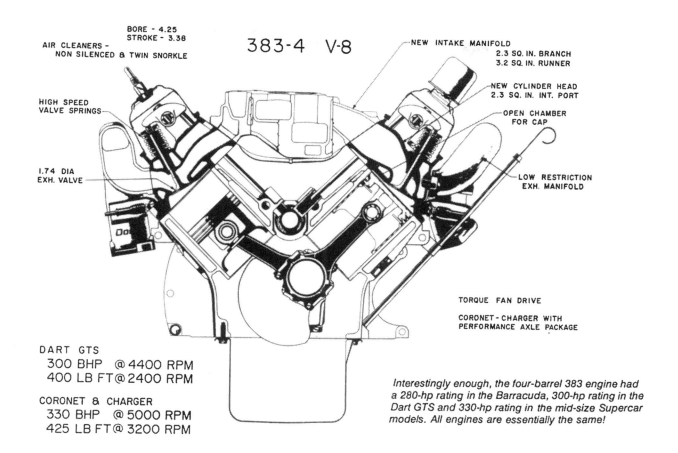

383-4 V-8

BORE - 4.25
STROKE - 3.38

AIR CLEANERS - NON SILENCED & TWIN SNORKLE

HIGH SPEED VALVE SPRINGS

1.74 DIA EXH. VALVE

NEW INTAKE MANIFOLD
2.3 SQ. IN. BRANCH
3.2 SQ. IN. RUNNER

NEW CYLINDER HEAD
2.3 SQ. IN. INT. PORT

OPEN CHAMBER FOR CAP

LOW RESTRICTION EXH. MANIFOLD

TORQUE FAN DRIVE

CORONET - CHARGER WITH PERFORMANCE AXLE PACKAGE

DART GTS
300 BHP @ 4400 RPM
400 LB FT @ 2400 RPM

CORONET & CHARGER
330 BHP @ 5000 RPM
425 LB FT @ 3200 RPM

Interestingly enough, the four-barrel 383 engine had a 280-hp rating in the Barracuda, 300-hp rating in the Dart GTS and 330-hp rating in the mid-size Supercar models. All engines are essentially the same!

compatible with the great bottom-end torque of the 383. Axle ring gear diameter is 8.75 in. Maximum stall ratio is 2.0:1. Manually shiftable. Console required.

MPH PER 1000RPM IN HIGH GEAR:

Tires:	Axle ratios:	2.93	3.23	3.55	3.91
D 70 x 14 Wide Oval			24.82	22.52	20.49	18.60

SUSPENSION:
Front: Heavy-duty torsion bars and ball-joints. Rate at wheel, 103 lbs. per in. Uses 0.88 in. dia. link-type front stabilizer bar.

Rear: Semi-elliptical, asymmetrical, leaf-type springs of chromium-alloy steel. Rate at wheel 136 lbs. per in.

Shock absorbers: Firm-Ride Oriflow type, with 1 in. dia. pistons.

STEERING:
Recirculating ball type. Standard ratio is 24.0:1 (5.3 turns, lock to lock). Fast-ratio steering option reduces this to 16.0:1 (3.6 turns, lock to lock). Power steering ratio is 15.7:1 (3.5 turns, lock to lock).

TURNING DIAMETER:
Curb to curb: Outside, front, 38.0 ft.   Inside rear, 22.5 ft.
Wall to wall: Outside, front, 40.0 ft.   Inside rear, 21.9 ft.

BRAKES:
Drum-type
Front: 10 in. x 2.25 in. cast iron. Self-adjusting.
Rear: 10 in. x 1.75 in. cast iron. Self-adjusting.
Total lining area: 156.2 sq. in.
Total swept area: 251.3 sq. in.

Disc (required with 383 V-8)
Front only: 10.79 in. diameter. Internally vented. Four pistons per caliper. Self-adjusting.
Total lining area: 102.3 sq. in.
Total swept area (with 10 in. rear drums): 314.7 sq. in.

WHEELS AND TIRES:
Wheel size and type: 5.5J x 14 in. Safety Rim.
Tire size and type: D70 x 14 in. Red Streak Wide Oval.
Recommended pressures (cold):

Front: 28 psi.
Rear: 30 psi.

DIMENSIONS:
Wheelbase	108.0 in.
Track, front	58.1 in.
Track, rear	56.3 in.
Length, overall	192.8 in.
Width, overall	71.6 in.
Height, overall	52.9 in.

Shipping weight	With 273	With 383
Hardtop	2868 lbs.	3120 lbs.
Fastback	2953 lbs.	3205 lbs.
Convertible	2973 lbs.	3225 lbs.

CAPACITIES:
Fuel tank	18 gals.
Cooling system	
273	18 qts.
383	17 qts.
Oil pan	5 qts. with filter
Transmission	
4-speed	8 pts.
273 Automatic	18.5 pts.

'Cuda Options.

Items of particular interest to you are shown on the left; others are listed below. Again, we've given you the order code for each one, in order to expedite matters.

1. #408: Our Sure-Grip differential. The standard ratio with Formula S is 3.23 to 1. Optional ratios are 3.55 and 3.91. Ring gear diameter is 7½ in., 8¼ in. or 8¾ in., depending on engine transmission combinations.
2. #367: The Formula S Package. Described in detail on page 11.
3. #294: Sport stripes. Fighting trim, if you like.
4. #583: Bolt-on type wheel covers.

5. #577: Tachometer. We mount it in the dash, right beside the speedo.
6. #479: Front disc brakes. Internally finned; four pistons per caliper; 10-in. diameter. Increase total swept area to 314.7 sq. in.

#360: Decor group. Contains pedal dress-up; 150 mph speedometer; simulated wood interior trim; rear armrests with ashtrays.

#411: Air conditioning. (NA with 383 V-8)

#621: 70 amp. battery.

#591: 46 amp. alternator.

#486: Console. (W. bucket seats only)

#418: Rear window defroster.

#521: Tinted glass—all windows.

The Barracuda achieved full Supercar status in 1967 with the addition of the 383-inch four-barrel engine as available in the mid-size models. With an extra 100 pounds over the front end, handling suffered as compared with 273-inch Formula S model.

The '67 Barracuda is longer, lower and wider than the previous model and has a two-inch-longer wheelbase at 108 inches. The fastback accounted for a larger portion of Barracuda production than the hardtop coupe which totaled 28,196 units.

#533: Headrests.

#544: Sill molding.

#451: Power brakes.

#456: Power steering. (NA with 383 V-8)

#568: Shoulder belts.

#579: Undercoating with underhood pad.

#574: Vacuum gauge. (in place of tach)

#708: Buffed metallic paint.

#588: Wheelhousing liners.

#628: Fast-steering ratio.

#589: Variable-speed windshield wipers.

For additional options, see your dealer.

THE SUPER CHARGER

The "Super Charger," Mr. Norm's newest entry into the fast and funny world of match racing, is based on a special tube chassis complete with a full roll cage. The one piece fiberglass Dodge Charger body is beautifully finished in a bright red with silver leaf trim. Power is developed by a blown 426 cu. in. fuel burning Dodge Hemi. Designed to exceed 180 mph, Gary Dyer has driven the 1920 lb. machine 175 mph on its first full power test runs.

1968—THE WIN-YOU-OVER BEAT GOES ON!

A new mid-displacement V-8 makes the Barracuda even more desirable

Minor grille trim changes set the '68 Barracuda off from the '67 model. Fastback models accounted for 22,575 units sold in the 1968 model year. Formula S package continues as the best handling Ponycar on the market.

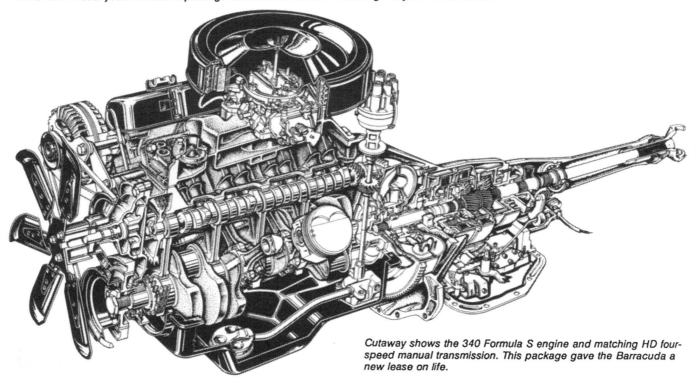

Cutaway shows the 340 Formula S engine and matching HD four-speed manual transmission. This package gave the Barracuda a new lease on life.

New for 1968 was limited-production Dodge Charger 500, built only to allow use of sleek
fastback rear window in NASCAR cars. Ford had Talladega; Dodge had Charger 500. This one,
like the racers, is Hemi-powered. Only 500 model had streamlined backlight treatment.

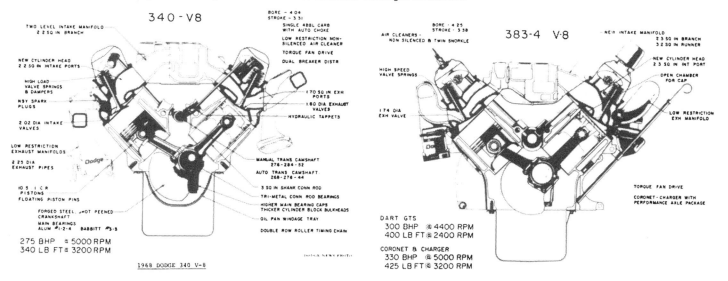

1968 HIGH-PERFORMANCE ENGINES

CUBIC INCHES	BORE	STROKE	HORSEPOWER	TORQUE	COMPRESSION	INDUCTION
340	4.040	3.310	275 @ 5000	340 @ 3200	10.50	FOUR-BARREL
383	4.250	3.380	300 @ 4400	400 @ 2400	10.00	FOUR-BARREL
383	4.250	3.380	350 @ 5000	425 @ 3200	10.00	FOUR-BARREL
383	4.250	3.380	335 @ 5200	425 @ 3400	10.00	FOUR-BARREL
426	4.250	3.750	425 @ 5000	490 @ 4000	10.25	DUAL-QUAD
440	4.320	3.750	350 @ 4400	480 @ 2800	10.10	FOUR-BARREL
440	4.320	3.750	375 @ 4600	480 @ 3200	10.10	FOUR-BARREL

Specifications:

Engines:	Standard 6	Standard V-8	Formula S 340 V-8	Formula S 383 V-8
Bhp @ rpm	145 @ 4000	230 @ 4400	275 @ 5000	300 @ 4200
Torque, lbs.-ft.	215 @ 2400	340 @ 2400	340 @ 3200	400 @ 2400
Bore, in.	3.40	3.91	4.04	4.25
Stroke, in.	4.125	3.31	3.31	3.38
Displacement, cu. in.	225	318	340	383
Compression ratio	8.4:1	9.2:1	10.5:1	10.0:1
Minimum allowable combustion chamber volume, cc.	53.8	60.6	63.3	79.5
Deck Height, in.	—.141 Min.	+.022 Max.	+.045 Max.	+.020 Max.
Carburetion	1-bbl Holley	2-bbl Ball & Ball	4-bbl Carter	4-bbl Carter
Throttle Bore, in.	1.69	1.44	P:1.44 S:1.69	P:1.44 S:1.69

Camshaft duration, deg.			Man. trans. / Auto. trans.	
Intake	240	240	276 / 268	256
Exhaust	236	248	284 / 276	260
Overlap	16	20	52 / 44	32
Camshaft Lift @ Zero Lash				
Intake	.394	.372	.445 / .430	.425
Exhaust	.390	.400	.455 / .445	.437
Valve Diameter				
Intake	1.62	1.78	2.02	2.08
Exhaust	1.36	1.50	1.60	1.74
Tappet Clearance				
Intake	.010 Hot	Hydraulic	Hydraulic	Hydraulic
Exhaust	.020 Hot	Hydraulic	Hydraulic	Hydraulic
Max. Valve Spring Pressure, lbs. (closed/open)				
Intake	74/154	103/142	114/245	128/240
Exhaust	74/154	103/142	114/245	128/240
Max. Spark Advance, deg.				
Manual	41.4	56.5	50.0	62
Automatic	41.5	59.0	50.0	62
Exhaust System	Single	Single	Low restriction dual	Low restriction dual

Aluminum steel strut elliptically-turned tin plated pistons. Low restriction air cleaner on 4-bbl. engines. Crankshaft: 318 is cast ductile iron, 225, 340, and 383 are forged steel. Full flow oil filter.

POWER TRAINS:

Engine:	Transmission:	Ratio 2.76	3.23	3.55	2.76	3.23	3.55	3.91
					(Sure-Grip)			
225 cu. in. 6-cylinder	3 speed manual		std.	opt.		std.		
	Automatic	std.	opt.	opt.	std.	opt.		
318 cu. in. 8-cylinder, 2-bbl.	3 speed manual		std.*			std.*		
	4 speed manual		std.*			std.*	opt.*	opt.*
	Automatic	std.	opt.*			opt.*		
340 cu. in. 8-cylinder, 4-bbl.	4 speed manual		std.*			std.*	rec.*	opt.*
	Automatic		std.*			std.*		opt.*
383 cu. in. 8-cylinder, 4-bbl.	4 speed manual		std.*			std.*	opt.*	opt.*
	Automatic		std.			std.*	opt.*	

*8.75 Ring Gear Dia. Others 7.25.

TRANSMISSIONS: A 3-speed manual transmission with column mounted lever is standard (but not available with Formula S).
The synchromesh 4-speed is extra cost for all V-8s and may be mounted on the floor or in the optional console. Ratios are 2.66:1, 1.91:1, 1.39:1, and 1.00:1.
The famous TorqueFlite automatic transmission is extra cost with all engines. It mounts on the column or console. With ratios of 2.45:1, 1.45:1 and 1.00:1. (It is manually-shiftable to boot.) The Sure-Grip differential puts all the power to the ground. Extra cost.

With Barracuda, safety is built in, not added on • Standard safety features • Improved fuel tank retention • Vehicle side marker lights • Folding seat back-latches • Instrument panel padding (full upper and lower) • Recessed instrument panel knobs and switches • Breakaway instrument panel ashtrays • Energy-absorbing front seat back tops • Safety armrests • Heavy laminate windshield glass • Non-override inside door locks • Soft, window crank knobs • Painted windshield garnish moldings (anti-glare) • Left outside rearview mirror • Energy-absorbing steering column • Dual brake system and warning light • Emergency flashers • Swing-away inside prismatic day/night mirror • Seat belts, 2 front, 2 rear • Padded sun visors • 2-speed windshield wipers with washers • Dull-finish windshield wiper arms and blades, horn ring, steering wheel hub, inside rearview mirror frame and bracket, turn signal and gear shift levers • Safety-Action inside door handles • Safety-Rim wheels • And the Plymouth win-you-over beat goes on.

DIMENSIONS: (In inches)

Body Style:	Fastback	Hardtop	Convertible
Wheelbase	108.0	108.0	108.0
Overall length	192.8	192.8	192.8
Overall width	71.6	71.6	71.6
Overall height*			
6-cylinder	52.8	52.6	53.2
V-8	52.8	52.7	53.2
Track, front wheels	57.4	57.4	57.4
Track, rear wheels	55.6	55.6	55.6

*Height dimensions are based on a five passenger load.

STANDARD SUSPENSION:

Engines:	Standard 6	Standard V-8	Formula S 340	Formula S 383
Front—Torsion bars. Rate at wheel, lbs./in.	85	100	103	115
Rear—2½ in. outboard mounted asymmetrical leaf springs. Rate at wheel, lbs./in.	108	132	132	150
Anti-Sway bar, diameter, in.	none	none	.88	.94
Shock Absorbers	Oriflow	Oriflow	Oriflow Firm-Ride	Oriflow Firm-Ride

ELECTRICAL: A 12 volt, 48 amp/hrs. (59 amp/hrs. with 383) battery produces a very hot spark when charged by a 37 amp alternator. Optional (and hotter yet) is Chrysler Corporation's 46 amp alternator. (If you buy air conditioning, you get one free.)

STEERING: Recirculating ball bearing steering gear. Standard ratio is 24.0:1 with 5.3 turns lock to lock. Fast manual steering (not recommended with 383 V-8) is 16.0:1, 3.6 turns lock to lock. Power steering is 15.7:1, 3.5 turns lock to lock.

TURNING DIAMETER: (In feet)

Curb to curb.................Outside Front 38.0		Inside Rear 22.5
Wall to wall..................Outside Front 40.8		Inside Rear 21.9

BRAKES:

Drum type....6-cylinder engine models have 9 in. diameter brakes with total lining area of 153.5 sq. in., swept area of 254.5 sq. in.
V-8 engine models have 10 in. diameter brakes with total lining area of 156.2 sq. in., swept area of 251.3 sq. in.
Disc brakes (front)....6-cylinder and V-8 both have 102.3 sq. in. total lining area, swept area of 314.7 sq. in. Rear brake is 10 in. diameter drum type.

CAPACITIES:

Fuel tank .... 18 gals.	
Engine crankcase requirement .... 4 qts.	
Coolant (with heater)	
6-cylinder engine (standard) .... 13 qts.	
318 cu. in. V-8 (standard) .... 18 qts.	
340 cu. in. V-8 Commando (optional) .... 18 qts.	
383 cu. in. V-8 Super Commando (optional) .... 17 qts.	

MPH PER 1000 RPM IN HIGH GEAR:

Tires	Axle ratios: 2.76	3.23	3.55	3.91
E 70 x 14 (optional)	27.04	23.10	21.02	19.08
D 70 x 14	26.35	22.52	20.49	18.60
6.95 x 14 (standard)	26.85	22.69	20.65	18.75

(A word for you buffs. When you go the 'Cuda route, you can join the **National Barracuda Owners Club.** Write them at Box 478, Detroit, Michigan for the address of your local Chapter.)

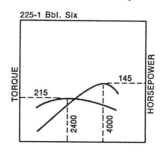

225-1 Bbl. Six

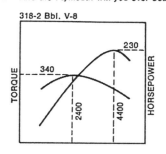

318-2 Bbl. V-8

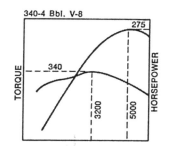

340-4 Bbl. V-8

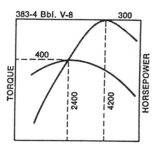

383-4 Bbl. V-8

Formula S

Take any Barracuda. Add the Formula S performance package. Call it King 'Cuda.

The Formula S is an optional performance package available on any model Barracuda. Fastback. Hardtop. Convertible. It comes in two winning ways—340-S and the super 383-S. Either way, Formula S makes driving a new experience. On city streets, or the open highway—this is where it's at.

The 340-S includes the brand-new 340 Commando V-8—the most exciting thing to happen to iron in years. It's loaded with a special cam, 4-bbl. carburetion, a dual breaker distributor and a low restriction dual exhaust. Pick up those good vibrations.

Basic hardtop coupe could be Formula-S-equipped, just like the fastback and convertible. Hardtop sales hit 19,997 units in 1968 model year. Convertible sales dropped almost in half for 1968, totaling 2,840 units.

Author Schorr testing a pre-production Formula S Barracuda at Chelsea during performance evaluation by factory engineers prior to setting up factory-sponsored racing programs for 1968.

Plymouth made it possible for the enthusiast to get real supercar power and performance for $500 to $1,000 less than competitive GM products.

ROAD RUNNER, A SUPERCAR FOR THE MASSES!

Plymouth packs status and power into its intermediate and ends up with a Supercar with a budget price tag

FOR 1968 Plymouth's Road Runner is available in one body style only—a two-door coupe. This keeps initial cost down and gives you the lightest body style in the line. Less weight means more go. Actually, the body style is the same as the Belvedere I but with different trim. It is handsome in a spartan kind of way. Side glass is frameless and the rear quarter windows flip out rather than roll down. The car looks lean and muscular. And it is.

Helping the power image is the special hood that is standard on both the Road Runner and GTX. It features twin side-facing air scoops—simulated, that border a raised section. Mounted in the hood scoops are the image numbers or words—either "383" or "Hemi." Chrome is used minimally on the body.

The interior is, again, outfitted functionally—almost spartan—to keep costs down. Bench seats are standard. You can't even get buckets as an option. If a manual transmission is fitted, a floor shift is optional. If you order an automatic, the level is column-mounted. Seats are upholstered in all-vinyl fabric and are available in three color combinations—two-tone blue, parchment and tan, and silver and black.

Under the skin is where the story really gets interesting. Suspension on the Road Runner is the same as you get on the GTX 440. That means heavy-duty springs, shocks, torsion bars, anti-sway bar and balljoints. It's the same suspension that came standard on Street Hemis last year and the same suspension that was standard on Super/Stocks a few years ago. Rear springs are 2.5-inches wide and come with six leaves.

Wide 5.5X14 wheels mount red streak F70-14s. If you order optional disc brakes, then F70-15 wide oval tires are fitted on 6.X15 wheels.

Brakes are the best. Standard are massive drum brakes that are fitted to big Chryslers and Imperials. Up front are 11X3 drums while 11X2½-inch drums are fitted to the rear.

Standard engine in the Road Runner is a 383 that is rated 335 horsepower at 5,200 rpm and 425 foot/pounds of torque at 3,400 rpm. The standard Plymouth 383 is rated 325 horsepower. After adding the 440 cylinder heads with bigger exhaust valves, a crankcase windage tray, intake manifold, exhaust manifolds and camshaft, Plymouth engineers came up with some extra power. In side-by-side drag races, the Road Runner with the 383 ran with a 440 GTX right through

Pre-production Road Runner with 383 engine during drag strip tests at the Chelsea Proving Grounds. Road wheels add a lot to this spartan stormer.

It didn't take long for Sox & Martin to get into the Road Runner and they made headlines with their 426 Hemi drag car. In 1969 they ran one with a Six-Pack 440 motor.

the quarter mile. And the 440 is rated 375 horsepower!

The cam in the Road Runner has 268 degrees intake duration and 284 degrees exhaust duration. Lift is .450-inch on intake and .465-inch for the exhausts. Intake valves are 2.08 inches. Exhaust valves are 1.74 inches. The new windage tray keeps oil right around the pick-up, and keeps the oil and air separated in the crankcase.

Standard transmission for the Road Runner is Chrysler's A-833 heavy-duty four-speed. Ring gear diameter is the standard 8.75 inches with the 383 engine. If the optional 426 Hemi is ordered with four-speed, the ultra-duty Dana rear axle assembly with 9.75-inch ring gear is fitted. Standard axle ratio is 3.23 with the manual trans.

Let's start right with performance options. There is only one engine option for the Road Runner—the 426 Street Hemi. It's option code 73 and costs $564 over the standard engine. The Street Hemi is improved this year. It also gets the new windage tray along with a new cam and other detail improvements. The new cam packs a full 284 degrees duration for both intakes and exhausts. The overlap is 60 degrees. This replaces the 276-degree stick. Everything else is the same, including the dual four-barrel carburetion.

There is only one option—the heavy duty Torqueflite automatic. It's option code 395 and costs approximately $40 extra in the Road Runner where the four-speed is standard. When you order the Torqueflite, you get the shift lever column-mounted.

You can order optional brakes. If the 11X3 drums aren't enough for you, check out option code 479, front disc brakes. They cost $69 extra, but are well worth it. If you order the discs, then you must order option code 451, power brakes, at $41.75. The power assist cuts braking effort up to one-third. And with the discs, they're an absolute necessity. If you order the front discs, you get 15-inch wheels and tires (F70-15) as part of the package.

There are a few rear axle assemblies.

Coming or going, the Road Runner was right for the times and an instant hit with the street freaks.

First, you can order the Sure-Grip limited-slip differential. It's option code 408 and costs $37.60. Then you can order the heavy-duty rear axle assembly that includes the 9.75-inch ring gear Dana center with Sure Grip. This is the same rear axle assembly you get as part of the Street Hemi package with the four-speed. It's option code 408-HD and costs $138.90. This is the strongest rear axle assembly in the industry.

A number of rear axle ratios are available at no extra cost. They are 2.76, 2.94, 3.23 and 3.55.

You can order a package especially tailored for the performance enthusiast. Or you can order any of the items separately. The package consists of a 3.55 rear axle ratio, Sure Grip (standard duty) differential, a heavy-duty radiator and fan shroud and a viscous fan drive.

The last option that you've just got to have is the optional tachometer, option code 577. It costs $48 and mounts in the dash in place of the clock. Who needs a clock, anyway?

THE
JUNIOR SUPERCAR
REBELLION

The trend is to ultra-efficient, small-displacement engines
and few can hold a candle to the new 340-inch Wedge

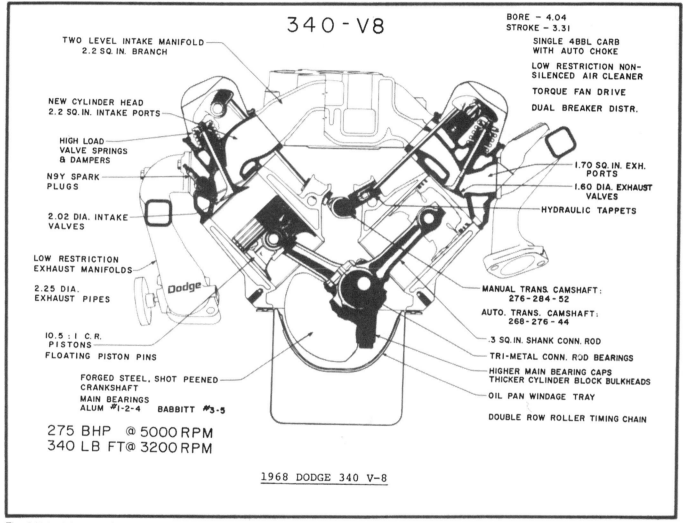

340 - V8

BORE – 4.04
STROKE – 3.31

TWO LEVEL INTAKE MANIFOLD
2.2 SQ. IN. BRANCH

NEW CYLINDER HEAD
2.2 SQ. IN. INTAKE PORTS

HIGH LOAD
VALVE SPRINGS
& DAMPERS

N9Y SPARK
PLUGS

2.02 DIA. INTAKE
VALVES

LOW RESTRICTION
EXHAUST MANIFOLDS

2.25 DIA.
EXHAUST PIPES

10.5 : 1 C.R.
PISTONS
FLOATING PISTON PINS

FORGED STEEL, SHOT PEENED
CRANKSHAFT
MAIN BEARINGS
ALUM #1-2-4   BABBITT #3-5

275 BHP @ 5000 RPM
340 LB FT @ 3200 RPM

SINGLE 4BBL CARB
WITH AUTO CHOKE

LOW RESTRICTION NON-
SILENCED AIR CLEANER

TORQUE FAN DRIVE

DUAL BREAKER DISTR.

1.70 SQ. IN. EXH.
PORTS
1.60 DIA. EXHAUST
VALVES
HYDRAULIC TAPPETS

MANUAL TRANS. CAMSHAFT:
276-284-52

AUTO. TRANS. CAMSHAFT:
268-276-44

.3 SQ. IN. SHANK CONN. ROD

TRI-METAL CONN. ROD BEARINGS

HIGHER MAIN BEARING CAPS
THICKER CYLINDER BLOCK BULKHEADS

OIL PAN WINDAGE TRAY

DOUBLE ROW ROLLER TIMING CHAIN

1968 DODGE 340 V-8

*The 340-inch high-performance engine was Chrysler's first serious attempt to
unseat the small-block Chevy and Ford engines from their top dog positions.*

THE MOPAR crew has a "mini-motor" that should cause a hassle on the street and strip. It's the 340-cube *Scat Pack* motor available in the Dart and Barracuda lines. Before going any farther we would like to mention that by going the super-efficient small-cube route, such powered cars fall out of the super premium insurance brackets which make it extremely difficult for the youth market to

cut it financially. And, a lower option price also helps sales.

The 340-cube high-performance engine is standard equipment in the GTS Dart and is probably the most sensible power package for this car. It's a light, responsive machine, capable, when properly tuned, of negotiating the quarter-mile in the high 14s with trap speeds ranging from 90 to 98 mph. When

properly prepared with headers, ignition and ultimate gearing, the GTS is good for high-13—low 14-second quarters with speeds over the century mark.

To get the 340 cubes, Mopar engineers resorted to a 3.31-inch stroke—4.04-inch bore configuration. Compression is a healthy, yet easy to nourish, 10.5-to-1 and horsepower checks out at 275 at 5,000 rpm with max torque coming in (340 foot pounds) at 3,200 rpm. Also standard with the 340 mill is a matching heavy-duty suspension and powertrain, making the GTS Dart one of the best balanced of the junior supercars. All that's missing is a fresh air intake package.

LOWER ENGINE ASSEMBLY

The comparatively light weight of the new 340 engine, 539 pounds (dry), can be attributed in great part to the progressive foundry techniques used in casting its block. These involve furan cores which provide greater dimensional accuracy, and the extra effort of gauging the position of the cores when they are assembled in the mold to make certain they are properly aligned before casting begins. This great care in the casting operation allows engineers to call for 340 CID block castings with a minimum cylinder wall thickness of 0.10-inch. The barrel slab, water jacket, tappet chamber, and crankcase cores are furan.

The 340 crankshaft is of drop-forged steel. Bob-weights weighing 2306.6 grams are used to balance the piston assemblies. The crankshaft, at 25 inches, is the same length as the 273/318 shafts.

The introduction and successful application of aluminum-tin alloy main bearings in the 340 V-8 may start a trend. The aluminum is alloyed with about 20 percent tin and 1 percent copper, applied to a steel back. Engineers specify it for the #1, #2, and #4 main bearing shells where its superior load carrying capacity (over twice that of babbitt) and resistance to fatigue at higher temperatures are most needed.

The aluminum-tin alloy has several other important qualities: 1) although not as soft as babbitt, it still is soft enough to allow dirt and metal particles to become imbedded in it, but not permanently, diminishing any effect these particles might have on crankshaft bearing surface; and 2) it has a very high resistance to corrosion.

The #3 and #5 main bearings are made of conventional leadbase babbitt on steel.

Like the 426 Hemi-engine, the 340 is equipped with a 68-link, double-roller timing chain whose greater strength and durability are particularly suited to high engine speeds. Chain width is 0.87 inches. This type of chain is preferable whenever an increased strength-to-weight ratio is desirable.

To increase net horsepower at higher engine speeds, the 340 is fitted with the windage tray—a large sheet metal baffle that is placed between the oil pan and the crankshaft. Its purpose is to prevent the crankshaft from whipping up a dense oil mist when it is rotating at high speeds, and sucking that mist into its rotating path where the increased friction would lower net horsepower. Crankcase capacity is four quarts.

Pre-production Barracuda with unique hood treatment was used to showcase the four-barrel 340 HP engine in 1969 by Plymouth prior to the new model introductions.

When installed in late-model Barracuda, the 340 four-barrel got a fresh air shaker-style air cleaner hood scoop just like its big-brother Hemi.

Pistons are made of aluminum alloy, tin-plated. They have flat tops notched in two places to give the valve heads extra clearance (which also means there are right- and left-hand pistons). Two opposing steel struts are cast into the skirts for control of thermal expansion. Piston weight is 719 grams.

Ring lineup consists of two compression rings, 0.078-inch wide, and a three-piece oil ring made up of two chrome-plated rails and a stainless-steel expander spacer. The top compression ring is a radius face twist design, Molybenum-filled for better scuff and wear resistance. The second compression ring has a reverse twist, and tapered face, and is lubrite-coated.

Connecting rods are new forgings, (larger and heavier than the 273 and 318 CID components especially across the big ends, where the extra strength is needed under the high-speed loadings of the piston assembly. A floating pin, held in place by spring-steel lock rings, connects the rod to the piston.

UPPER ENGINE ASSEMBLY

The new 340 cylinder head looks similar to the 318 engine, but it has larger intake and exhaust ports. Intake port area is 2.2 square inches, with 1.70 square inches provided for the exhaust ports. Combustion chambers are of modified wedge-shape with an open "squish" area purposely designed to reduce unburned hydrocarbons.

The 340 has two different camshafts—one for use with manual transmissions, the other with automatic. This is done to maximize engine performance while still maintaining the low emissions and acceptable quality of idle demanded of both engine-transmission combinations.

The manual transmission camshaft has an intake valve duration of 276 degrees with a lift of .445-inch lift at zero lash, an exhaust valve duration of 284 degrees with a .455-inch lift at zero lash, and 52 degrees of valve overlap.

The automatic transmission camshaft has an intake valve duration of 268 degrees with a .430-inch lift at zero lash, an exhaust valve duration of 276 degrees plus .445-inch lift and 44 degrees overlap.

Hydraulic tappets and solid, 0.28-inch diameter steel push rods drive the valves. Rocker arms are one-piece steel stampings (common with those of the 318 engine) and, they are arranged in pairs so that a small shoulder on one arm is butted against a similar shoulder on the other to provide proper spacing between them automatically.

High load springs with surge dampers help prevent valve float at higher engine

INDIANAPOLIS RACE

Drag racers like Hamburger and Coletti Plymouth firmly established the 340 engine as a very serious small-displacement powerplant. Lower class Super/Stock ranks were dominated by 340 cars and Hamburger went on to market a full line of 340 speed equipment.

speeds; the same springs are used for both intake and exhaust valves. Their load specifications are 96 pounds at 1.65-inch height with the valves closed, and 242 pounds at 1.21 inches with the valves open.

Intake valves are 4.99 inches long and have an over-all head diameter of 2.02 inches, almost 20 percent greater than those used in the 273-318 engines. Exhaust valves are 5.00 inches long and have a 1.60-inch head diameter.

A new, cast-iron double-level intake manifold has intake ports arranged in adjacent pairs. Branches are 2.2-square inches of basic area versus 1.63 for the 318 and 1.60 for the 273/V-8. Basic runner area also is made up of a generous 2.9-square inches for good breathing characteristics.

To allow the 340 engine to fit comveniently within the Dart engine compartment, the left exhaust manifold is a high runner that extends back to the rear of the engine before dipping down quickly to meet the exhaust pipe, thus clearing the steering gear.

The right exhaust manifold is the conventional. three-branch, low-runner type. Mating flanges between the exhaust manifold outlets and the exhaust pipes are flat instead of ball joint, a construction which also takes up less room.

An important feature is a heat control valve at the right exhaust manifold outlet. Both ends of the valve shaft and its bushings are protected from the hot, escaping exhaust gasses whose deposits could cause the valve to stick. A new design, spring-type inertia weight and return spring help the heat valve operate quieter and with greater efficiency.

The fuel system operates through a low-restriction, unsilenced air cleaner and high-flow, single four-barrel Carter carburetor with air valve controlled secondary barrels. This carburetor is specially calibrated for the lean mixtures used in the Cleaner Air System. In fact, the 340 carburetor incorporates a number of features introduced primarily for exhaust emission control. Primary bore diameters are 1.44 inches each, while secondary barrels measure out at 1.69 inches. The secondaries are straight bores without venturis.

DOUBLE BREAKER DISTRIBUTOR

The ignition system features a double-breaker distributor for smooth performance and full power output at high-speed operation. It is the same type distributor as used in other Dodge high-performance engines.

Basic ignition timing with the manual transmission is set at TDC; with automatic transmission, at five degrees BTC. Spark plugs are Champion N9Ys, and the battery is a conventional 48-ampere-hours capacity unit.

A torque-limiting fan drive limits power loss from the fan at high speeds. Essentially a fluid coupling connecting the fan to its driving element—the water pump shaft, it is made up of two plates set face-to-face in a housing filled with high viscosity silicone oil.

As the water pump shaft revolves, it turns the first plate, which transfers torque to the second plate via the silicone oil, turning the fan to which the second plate is connected. As engine speed increases, fan speed begins to lag further and further behind the speed of the water pump shaft until at about 2,200 rpm, it levels off and there is no more increase in speed.

The importance of the torque-limiting fan is that fan horsepower at high rpm is reduced drastically, with the following advantages to the vehicle:

    a. faster acceleration,
    b. higher top speed,
    c. greater fuel economy,
    d. a marked reduction in fan noise.

The torque type fan drive also enables the 340 to be equipped with a larger fan for better low-speed cooling.

The little Mopar also makes for a dynamite street rod engine, especially when fitted with four Weber carbs and mounted in a lightweight tube-chassic T-bucket.

1968 SUPER/STOCK PROGRAM

Chrysler Corporation made an unprecedented move to corner a piece of the Super/Stock action by contracting with Hurst Performance to build a limited-number of Hemi-powered Dodge Darts and Hemi Cudas for sale to racers. These were not street cars and were built on Hurst's small assembly line in Michigan. Cars were delivered in "white" to be finished by the purchasers. They proceded to dominate NHRA's Super/Stock class.

SUPERCARS

DODGE STYLE

CHARGER R/T · CORONET

- High Performance 440 cu. in., 375 hp, 4-bbl Wedge engine is standard equipment. Stage II 426 cu. in., 425 hp, dual 4-bbl Street Hemi is the only engine option. Standard or economy engines *not available.*
- High-upshift, competition-type Torqueflite automatic or heavy duty 4-speed (with mandatory axle package), standard.
- Hurst Competition-Plus floor shift with simulated wood grain knob and reverse engagement warning light, standard with 4-speed.
- Heavy-duty Hemi suspension, standard.
- Heavy-duty 0.92-in. diameter front torsion bars, standard.
- Heavy-duty shock absorbers, standard.
- Heavy-duty 0.94-in. diameter front stabilizer anti-sway bar, standard.
- Heavy-duty ball-joints, standard.
- Heavy-duty 11-in. drum brakes, standard.
- 150 m.p.h. speedometer, standard.
- Heavy-duty radiator, standard.
- High performance dual exhaust system with 2½-in. exhaust pipes and tuned mufflers and 2¼-in. tail pipes and chromed, exposed exhaust tips, standard.
- High flow cylinder heads and intake manifold, standard.
- High performance Carter AVS 4-bbl carburetor, standard.
- Heavy duty 6-leaf left rear spring, standard.
- Special heavy-duty 6½-leaf right rear spring, standard.
- Heavy-duty driveshaft and U-joints, standard.
- Heavy-duty rear axle, standard.
- Heavy-duty battery, 70-amp-hour, standard.
- Red Streak wide tread F70 x 14 tires, standard.
- Extra-wide 5½-in. Safety-Rim wheels, standard.
- Dual fuel filtration, standard.
- Dual breaker distributor and viscous fan, standard, with 4-speed.
- High flow, unsilenced air cleaner, standard.
- Power disc brakes, optional.
- Torqueflite oil filter, standard.
- Dual braking system, standard.
- Performance hood, standard.
- Bucket seats, standard.
- Unitized construction, standard.
- Acrylic enamel, standard.
- 23 safety equipment items, standard.

SUPER BEE

- Special high performance 383 cu. in., 335 hp, 4-bbl Wedge engine is standard equipment. Stage II 426 cu. in., 425 hp, dual 4-bbl. Street Hemi is the only engine option. Standard or economy engines, *not available.*
- Heavy-duty 4-speed manual transmission, standard.
- Hurst Competition-Plus floor shift with simulated wood grain knob and reverse engagement warning light, standard.
- High upshift, competition-type Torqueflite automatic optional at low cost.
- Heavy-duty suspension, standard.
- Heavy-duty 0.90-in. diameter front torsion bars, standard.
- Heavy-duty shock absorbers, standard.
- Heavy-duty 0.94-in. diameter front stabilizer anti-sway bar, standard.
- Heavy-duty ball-joints, standard.
- Heavy-duty 11-in. drum brakes, standard.
- High flow, unsilenced air cleaner, standard.
- Heavy-duty radiator, standard.
- High performance Carter AVS 4-bbl carburetor, standard.
- High flow cylinder heads and intake manifold, standard.
- High performance exhaust system with 2¼-in. exhaust pipes and tuned mufflers and 2¼-in. tail pipes, standard.
- Heavy-duty 6-leaf rear springs, standard.
- Heavy-duty driveshaft and U-joints, standard.
- Heavy-duty rear axle, standard.
- Heavy-duty battery, 59-amp-hour, standard.
- Red streak wide tread F70 x 14 tires, standard.
- Extra-wide 5½-in. Safety-Rim wheels, standard.
- Dual fuel filtration, standard.
- Power disc brakes, optional
- Torqueflite oil filter, standard.
- Dual braking system, standard.
- Performance hood, standard.
- Unitized construction, standard.
- Acrylic enamel, standard.
- 23 safety equipment items, standard.

DART GTS

- All new special high performance 340 cu. in., 275 hp, 4-bbl lightweight Wedge engine is standard equipment. High performance 383 cu. in., 300 hp, 4-bbl Wedge engine is optional. Standard or economy engines *not available.*
- Heavy-duty 4-speed manual transmission or High-upshift competition-type Torqueflite automatic transmission, standard options.
- Hurst Competition-Plus floor shift with simulated wood grain knob and reverse engagement warning light, standard with 4-speed.
- Heavy-duty suspension, standard.
- Heavy-duty 0.87-in. diameter (340) and 0.94-in. diameter (383) front torsion bars, standard.
- Heavy-duty shock absorbers, standard.
- Heavy-duty 0.88-in. diameter (340) and 0.94-in. diameter (383) front stabilizer anti-sway bar, standard.
- Heavy-duty ball-joints, standard.
- 10-inch drum brakes, standard.
- Power disc brakes, optional.
- High flow cylinder heads and intake manifold, standard.
- High performance Carter AVS 4-bbl carburetor, standard.
- High performance dual exhaust system with 2¼-in. exhaust pipes (2½-in. on 383) and tuned mufflers and 2¼-in. tail pipes with chromed, exposed exhaust tips, standard.
- High flow, unsilenced air clearner, standard.
- Heavy-duty 6-leaf rear springs, standard.
- Heavy-duty driveshaft and U-joints, standard.
- Heavy-duty rear axle, standard.
- Red Streak wide tread E70 x 14 tires, standard.
- Extra wide 5½-in. Safety-Rim wheels, standard.
- Dual fuel filtration, standard.
- Torqueflite oil filter, standard.
- Dual breaker distributor, standard.
- Bucket seats, standard.
- Dual braking system, standard.
- Performance hood, standard.
- Unitized construction, standard.
- Acrylic enamel, standard.
- 23 safety equipment items, standard.

PROJECT SUPER/STOCK

Tom Hoover on the 1968 Hemi racer program that netted the Corporation with "ownership" of NHRA's SS/B class

DATE February 20, 1968
TO: All Plymouth Dealers

FROM: R.D. McLaughlin, National Sales Manager

RE: 1968 Hemi Barracuda Super/Stock

The Chrysler-Plymouth Division offers for 1968 a 426-Hemi-Powered Barracuda Fastback for use in supervised acceleration trials. Hemi-Powered Barracudas will be available through production in limited quantities in March. To order this vehicle use the Barracuda Order Form and specify Body Code B-029 and Transmission Code 393 for four-speed or Code 395 for automatic. No other specifications are necessary.

Please note that the following items are deleted on this model: Heater, Body Sealer and Sound Deadeners, Silencing Pads, Outside Mirrors, Right Side Seat Belt and Body Color Paint. NO OPTIONAL EQUIPMENT OF ANY KIND CAN BE ORDERED.

These vehicles will be sold without warranty and will display special stickers which will read as follows: "This vehicle was not manufactured for use on public streets, roads or highways and does not conform to Motor Vehicle Safety Standards." All customer orders must be accompanied by a signed disclaimer indicating that the purchaser understands the above.

The cost of such vehicle— $5,495.00.

WHEN WE set out early last winter to built the drag car everyone was asking for, we had several general guidelines in mind. First, of course, were NHRA rules. Once past them, the car could, with minor modifications, compete almost anywhere. That was 1967.

Second was cost. We wanted to build a car with a price that made sense. For instance, we could have put aluminum heads on the Hemi to cut the weight if we weren't thinking economics, but it would have cost about 20 dollars a pound for the weight saved. We found cheaper ways to reduce the weight, and the car still fits in the 'B' class.

Third, we had to make sure the car could be shipped conveniently, so we had to forego installing racing cam and high-capacity oil pan because of driving and ground clearance problems that could develop at the factory.

The car requires some home work between delivery and the drag strip (for one thing, it is painted only in primer, to allow for inevitable custom jobs). But less needs to be done to this car than any other than has been factory-built strictly for the drags. To make it race-ready, it needs only slicks, racing cam and valve gear, bigger oil pan and colors.

We have tried to take care of everything else, including painstaking development of the proper torque converter set-up for the automatic version and proper rear suspension, two of the biggest adjustments drivers face in setting up a drag car.

The Hemi-Barricuda weighs just over 3,000 pounds with an engine rated at 500 horsepower, qualifying for the 6.00-6.99 pounds per horsepower SS/B bracket.

On the shell of the car, weight has been cut to a minimum. The hood and fenders are fiberglass, the front bumper and doors light gauge steel. The Chemcor glass in the car is only .080-inch thick, strange to look at the first time, but as

Awesome Barracuda is pre-production unit which Hoover drag tested at Irwindale prior to introduction of the program. Front fenders, scooped hood are fiberglass.

Cars came through with your basic drag Hemi engine complete with cross-ram induction, Holleys, 12.5-to-1 pistons and headers by Hooker.

Helping keep the weight down to a minimum are lightweight side window glass, lightweight steel doors, trick front bumper and a lack of any sealers or silencers normally installed on the assembly line.

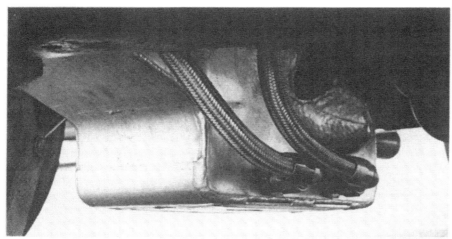

Hoover's test car was fitted with a special deep oil pan, pump and braided-steel lines with aircraft high-pressure fittings.

durable as the heavier real stuff. The battery is in the trunk, the back seat is gone and the interior is the clean Plymouth business coupe treatment.

To fit the 426-cubic-inch Hemi into Barracuda's tight engine compartment, some rearranging was necessary. The master brake cylinder has been shifted forward and to the left, the right front shock tower has been relocated and several other space-making modifications have been adopted. It is a car full of engine.

It breathes with the help of a hood scoop that is a little on the monstrous size, but functional. It's the result of about a year and a half of experimentation. Carburetion is by two four-barrel Holleys with 1.68-inch barrels on a cross-ram manifold.

Dodge also offered its loyal followers the same package wrapped in a Dodge Dart shell. This is one of the early Hurst-built Hemi-Darts campaigned during the late-Sixties by Charlie Castaldo.

The parking lot at Hurst's Motown facility, with a full array of both Hemi-Barracuda and Dart models ready for racer pickup. The package was designed by Chrysler and the semi-finished cars shipped to Hurst for completion.

Compression is 12.5-to-1, a sizable jump from the 10.25 ratio with standard Street Hemi pistons. The exhaust system is "simulated" with Hooker headers, pipes and mufflers. And the engine is equipped with a viscous drive fan.

Most of the characteristics of the power plant are familiar to enthusiasts who recall special Plymouth drag products built between 1964 and 1966. No revolutionary innovations have been applied, only time-tested features put together in the strongest package to come out of Detroit for production drag purposes so far.

Along the driveline, the four-speed manual Hemi-Barracuda carries a 10½-inch diameter Hemi race clutch with a cast steel housing that eliminates the need for a flywheep shield. The rear axle is a heavy-duty 9.75-inch Dana 60, ratio

Photo taken in May of 1968 shows some of the paperwork which was attached to each Super/*Stock car.*

Continued

Loading up at the Hurst facility. Loyal to Dodge for many years, Castaldo towed his Dart with a loaded Monaco wagon.

Charlie Castaldo checks out the Hemi engine in his Dart before loading up for the trip back to New York City.

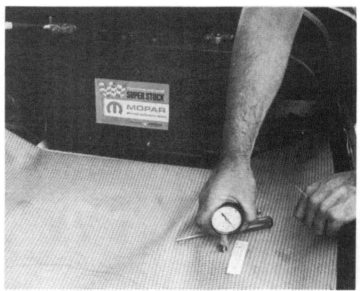

The Dart and Barracuda Hemi cars came with a special Mopar Super/Stock battery mounted over the right rear wheel. Castaldo installed air shocks at the rear.

Trackside at Englishtown in 1968 for the NHRA Summernationals, Castaldo and Speedwin's Joe Jill do some last minute tuning.

4.89-to-1.

The Torqueflite has a high-stall-speed B & M torque converter on which we spent a lot of effort at Irwindale, setting it-up for optimum performance. Rear axle on the automatic is the 8.75-inch Belvedere version with a 4.86-to-1 ratio. Like the manual, the automatic has a Sure-Grip limited-slip differntial, and both manual and automatic are equipped with Hurst shifters.

The rear suspension is all special, and moved inboard to accommodate big slicks. Front and back bolt circles are 4.5 inches instsad of the standard four, to fit racing wheels. Brakes are Kelsey-Hayes discs in front, drums in the rear.

Most of the creative work on the Hemi Barracuda wasn't the product of a formal design program. Instead, engineer Bob Tarozzi, drag mechanics Dan Knapp, Larry Knowlton and John Bauman and I collaborated on the car, using lab specialists and engineering departments only on special problems.

We had a "mule" car, a slightly overweight prototype built for 50 or 60 runs a day, ready to go in January, and during several weeks at Irvindale worked out the last bugs in the system.

All the cars were delivered in early May, in time to qualify for the NHRA Springnationals at Englishtown, N.J., in June. The Hemi Barracuda is quick and strong, the hottest drag special SS/B has ever seen.

IT'S THE YEAR OF THE MOPAR REVOLUTION

With late-intro Dodge 'Winged' Thing' Charger Daytonas, Six-Pack screamers and a whole new line of NASCAR cars, Dodge & Plymouth revolutionize the street performance scene

To hype the new Dodge econo-supercar (Dart Swinger), they built a customized job with rectangular headlamps and a bug-catcher-style injection scoop on the hood. Plymouth GTX with 440 Wedge power proved to be ideal street supercar, priced right for the marketplace.

CAPSULE COMMENTS

PERFORMANCE for a buck is the word at Mopar. Plymouth's Road Runner has been face-lifted and then expanded to include both a hard top and a convertible. It's not only a strong car, but also one with class. Beep-Beep is spelled out on the steering and the horn is painted purple, but there is also a functional Air-Grabber. Air comes in through two grilles in the top of the hood, and travels through plastic duct work that completely encloses the air cleaner. When you're ready for action, pull out the big red knob under the dash and the Air-Grabber opens up. In a rain storm or snow you are welcome to push the button back in.

The Road Runner is available with either the standard 383, or with an optional Hemi engine. A four-speed is standard while the automatic is less than $40 extra. Where last year you had to fight to get worthwhile gear ratios, for 1969 a 3.55, 3.91 and the 4.10 can be ordered directly from the factory or bought over the counter.

Dodge's answer to the Road Runner, the Super Bee is mechanically similar to Road Runner. Both cars represent a basic performance level, but for the guy with more money in his pocket and a heavier foot there is a GTX in which a 440 engine and automatic is standard equipment. The 440 is a torque machine which, properly geared, will run away and hide from the 383 or the Hemi up to 60 mph. Above that, the Hemi is still king. All of the Road Runners and Super Bees come through with a heavy-duty Hemi suspension package; the GTX in the Coronet RT also have the suspension. However, you can go beyond this and acquire a Performance Axle package, with a 3.55 Sure-Grip limited slip rear, a larger fan with a viscose drive a fan-shroud and a big radiator. Next step up the ladder is the high-performance package that includes 3.91 gear set plus all of the above. Topping it all is the super performance Dana axle with 4.10 gears.

The guys in the white hats may have come in Second with

the Super Bee, but they certainly out-foxed the Plymouth clan with a new machine all of their own. In a way, the new Swinger is a poor man's Road Runner. Engine power is a 340, a mill with big valves and lots of top end breathing. It also costs less than the Road Runner and, for that matter, less than the Formula S Barracuda. At 3,100 to 3,200 pounds, the Swinger weight falls between the fastback and notchback Barracuda, and its 111 inch wheelbase gives a smooth ride and quick response.

What the Dodge boys produced is a showroom stock racer ready to get off at the light. By spending a little money for headers and blueprinting, you get 108 mph on the quarter-mile.

Standard carburetion includes a Carter AVS with 1-7/16 primaries, and 1-11/16 secondaries, same size as the one used in the Super Bee and is mounted on a high-riser man-

ifold. With large 735 Holley, an Edelbrock manifold, and going through the engine, ets will drop to the 12-second bracket while the top speed will increase to 115 mph. Both the Swinger 340 and its more elegant GTS counterpart have their own heads, forged 10.5-to-1 pistons, 2.02 intakes and a 1.60 inch exhaust. To go with these goodies is a split-pattern cam with 276 degrees intake duration and 284 degrees exhaust duration.

The four-speed has a 2.66 First and fine-pitched gears, quieter than the ones used on the 440-powered cars. Also standard equipment on the Swinger is a Hurst stick and a Borg and Beck 10½-inch clutch. The rear axle has 8¾-inch gears with 3.23 standard, and 3.55 or 3.91 optional at no extra cost. Standard tires are red line E 70 14's. Optional, are the Polyglas E 70's. ●

Dodge Charger R/T offered the best of both worlds with sleek styling, luxurious appointments and power to handle any possible situation. Plymouth had its version of fresh air induction known as Air Grabber, right.

Dodge Coronet R/T with cold air Ramcharger induction gave the performance enthusiast everything at a price that was affordable. Ramcharger package, right, hid engine from view making tuneups extremely difficult.

1969 HIGH-PEFORMANCE ENGINES

CUBIC INCHES	BORE	STROKE	HORSEPOWER	TORQUE	COMPRESSION	INDUCTION
340	4.040	3.310	275 @ 5000	340 @ 3200	10.50	FOUR-BARREL
383	4.250	3.380	335 @ 5000	425 @ 3400	10.00	FOUR-BARREL
426	4.250	3.750	425 @ 5000	490 @ 4000	10.25	DUAL-QUAD
440	4.320	3.750	350 @ 4400	480 @ 2800	10.10	FOUR-BARREL
440	4.320	3.750	375 @ 4600	480 @ 3200	10.10	FOUR-BARREL

SUPERCARS
PLYMOUTH STYLE

GTX

- High Performance 440 cu. in., 375 hp, 4-bbl Wedge engine is standard equipment. Stage II 426 cu. in., 425 hp, dual 4-bbl Street Hemi is the only engine option. Standard or economy engines *not available.*
- High-upshift, competition-type Torque-flite automatic or heavy duty 4-speed (with mandatory axle package), standard.
- Hurst Competition-Plus floor shift with simulated wood grain knob and reverse engagement warning light, standard with 4-speed.
- Heavy-duty Hemi suspension, standard.
- Heavy-duty 0.92-in. diameter front torsion bars, standard.
- Heavy-duty shock absorbers, standard.
- Heavy-duty 0.94-in. diameter front stabilizer anti-sway bar, standard.
- Heavy-duty ball-joints, standard.
- Heavy-duty 11-in. drum brakes, standard.
- Heavy-duty radiator, standard.
- High performance dual exhaust system with 2½-in. exhaust pipes standard.
- High flow cylinder heads and intake manifold, standard.
- High performance Carter AVS 4-bbl carburetor, standard.
- Heavy duty 6-leaf left rear spring, standard.
- Special heavy-duty 6½-leaf right rear spring, standard.
- Heavy-duty driveshaft and U-joints, standard.
- Heavy-duty rear axle, standard.
- Heavy-duty battery, 70-amp-hour, standard.
- Red Streak wide tread F70 x 14 tires, standard.
- Extra-wide 5½-in. Safety-Rim wheels, standard.
- Dual fuel filtration, standard.
- Dual breaker distributor and viscous fan, standard, with 4-speed.
- High flow air cleaner, standard.
- Power disc brakes, optional.
- Torqueflite oil filter, standard.
- Dual braking system, standard.
- Performance hood, standard.
- Bucket seats, standard.
- Unitized construction, standard.
- Acrylic enamel, standard.
- 23 safety equipment items, standard.

ROAD RUNNER

Special High Performance 383 cu. in., 335 HP, 4-bbl Wedge engine is standard equipment. 440 cu. in., 3—2 bbl Wedge, 390 HP, and Stage II 426 cu. in., 425 HP, Dual 4-bbl Street Hemi are the only engine options. Standard or economy engines, not available.

- Heavy-duty 4-speed manual transmission, standard.
- Hurst Competition-Plus floor shift with simulated wood grain knob and reverse engagement warning light, standard.
- High upshift, competition-type Torque-flite automatic optional at low cost.
- Heavy-duty suspension, standard.
- Heavy-duty 0.90-in. diameter front torsion bars, standard.
- Heavy-duty shock absorbers, standard.
- Heavy-duty 0.94-in. diameter front stabilizer anti-sway bar, standard.
- Heavy-duty ball-joints, standard.
- Heavy-duty 11-in. drum brakes, standard.
- Heavy-duty radiator, standard.
- High performance Carter AVS 4-bbl carburetor, standard.
- High flow cylinder heads and intake manifold, standard.
- High performance exhaust system with 2¼-in. exhaust pipes and tuned mufflers and 2¼-in. tail pipes, standard.
- Heavy-duty 6-leaf rear springs, standard.
- Heavy-duty driveshaft and U-joints, standard.
- Heavy-duty rear axle, standard.
- Heavy-duty battery, 59-amp-hour, standard.
- Red streak wide tread F70 x 14 tires, standard.
- Extra-wide 5½-in. Safety-Rim wheels, standard.
- Dual fuel filtration, standard.
- Power disc brakes, optional
- Torqueflite oil filter, standard.
- Dual braking system, standard.
- Performance hood, standard.
- Unitized construction, standard.
- Acrylic enamel, standard.
- 23 safety equipment items, standard.

BARRACUDA

- All new special high performance 340 cu. in., 275 hp, 4-bbl lightweight Wedge engine is standard equipment. High performance 383 cu. in., 330 hp, 4-bbl Wedge engine is optional. Standard or economy engines *not available.*
- Heavy-duty 4-speed manual transmission or High-upshift competition-type Torqueflite automatic transmission, standard options.
- Hurst Competition-Plus floor shift with simulated wood grain knob and reverse engagement warning light, standard with 4-speed.
- Heavy-duty suspension, standard.
- Heavy-duty 0.87-in. diameter (340) and 0.94-in. diameter (383) front torsion bars, standard.
- Heavy-duty shock absorbers, standard.
- Heavy-duty 0.88-in. diameter (340) and 0.94-in. diameter (383) front stabilizer anti-sway bar, standard.
- Heavy-duty ball-joints, standard.
- 10-inch drum brakes, standard.
- Power disc brakes, optional.
- High flow cylinder heads and intake manifold, standard.
- High performance Carter AVS 4-bbl carburetor, standard.
- High performance dual exhaust system with 2¼-in. exhaust pipes (2½-in. on 383) and tuned mufflers and 2¼-in. tail pipes, standard.
- High flow, unsilenced air clearner, standard.
- Heavy-duty 6-leaf rear springs, standard.
- Heavy-duty driveshaft and U-joints, standard.
- Heavy-duty rear axle, standard.
- Red Streak wide tread E70 x 14 tires, standard.
- Extra wide 5½-in. Safety-Rim wheels, standard.
- Dual fuel filtration, standard.
- Torqueflite oil filter, standard.
- Dual breaker distributor, standard.
- Bucket seats, standard.
- Dual braking system, standard.
- Performance hood, standard.
- Unitized construction, standard.
- Acrylic enamel, standard.
- 23 safety equipment items, standard.

1969—SOMETHING FOR EVERYONE!

There's a Formula S 340 Barracuda for the sporty car set, econo models for grocery-getting and even a 440-inch version designed to blow the doors off anything the competition has to offer

1969 440 BARRACUDA SPECIFICATIONS

BASE LIST PRICE $2,813.00
CUDA-440 OPTION ....$ 345.00
WEIGHT (W/Driver) ....3,740 pounds
WEIGHT DISTRIBUTION (F/R) 57.2/42.8%
DISPLACEMENT ....440 cubic inches
COMPRESSION RATIO 10.1-to-1
HORSEPOWER ....375 at 4,600 rpm
TORQUE ....480 at 3,200 rpm
CARBURETION ....Single Carter AFB
CAMSHAFT ....Hydraulic
DURATION ....268/284 degrees
EXHAUST ....Reverse flow, duals
0-to-30 MPH ....2.5 Seconds
0-to-60 MPH ....5.6 Seconds
0-to-100 MPH ....13.8 Seconds
QUARTER-MILE ....104 MPH/14.10 Secs.

NOTE: The Cuda-440 Group consists of a 375-hp 440-inch engine, Torqueflite transmission, Heavy-Duty suspension, Heavy-Duty 14x5½-inch wheels with E-70 Wide Oval tires. Recommended extras include Sure-Grip differential ($42.00) and Electric Tach ($50.00). Options that are not available with the Cuda-440 package are Four-Speed, Power Brakes, Power Steering and Disc Brakes. There is no underhood room for the booster needed for the brakes. The Cuda-440 option was a mid-1969, limited-production package.

THE '69 Barracuda has more versions than ever, enhancing the possibilities of its dominance in the stock classes. Its body shell remains the same, with hood, trim, grille, and rear end updating making the big difference.

Besides the basic Barracuda series, in fastback, notchback, and convertible, there's the Formula-S, with 340 or 383 engines, HD front and rear suspensions, shocks, and front sway bar, 14 x 5½ wheels and E70-14 redline tires, along with the familiar emblems.

The newest Barracudas are the slickly-painted and nicely appointed Cuda-340 and Cuda-383 models, with big, bold side striping and rear deck paint treatments. These cars are bench-seat models, using the two lightweight engines, standard four-speeds with Hurst linkage, status E70-14 tires, HD suspension, and decorative hood scoops for less money than the Formula S package.

Those interested in the 383, in Cuda or Formula S cars, should know that it is the same engine as used in the Road Runner, with 440 cam, heads, and dual-point distributor, but rated at 300 hp. The 340 is tagged at 275 hp.

All Barracudas are drivers' cars, be it in a straight line or through a slalom course. Good, if not perfect weight distribution, a 108-inch wheelbase, and newer, more powerful engines give the Barracuda balance and driving ease not found in too many American cars.

The fastback model was the most popular in the lineup for 1969. They sold 17,788 of these during the 1969 model year buildout. For just $309.35 extra you could turn a stock Barracuda into a 340-inch Formula S screamer.

The rarest of the rare are the convertibles fitted with optional high-performance powerplants. This one is slightly modified via later model accessories, oversize tires, stereo speaker installation and some engine dress-up goodies.

What the well-stocked engine compartment is showing this year.

The 340:

(As found in the 'Cuda 340)'

Bhp @ rpm	275 @ 5000
Torque @ rpm	340 @ 3200
Bore	4.04 in.
Stroke	3.31 in.
Displacement	340 cu. in.

Compression Ratio
- Nominal .... 10.5 to 1
- Maximum .... 11.79 to 1

Minimum Combustion
- Chamber Volume .... 63.3 cc.

Minimum Deck Clearance .... +.045 in.

Carburetion .... Single AVS

Throttle
- Primary .... 1-7/16 in.
- Secondary .... 1-11/16 in.

Cam Duration
- Intake .... 276°
- Exhaust .... 284°
- Overlap .... 52°

Lift at Zero Lash
- Intake .... 430 in.
- Exhaust .... 445 in.

Valve Diameter
- Intake .... 2.02 in.
- Exhaust .... 1.60 in.

Tappet Type .... Hydraulic

Tappet Clearance
- Intake .... Zero
- Exhaust .... Zero

Max. Valve Spring Pressure
- Closed .... 110.2 lb. @ 1.62 in.
- Open .... 240 lb. @ 1.24 in.

Crankshaft Journal Diameter
- Mains .... 2.50 in.
- Rods .... 2.13 in.

Rod Bearing Material .... Tri-Metal

Ignition Type
- TorqueFlite .... Single Breaker
- 4-Speed .... Dual Breaker

Point Gap .... 014-.019 in.

Dwell
- Single Breaker .... 30°-35°
- Dual Breaker .... 27°-32° each
  - 37°-42° total

Timing
- TorqueFlite .... Single Breaker: 5° BTC
- 4-Speed .... Dual Breaker: TDC

Plug Type .... Champion

Range N-9Y

Gap .... 035 in.

The 383:

(As found in the 'Cuda 383)

Bhp @ rpm	330 @ 5200 rpm
Torque @ rpm	410 @ 3600 rpm
Bore	4.25 in.
Stroke	3.38 in.
Displacement	383 cu. in.

Compression Ratio
- Nominal .... 10.1 to 1
- Maximum .... 10.8 to 1

Minimum Combustion
- Chamber Volume .... 79.5 cc.

Minimum Deck Clearance ..... +.0205 in.

Carburetion .... Single AVS

Throttle
- Primary .... 1-7/16 in.
- Secondary .... 1-11/16 in.

Cam Duration
- Intake .... 276°
- Exhaust .... 292°
- Overlap .... 54°

Lift at Zero Lash
- Intake .... 450 in.
- Exhaust .... 465 in.

Valve Diameter
- Intake .... 2.08 in.
- Exhaust .... 1.74 in.

Tappet Type .... Hydraulic

Tappet Clearance
- Intake .... Zero
- Exhaust .... Zero

Max. Valve Spring Pressure
- Closed .... 131 lb. @ 1.83 in.
- Open .... 248 lb. @ 1.41 in.

Crankshaft Journal Diameter
- Mains .... 2.63 in.
- Rods .... 2.37 in.

Rod Bearing Material .... Tri-Metal

Ignition Type .... Dual Breaker

Point Gap .... 014-.019 in.

Dwell .... 27°-32° each

Timing
- TorqueFlite .... 5° BTC
- 4-Speed .... TDC

Plug Type .... Champion

Range J-11Y

Gap .... 035 in.

Car tested: 1969 'Cuda 340 Fastback

Equipment on test car:

"340" engine; 4-speed transmission; 3.91:1 Sure-Grip rear axle; E70 x 14" "Polyglas" tires; power disc brakes; power steering; AM/FM; folding rear seat; heater/defroster.

Test results:

Run #	Elapsed time / secs.	Trap speed / mph
1.	13.88	102.50
2.	13.94	101.46
3.	13.95	101.01
4.	14.01	100.44
5.	13.86	102.50
6.	13.98	101.35
7.	14.04	100.89
Average:	13.95	101.45

Seldom-seen dual-scooped hood is shown here on one of the rare Cuda-440 models. This is a pre-production pilot model first shown to the Press in June of 1968. Total hardtop coupe production hit 12,757 units for the 1969 model year.

The '69 Barracuda convertible is the rarest of the first series open-top models with production tagged at 1,442 units.

'Cuda 340

Front suspension:

Type . . . . Torsion bar; heavy-duty
Diameter. . . . . 0.87 in.
Rate at wheel . . . . 100 lbs. per in.
Stabilizer bar . . . . Heavy-duty
Diameter . . . . 0.88 in.
Shock absorbers . . . . Heavy-duty
Caster . . . . −1/2°±9/16° (Manual),
+3/4"±9/16° (Power)
Camber +1/2°±1/4° (Left), +1/4°±1/4° (Right)
Toe-in . . . . 1/8"±1/32"

Rear suspension:

Type . . . . .Asymmetrical; heavy-duty; multiple-leaf
No. of leaves on left 6
No. of leaves on right 6
Rate at wheel, both sides . . . . 130 lbs. per in.
Shock absorbers . . . . Heavy-duty

'Cuda 383

Front suspension:

Type . . . . Torsion bar; heavy-duty
Diameter . . . . 0.89 in.
Rate at wheel . . . . 110 lbs. per in.
Stabilizer bar . . . . Extra-heavy-duty
Diameter . . . . 0.94 in.
Shock absorbers . . . . Heavy-duty
Caster . . . . −1/2°±9/16° (Manual),
+3/4°±9/16° (Power)
Camber −1/2°±1/4° (Left), +1/4°±1/4° (Right)
Toe-in . . . . 1/8"±1/32"

Rear suspension:

Type . . . . Asymmetrical; heavy-duty; multiple-leaf
No. of leaves on left 6
No. of leaves on right 6
Rate at wheel, both sides . . . . . . 150 lbs. per in.
Shock absorbers . . . . Heavy-duty

The Brakes.

'Cuda 340 and 383 Standard front brakes:

Type . . . . Drum; self-adjusting
Diameter . . . . 10 in.
Width . . . . 2.25 in.
Lining material, High-temperature, fade-resistant
Lining area per wheel . . . . 43.93 sq. in.
Swept area per wheel . . . . 70.69 sq. in.

Standard rear brakes:

Type . . . . Drum; self-adjusting
Diameter . . . . 10 in.
Width . . . . 1.75 in.
Lining material, High-temperature, fade-resistant
Lining area per wheel . . . . 34.16 sq. in.
Swept area per wheel . . . . 54.98 sq. in.
Total lining area . . . . 156.2 sq. in.
Total swept area . . . . 251.3 sq. in.

'Cuda 340 and 383 Optional front brakes:

Type . . . . Disc; self-adjusting
Diameter . . . . 10.79 in.
Features . . Internally vented; full floating caliper
Lining material, High-temperature, fade-resistant
Lining area per wheel . . . . 17.0 sq. in.
Swept area per wheel . . . . 51.18 sq. in.

Standard rear brakes:

Type . . . . Drum; self-adjusting
Diameter . . . . 10 in.
Width . . . . 1.75 in.
Lining material, High-temperature, fade-resistant
Lining area per wheel . . . . 34.16 sq. in.
Swept area per wheel . . . . 54.98 sq. in.
Total lining area . . . . 102.3 sq. in.
Total swept area . . . . 314.7 sq. in.

For an extra $344.75 you could get the 383 Group which offered more straightline performance per-buck than any of the competition. The 383 Wedge boasted 440-type heads, cam and dual-point ignition.

What's standard? Optional? Which engine? Which gear? Plymouth tells it like it is.

Barracuda

Basic Equipment (with 'Cuda 340 or 383 package):
• High-performance 340 or 383 cu. in. Wedge V-8, standard. ("Economy" versions not available.)
   High-performance camshaft, standard.
   High-flow cylinder heads and intake manifold, standard.
   High-performance Carter AVS 4-bbl. carburetor, standard.
   High-flow air cleaner, standard.
   Dual breaker distributor, standard.
   Oil pan windage tray, standard.
• Heavy-duty 4-speed manual transmission, standard.
• Hurst Competition-Plus floor shift with reverse gear indicator light, standard.
• Heavy-duty suspension, standard.

Heavy-duty 0.87" diameter (with 340) and 0.94" diameter (383), front torsion bars, standard.
Heavy-duty 6-leaf rear springs, standard.
Heavy-duty shock absorbers, standard.
Heavy-duty 0.88" diameter front anti-sway bar, standard.
Heavy-duty ball joints, standard.
• 10-inch drum brakes, standard.
• High-performance dual exhaust system with 2¼ in. exhaust pipes (2½ on 383), twin mufflers and 2¼ in. tail pipes, standard.
• Heavy-duty driveshaft and U-joints, standard.
• Heavy-duty rear axle, standard.
• Red Streak wide tread E70 x 14" tires, standard.
• Extra-wide 5.5 in. Safety-Rim wheels, standard.
• Dual braking system, standard.
• Full instrumentation, standard.

DODGE'S FLYING MACHINE!

The public
really benefitted from
Dodge being forced
to produce over
500 replicas of their
outrageous 'winged-thing'
Charger Daytona,
The World's
Fastest Stock Car

Dave Marcis in his Hemi-Daytona Charger leads the pack around Riverside during the big annual NASCAR event. Another Daytona brings up the rear.

IN STOCK CAR racing circles it has generally been considered a truth that if you want to go faster you either increase cubic inches or reduce weight—both if you can.

There have been cliches covering the alleged fact that "you can't beat cubic inches . . ."

In the latter part of the 1969 racing season, the pinnacle of an iceberg was viewed on the racing scene. It is possible that it could have sub-surface proportions of milestone importance. The activity concerned making the "prime mover" more efficient by changing the shape of the object that was being pushed through the air. The new direction is also coupled with a belief that not only can you beat cubic inches, but you can do it efficiently and in a manner pleasing to the public.

In the past when an automotive company developed a new engine, it was generally known *only* to the insiders. . . . It was up to the "buffs" to get the word out on the development— and then—in a good share of the cases, the people really didn't know what it was all about.

There are still a lot of automotive enthusiasts who know what a Hemi is for instance, but are hard pressed to tell you what it does and/or why.

There are a lot fewer automotive enthusiasts or, for that matter, even members of the general car citizenry that have had their mind blown at the sight of a Charger Daytona and are unable to recognize one a second time and realize at least that it is an aerodynamically-fashioned machine— "probably for racing."

The first overt action in the direction of finessing the car form came with the Charger 500. The very competitive Dodge boss Bob McCurry was faced with the simple fact that a new engine would be necessary to meet the drastically reduced 366 cubic-inch limit for 1971—down from the current max of 426 cubes—and that it wouldn't be very sound economics to put a lot of development money into a power plant that was due to be dropped.

The Charger 500 with flush grille and covered backlight produced a faster car without major engine change. It was at once obvious that a real aerodynamic machine ought to produce that much more.

Enter the Daytona Charger—the fastest stock car in the world at 199.985 miles per hour. (A record set in practice for the inaugural race at Talladega, Ala. in September.) Charlie Glotzbach who put the Charger Daytona on the pole at Talladega and cut the record lap—and a gentleman who is well-known in the racing fraternity as one not given to public relations puffery said:

"It's like a whole new world. There's no comparison to what other cars handle like. This one is a lot more stable. You go right down into the corner and then with one hand you go right through.

"You just point it where you want to go and that's where it goes.

"With a regular race car when you go into the corner there's lots more pull on the wheels—you have to work at it. With the Daytona you can go around all day and never need to use more than one hand.

"It's easier to drive and that rear stabilizer sure helps it handle better. Overall it's the safest race car I ever drove."

"I honestly think that any average citizen could go out and drive the Daytona around Talladega at 180 miles-per-hour without any trouble at all."

At 180 miles-per-hour and up about 17 additional horsepower are required to make a stock car go one mile-per-hour faster in the straightaway, and about 20 to 25 additional horsepower to pick up one mile-per-hour in the curves according to aerodynamicists.

The design changes incorporated in the Charger Daytona were made to "overcome the aerodynamic forces which tend to unstabilize the car and slow it down."

For example, the wedge-shaped nose reduces drag. The front spoiler reduces it further by counteracting front end lift. At 70-miles-per-hour, tests showed the movement of air created about 180 pounds of front end lift on the Charger—or enough to lift the whole nose of the car by about one-half inch. The new design gets lift back down to zero or a slight downforce. The front design pierces the air lower and lets less air get underneath the car.

The rule of thumb is that the less air you have passing under the car the better the performance and stability. This is especially true when the vehicle is operating on today's superspeedways.

Jack McCoy pulls in for a pit stop during Riverside NASCAR bash. Note top section of rear wing has been angled to create the needed aerodynamic assist. Car is a veteran of many roundy-round bouts.

The flush rear window configuration of the Charger Daytona eliminates turbulence and decreases rear drag. The vertical stabilizers, like the feathers on an arrow, will tend to keep the car going straight, while the horizontal stabilizers improve rear traction and stability.

In addition to the obvious benefits brought to the racing scene the attributes of the Dodge Charger Daytona design are also applicable to the passenger car version, especially in the areas of fuel economy, stability and handling.

At 50-miles-per-hour engineers estimate improved performance is about half aerodynamics and half chassis efficiency including engine output.

At speeds above 50-miles-per-hour aerodynamics becomes the most important single influence on performance.

The design of the Daytona moves the center of pressure of the car back to approximately the center of gravity, stabilizing the balance of the whole automobile while generally enhancing its handling characteristics.

While Charlie Glotzbach discussed the "pull on the wheels and his ability to drive the Daytona one-handed" the aerodynamic folks discuss the reduced sensitivity to side air pressure as a result of the raised rear stabilizer.

"Side air pressures" are also those created by cross winds

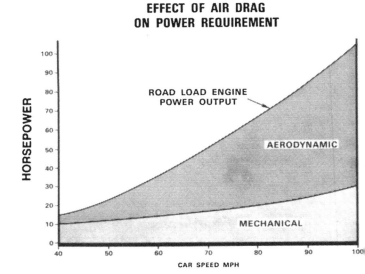

EFFECT OF AIR DRAG ON POWER REQUIREMENT

Bob Rodger, special car chief engineer for Corporation's high-performance program, demonstrates the strength of the stabilizer bar used on the Daytona, left. Author, above, test drives one of earliest production Daytonas.

. . . on a race track or on a highway . . . or in a drafting situation when you are passing a truck on a highway or a race car on a superspeedway.

There has already been some cross pollination from race car development to passenger car use but the possibilities held out for progress in the area of aerodynamics for the highway vehicle are considered most interesting by many authorities.

Aerodynamic developments and resultant improvements in the direction of economy and handling for the passenger car could be most beneficial for the future need to move more people in an expeditious manner at less cost.

In any event it has started a new direction of thinking and if the radical Daytona Charger is only responsible for a new perspective on old and/or new problems it will be beneficial to the motoring public.

In order to go racing Dodge Division produced 503 '69½ Charger Daytonas (433 with single-quad 440 wedges and 70

with 426 Street Hemi engines) which ended up costing its purchasers just $300 to $350 over the cost of a basic Charger R/T with the same options. Actually, the Daytonas were hand-finished Charger R/T models set up to run sans air conditioning. You could not get AC in a Daytona.

While Creative Industries in Detroit, was the outside vendor on this project (special parts and the conversion work), Chrysler Corporation had put together a team of experts to see the program through. Bob Rodger, Special Car Chief Engineer for the corporation's High-Performance Program was involved in the Daytona deal along with some key engineers: George Wallace, Special Vehicle Engineering; Gary Romberg, Race Car Aerodynamicist and Bill McNulty, the High-Performance Supervisor at the Chelsea, Michigan Proving Grounds.

The Dodge Charger Daytona took over the spot held by the fastback-roof Charger 500 and became the fastest stock car in the world. ●

SIX-PACK TO GO!

Introduced late-1969 for use in 1969½-'70 model cars, the tri-power 440 was designed to offer the enthusiast an alternative to the Hemi for the ultimate in street performance

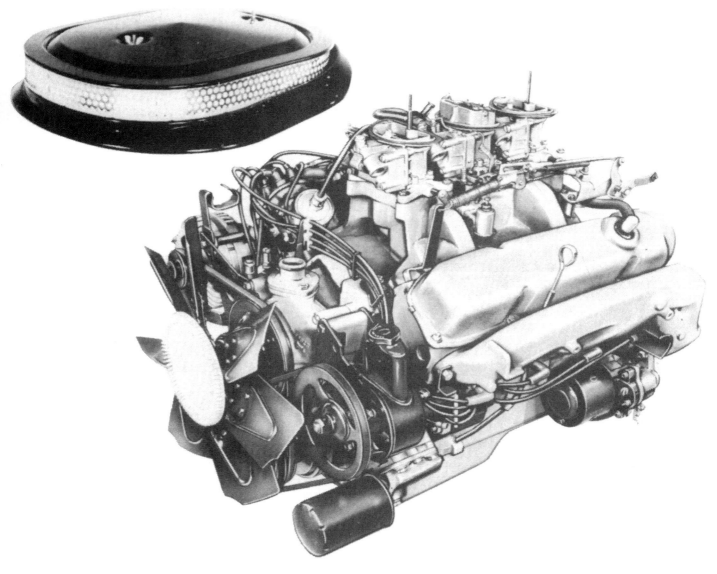

HP version of 440-inch Wedge boasts new-design 10.5 pistons and three-two-barrel Holley carburetors on a high-rise manifold casted by Edelbrock. Center carburetor is operated by the gas pedal and the other two controlled by vacuum. Dodge intake manifold carries part number 3412048. Later manifolds were casted by Mopar.

Early road tests of Super Bee with tri-power 440 mill was conducted by author while at CARS Magazine. First Super Bee model had NASCAR-pinned fiberglass hood finished in matte black with functional super-wide air scoop. With a 4.320-inch bore and 3.750-inch stroke, Six-Pack Wedge is rated at 390 hp at 4,700 rpm and 490 foot pounds of torque at 3,200 rpm. It's a real torquer.

The twin-scooped, matte-finished hood on the Challenger was a lot more sedate than the Shaker setup, but the engine was just as outrageous.

SIX BARRELS, NO WAITING!

Chrysler's tri-power 440-inch Wedge established itself almost overnight as the street engine to beat

With 440-Six-Pack power and either four-speed or the excellent Torqueflite, the Chrysler Ponycars for 1970 were unbeatable.

INTRODUCTION on August 28, 1969, of the new special-high-performance 440-cubic-inch, six-barrel engine into regular high-volume production for 1970 marked another engineering-plus for Plymouth & Dodge's well-respected lineup of performance cars. The 440-six barrel first created interest among performance enthusiasts following its limited-production, mid-1969 introduction in special Road Runner and Super Bee models.

For 1970, it is available as a Regular Production Option in a full array of models. It is designed to deliver exceptional power, and yet retain favorable operating characteristics and ease of maintenance for street driving. Moreover, it is priced attractively, in line with the Mopar performance car policy of offering maximum performance-per-dollar vehicles ready to be driven off the floor.

The 440-six-barrel is rated at 390 horsepower at 4,700 rpm, and 480 foot pounds of torque at 3,600 rpm. It carries a new Mopar-manufactured intake manifold to mount three high-flow Holley carburetors in-line. The primary two-barrel has 1-½-inch throttle bores, the secondary two-barrels have 1-¾-inch throttle bores. The center carburetor is operated mechanically directly by the accelerator pedal, while the front and rear carburetors are vacuum-operated. They open *only* when air flow in the center carburetor is high.

Because of the greater power and rpm capability of this engine, many internal modifications have been made. Contributing to this power increase is a new piston design which gives the engine a 10.5-to-1 compression ratio. The new piston ring line-up has a moly-faced top ring and a high tension oil ring. A new connecting rod forging has a heavier cross section for greater strength.

The valve train is considerably different from the other 440 cubic-inch engines. The camshaft has a lubrite treatment to prevent scuffing. Flat-face hydraulic tappets and low taper camshaft lobes are used to reduce stresses. Rocker arms are specially selected, and valve springs are the same high-rpm units as used on the 426 Hemi engine. The valves have hardened tips and chrome-plated stems to reduce wear.

The ignition system uses a double-

1969-1971 SIX-PACK/SIX-BARREL ENGINE

There are many special features about this engine other than just the intake manifold and carbs. Some of these items are heavy-duty rods, external balancing, heavy-duty rocker arms, special low-taper cam and special lifters and a higher compression ratio. All of these cars in 1969 were built with aluminum manifolds, while in 1970 and 1971 the manifolds were both cast-iron and aluminum.

PART NUMBERS

Crankshaft	PN-3512036
Crank Sprocket	PN-2205568
Cam	PN-3512905 (71)
Camshaft Sprocket	PN-2780572
Screw (3 Required)	PN-2120930
Timing Chain	PN-2205569
Connecting Rod	PN-2951906
Piston (Notched—Std. Bore)	PN-3420218
Rings (Std. Bore)	PN-3420228
Intake Valve	PN-3418475
Exhaust Valve	PN-3418479
Valve Springs	PN-3418491
Cam Tappet	PN-3420039
Rocker Arms	PN-2946033
	PN-2946034

The Six-Pack 440 was available complete with "shaker" induction.

The '69½ Six-Pack motors featured Edelbrock high-rise alloy intake manifolds, while the later cars made use of Chrysler-manufactured manifolds.

The tri-power 440-inch Wedge still rates as one of the most outstanding street performers ever to come out of Motown.

The last advertised availability of the Six-Pack engine was in 1971.

breaker high-performance distributor.

To obtain acceptably low exhaust emissions during idle and deceleration according to the new, more stringent 1970 standards, the engine employs a higher—800 rpm—idle speed. In order to prevent running on with the higher idle speed, the engine has an electrical solenoid throttle stop which holds the throttle at the correct idle position when energized, but de-energizes when the ignition is turned off, allowing the throttle blades to close more completely.

The 440-six-barrel is intended to be a step between the high-performance 440 four-barrel and the legendary Hemi, first introduced as a street package in 1966, and subsequently updated in 1968, and again in 1970 with hydraulic tappets.

Two unique all new fresh air scoop systems, available on Intermediate and Ponycar models, further increase the performance potential of the new engine. The optional air scoop systems direct fresh, cooler-denser air to the carburetors, thus enabling the engine to produce even more power.

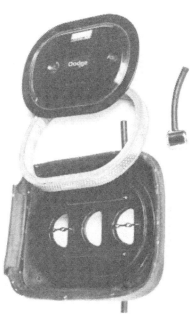

Air cleaner fixture for original Six-Pack Super Bee which was designed to work with a functional Super/Stock-style hood scoop.

Tight installation of Six-Pack motor in Mopar Ponycar.

133

DODGE BUILDS A Q-BOAT!

Contrary to popular belief, Dodge did build a limited-number of 375-hp 440-cube Dodge Darts in 1969. This was one of the first off the line

QUARTER MILE TEST LAB

In 1969 Chrysler Corporation moved its research lab to the drag strip
to help develop genuine high-performance products—it worked!

THESE quarter-mile runs were conducted in private at a sanctioned drag strip by Chrysler Engineering, as part of a constant program of test and evaluation—both in the lab and on the track. The four cars tested were in pure stock condition, using street tires, stock exhaust systems and clean-air packages.

The results are impressive—particularly as an indication of potential. All four cars tested turn the quarter in the 13-14-second bracket with speeds in the 100-105 mph range.

1969 ROAD RUNNER COUPE

Equipped with 383-cubic-inch engine, four-speed transmission, 3.90-to-1 Sure-Grip rear end with Track-Pack, Air-Grabber, Decor package, radio, road wheels, F70x14-inch Polyglas tires, power steering, heater/defroster.

RUN #	ELAPSED TIME	TRAP SPEED
1	14.01	101.23
2	14.06	101.01
3	14.06	100.55
4	13.98	101.80
4	13.95	101.69
6	14.00	101.46
7	14.03	101.12

Average Quarter-Mile Performance: 101.26 mph in 14.01 seconds

---

1969 ROAD RUNNER COUPE

Equipped with 426 Street-Hemi engine, TorqueFlite transmission, 4.10-to-1 rear end with Super-Track-Pak, Air Grabber, Decor package, F70x14-inch Polyglas tires, radio, heater/defroster.

RUN #	ELAPSED TIME	TRAP SPEED
1	13.44	106.25
2	13.53	105.38
3	13.69	104.28
4	13.43	105.88
5	13.50	105.50
6	13.56	105.14
7	13.35	107.39

Average Quarter-Mile Performance: 105.68 mph in 13.50 seconds

---

1969 PLYMOUTH GTX HARDTOP

Equipped with 440-cubic-inch, four-speed transmission, 4.10-to-1 Sure-Grip rear end with Super-Track-Pak, F70x14-inch Polyglas tires, road wheels, AM/FM radio, Air Grabber, power steering, heater/defroster.

RUN #	ELAPSED TIME	TRAP SPEED
1	14.04	102.04
2	13.87	102.27
3	14.02	102.04
4	13.92	102.38
5	13.82	102.62
6	13.77	102.50
7	13.80	102.38

Average Quarter-Mile Performance: 102.32 mph in 13.89 seconds

1969 'CUDA 340 FASTBACK

Equipped with 340-cubic-inch engine, four-speed transmission, 3.91 Sure-Grip rear end, E70x14-inch Polyglas tires, power disc brakes, power steering, AM/FM radio, folding rear seat, heater/defroster.

RUN #	ELapsed tIME	TRAP SPEED
1	13.88	102.50
2	13.94	101.46
3	13.95	101.01
4	14.01	100.44
5	13.86	102.50
6	13.98	101.35
7	14.04	100.89

Average Quarter-Mile Performance: 101.45 mph in 13.95 seconds

RARE
AND
WELL DONE!

Hemi-fired Charger 500 was the first propane-powered car
set up exclusively for the quarter-mile

Al Pulliam on the line ready for a shakedown run. Charger ran in the 11s at speeds over 121 mph which
wasn't bad for a 4,200-pound car loaded with full power accessories.

Powered by a unique
Propane-fed 426 Hemi,
this limited-production
Charger 500 (originally
designed so that rear
window configuration
could be used on
NASCAR racers for
additional streamlining)
was the first Propane
car to be drag-raced.

Don Bass supervises the filling of the Charger's trunk-mounted 23-gallon tank. There's not much trunk left over!

Engine-builder Don Bass sets up the Charger's Hemi on an engine dyno, working closely with the Impco people and the Western Liquid Gas Association.

Impco propane carburetion and alloy air box manifolding specially made for this application.

PROPANE X looks quite like any stock-bodied Dodge Charger 500. From the stands only a few people might notice the odd carburetors punching through the fiberglass hood. And in the pits only the most interest and observant would note that they are different.

But Propane X is an unusual machine. It is the only drag car anywhere running on propane gas. Many cars and trucks in business and industrial fleets have been converted from gasoline to propane, but none has been done with an eye entirely to performance.

To say the conversion of the big Dodge 426 Hemi engine for propane use was easy, would be basically true. But Don Bass, who blueprinted the big mill is quick to point out that though the conversion was relatively simple, going through the engine for use of propane was no less simple or different than working-over any engine intended to be competitive on

the strip.

Obviously the most unusual aspect of Propane X is its unique carburetion set-up. The two carburetors are by Impco, not a manufacturer readily recognized around the drag strip, but an established name in the propane world. The source of the fuel is a 23-gallon Manchester tank mounted in the truck. Fuel in liquid form feeds via 3/8-inch fuel line into two converters mounted aside and just below the carburetors. Here it becomes a gas and if fed via pipes that look for all the world like they came out of someone's bathroom, into the carburetors, where, like gasoline, it is mixed with air. At this point the gas-air mixture flows into a well-bolted and welded steel holding box, which is, in effect, the intake manifold.

Although the valves are stock (2.250-inch intakes and 1.940-inch exhaust) most of the other valve train components are not. The roller camshaft and lifters, as

well as springs and retainers, are by Moon. The pushrods are Smith Brothers Chromemoly while the rocker arms remain stock.

The bores have been trued and run Forge True pistons banded by Perfect Circle rings and pushed by a stock crankshaft and stock connecting rods. Both the main bearings and the rod bearings are by TRW. The ignition system is a Mallory and furnishes fire to Autolite AG901 plugs.

The big propane-powered Dodge Hemi relays its torque to a 4.88-to-1 rear axle through a B & M Torque Flite transmission, guided via a B & M shifter.

The rare fastback Charger which rolls on Cragar mag wheels front and rear is equipped with radio, heater, power windows, power steering, and power brakes. It also has been completely undersealed. The machine tips the scales, sans 210 pound driver, at almost 4,200 pounds.

THE RAPID TRANSIT SYSTEM!

Total Performance takes on a whole new meaning as a Superbird and third-generation poneycars with exotic Six-Pack powerhouses join the group

Available in both intermediate and ponycar models, the tri-power Six-Pack engine became the street performance standard of the Seventies. It was tame enough for everyday driving in a luxurious Dodge Charger and strong enough for street-pounding in a Cuda.

CAPSULE COMMENTS

THE NEW Barracuda is indeed a sharp machine, and its Dodge counterpart, the equally new Challenger, is every bit as wild. Though based on similar 110-inch wheelbase chassis, the two are different enough in styling to have the makings of a head-on battle in which both ought to win handsomely over much of the competition. The general thought was to offer competitive low-slung option in answer to the Camaros, Firebirds and Mustangs. A little game of switch-the-name tag took place at Plymouth and it all started with the old Barracuda being given the DeSoto treatment—the heave-ho. The new Barracuda, being a completely different series, doesn't even bear a nodding

acquaintance with the old one. It didn't take the Plymouth boys long to figure out that their Valiant didn't quite cut it at the drive-in. However, here was a lightweight 108-inch wheelbase machine, which would accept a 340 V8 and make it into a decent performance package. This has now become the 340 Duster. Buddy Martin and Ronnie Sox point out that the Duster has exceptionally good traction and that the 340 engine potential is still untapped. A vinyl hardtop did absolutely nothing for the Duster except make the body look bulky. On the other hand, a Duster painted in bright orange, complete with racing stripes, was just great.

The Cuda and Challenger will accept any of the Mopar

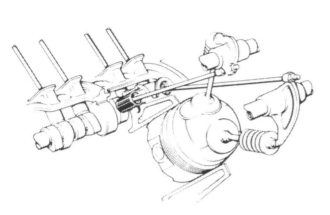

engines up to and including the Hemi, without having to make detours to Hurst performance. For the Hemis and the Six Packs, Dodge and Plymouth came up with brand new shaker air cleaners that poke right through the hood. Smaller engines in the Challenger and the Barracuda are going to be covered up with a special sloping hood complete with a power bulge but without a cold air intake. Unless, of course, you are ingenious and decide to readapt the vacuum operated trap door of the GTX onto a Barracuda or a Challenger.

Chrysler offered the biggest, most-macho four-speed shifter in history. For 1970 the Street Hemi got treated to hydraulic lifters, right, for more sensible street durability and maintenance. The Yellow Jacket, a tricked-out Dodge Challenger, thrilled Mopar fans on the auto show circuit.

Wildest of the Plymouth machines is the new Superbird which comes with a streamlined nose, giant tail fins and a wing. It's running proof that the wind tunnel boys can come up with wilder things than the crew at Styling.

All engines except the 340 and 440 have had compression lowered by about a half a point. The Six Pack, by offering a very small carburetor throttle area at idle, turns out to be a life saver in meeting the emissions requirements without affecting the performance. Also, all street Hemis for 1970 will have hydraulic tappets and minimum overlap cams, again to cut down on emissions. ●

Dodge offered ponycar enthusiasts more choices than any other maker in 1970. You could buy a plain jane Challenger or a loaded R/T with max power and show goodies. Window louvers and rear wing were available as aftermarket accessories from Mopar dealers.

If supercars were your bag, Plymouth and Dodge had all the machinery you could possibly ask for. Dodge's Super Bee, like the GTX and Road Runner from Plymouth, were available with Wedge or Hemi options.

1970 HIGH-PERFORMANCE ENGINES

CUBIC INCHES	BORE	STROKE	HORSEPOWER	TORQUE	COMPRESSION	INDUCTION
340	4.040	3.310	275 @ 5000	340 @ 3200	10.50	FOUR-BARREL
340	4.040	3.310	290 @ 5000	340 @ 3200	10.50	TRI-POWER
383	4.250	3.380	330 @ 5000	425 @ 3200	9.50	FOUR-BARREL
383	4.250	3.380	335 @ 5200	425 @ 3400	9.50	FOUR-BARREL
426	4.250	3.750	425 @ 5000	490 @ 4000	10.20	DUAL-QUAD
440	4.320	3.750	375 @ 4600	480 @ 3200	9.70	FOUR-BARREL
440	4.320	3.750	390 @ 4700	490 @ 3200	10.50	TRI-POWER

1970—THE RAPID TRANSIT AUTHORITY!

That's what Plymouth called its Hemi-Cuda. It was also known as the King Kong Ponycar

During the 1970 model year, Plymouth built 14 Hemi-powered soft-top Ponycars, nine with automatic and five with four-speed. By the end of the year, there were 666 Hemi-Cudas, the bulk of those being automatic hardtops (368).

The prototype in action on the Chrysler skid pad. The factory drivers were Dan Gurney (All-American Racers) and Swede Savage. Sponsorship came from Plymouth and Mattel (Hot Wheels).

Using a shoehorn, Plymouth engineers stuffed the hydraulic-lifter 426-Street-Hemi, complete with Shaker scoop, into the short-wheelbase Barracuda. It was an awesome performer.

IT TOOK Plymouth a lot longer than most manufacturers to get its Ponycar accepted, but it looks like the *Mayflower Men* made it. The '70 Barracuda is Plymouth's Third Generation Ponycar and unquestionably the finest since they got into this field in 1964. Few people realize that Plymouth was out with a Ponycar along with Ford in 1964, and actually had the *first* fastback machine. Ford didn't come out with the fastback Mustang until mid-1965. Unfortunately, the 1964-'66 Barracuda models were not sporty or powerful enough to compete with Mustang in the early Ponycar market. There was too much of a Valiant influence in the original Barracuda, and while the car was extremely sensible (lots of room, fold down rear seat), it just didn't make it. The Second Generation '67 Barracuda also failed as a Mustang-Camaro-Firebird beater.

For 1970 Plymouth introduced an all-new, super-sporty Barracuda with enough options and models to cover all phases of the marketplace. Under its skin is exactly what Dodge has in its Challenger. The suspension, powerplants and powertrain is exactly the same. The cars accelerate, handle, stop and perform in general exactly as the Challenger does. All performance data on the Challenger can be directly applied to the Barracuda.

The sheetmetal and trim are different, as are some of the model designations. For 1970 Plymouth offered three models—the basic Barracuda and the Gran Coupe and Cuda series. The front end is clean and functional, with turn signals recessed into the grille. On the Cuda there are four-inch road-fog lamps and optional color-keyed molded urethane foam bumpers. As in the Challenger, there are flush-mounted door handles, ventless side glass, tall integrated buc-

Specifications: 'Cuda

Engine	340	383	440	440 6-bbl.	Hemi
Displacement, cu. in.	340	383	440	440	426
Horsepower @ rpm	275 @ 5000	335 @ 5200	375 @ 4600	390 @ 4700	425 @ 5000
Torque, lbs.-ft. @ rpm	340 @ 3200	425 @ 3400	480 @ 3200	490 @ 3200	490 @ 4000
Compression ratio	10.5:1	9.5:1	9.7:1	10.5:1	10.25:1
Camshaft	High lift, long duration, high overlap				
Cam duration, intake/exhaust/overlap	276°/284°/52°	276°/292°/54°	276°/292°/54°	276°/292°/54°	292°/292°/68°
Lifter type	Hydraulic	Hydraulic	Hydraulic	Hydraulic	Hydraulic
Valve dia., int.	2.02"	2.08"	2.08"	2.08"	2.25"
Valve dia., exh.	1.60"	1.74"	1.74"	1.74"	1.94"
Carburetion	Single Carter AVS 4-bbl.	Single Holley AVS 4-bbl.	Single Carter AVS 4-bbl.	Triple Holley 2-bbl.	Dual Carter AFB 4-bbl.
Distributor	Dual-Breaker	Single-Breaker	Single-Breaker	Dual-Breaker	Dual-Breaker
Air induction (standard)	Under hood	Under hood	Under hood	Under hood	Air Grabber
(optional)	n.a.	n.a.	n.a.	Air Grabber	
Exhaust system	Dual, low restriction, with cast iron headers and high-flow mufflers				
Transmission (standard)	Heavy-duty 3-speed		High-upshift TorqueFlite automatic		
Transmissions (optional)	Heavy-duty 4-speed		Heavy-duty 4-speed		
	High-upshift TorqueFlite				
Suspension					
Torsion bars, front	Heavy-duty 0.90" dia.	Heavy-duty 0.90" dia.	Extra-heavy-duty 0.92" dia.	Extra-heavy-duty 0.92" dia.	Extra-heavy-duty 0.92" dia.
Rate at wheel, lbs. per in.	113	113	124	124	124
Shock absorbers	Heavy-duty	Heavy-duty	Extra-H-D	Extra-H-D	Extra-H-D
Stabilizer bar, front	Heavy-duty, 0.94" dia.	Heavy-duty, 0.94" dia.	Heavy-duty 0.94" dia.	Heavy-duty 0.94" dia.	Heavy-duty 0.94" dia.
Stabilizer bar, rear	0.75" dia.	0.75" dia.	n.a.	n.a.	n.a.
Rear springs, right	Heavy-duty, 4½ leaves	Heavy-duty, 4½ leaves	Extra-H-D; 5 leaves + 2 half-leaves	Extra-H-D; 5 leaves + 2 half-leaves	Extra-H-D; 5 leaves + 2 half leaves
Rear springs, left	Heavy-duty, 4½ leaves	Heavy-duty, 4½ leaves	Extra-heavy-duty, 6 leaves	Extra-heavy-duty, 6 leaves	Extra-heavy-duty, 6 leaves
Rate at wheel, lbs. per in.	129	129	148	148	148
Brakes, front	11 x 3" cast iron drums; self-adjusting				
rear	11 x 2½" cast iron drums; self-adjusting				
Optional brakes, front	Discs; full-floating calipers				
Driveshaft dia.	3.0"	3.0"	3.0"	3.0"	3.0"
U-joints	H-D	H-D	H-D	H-D	H-D
Rear axle	Heavy-duty, Chrysler-built 8¾" dia. ring gear		Extra-heavy-duty, Dana-built 9¾" dia. ring gear		
Axle ratios	See chart				
Rim size (std.)	15 x 7"	14 x 6"	14 x 6"	14 x 6"	15 x 7"
Tire size (std.)	E-60 x 15"	F-70 x 14"	F-70 x 14"	F-70 x 14"	F-60 x 15"

kets with headrests, boxed roof rails on the hardtops and a host of safety theft-protection features. The rear end completes the general racy, long-hood/short-deck theme and has a horizontal emphasis via tail blinkers and a thin bumper. Optional extra-wide wheels and glass-belted tires complete the sporty car styling.

The Cuda series is the one for performance enthusiasts, as the Gran Coupe is basically a super-luxury package aimed at an older audience. The standard Cuda is powered by a 383 four-barrel engine. Optional are Cuda 340 with 340 four-barrel, the Cuda 440 with single four-barrel 440 power, Cuda six-barrel with tri-power 440 power and the Hemi-Cuda with 426 dual-quad Street-Hemi power. The only two that really make sense for the daily-use street performance market are the tri-power 440 and the 340 four-barrel. The Hemi-Cuda, even with its improved low-end performance hydraulic-lifter 426, is still too radical for practical street use. The tri-power Wedge has all the straightline performance you could ask for, and it handles pretty well. All Cuda models come with HD suspension packages and beefy 11-inch brakes. Discs are optional as are a full instrumentation cluster and racing-styled mirrors.

In keeping with the trend to Ram-Air setups, Plymouth offered a "shaker" job as standard on the Hemi and optional on the tri-power 440. Its operation is driver-controlled so that you can select normal underhood air during the winter. Its effect on performance is almost nil at normal speeds, however.

The '70 Barracuda is a totally integrated sporty car that's right for the times. There's no trunk space (collapsible spare available) and the hood is super long. Plymouth was about six years late with the design, but it did put them back into the market that they, along with Ford, started in 1964.

The Hemi-Cuda was much better suited for drag strip performance than for daily driving. This is one of the rare five four-speed Hemi-Cuda convertibles built during 1970.

The only reason the owner of this Hemi-Cuda ordered the optional luggage rack was to add weight over the rear wheels! The Street-Hemi was an expensive option, costing the dealer $706.65 over base. For just $202.35 the dealer could get the excellent

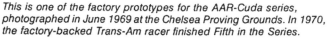

Plymouth was right on target with the Barracuda, especially the convertible model. Convertible production for the three models were as follows: Barracuda—1,554; Gran Coupe—596; Cuda—635.

This is one of the factory prototypes for the AAR-Cuda series, photographed in June 1969 at the Chelsea Proving Grounds. In 1970, the factory-backed Trans-Am racer finished Fifth in the Series.

For 1970 the Barracuda offered a clean, modern interior with minimal frills. Production of hardtops for three model series broke down as follows: Barracuda—26,651; Gran Coupe—8,183; Cuda—18,880.

1970—DODGE CHALLENGES THE WORLD!

From its mini-cube 340 to the maxi-inch scalding Street-Hemi,
the Challenger was truly the Ponycar for all seasons

Because of the limited T/A production, So-Cal dealers and customizers were converting well-optioned Challengers into T/A models, right down to 340 tri-carb engines. This is a a converted car photographed right after new model announcement in 1969. On the race circuit, Sam Posey drove the factory (and Classic Car Wax)-sponsored Autodynamics Trans-Am racer. Dodge finished Fourth with the Posey car.

THE Challenger is here! Dodge waited over five model years to meet the Mustang on the youth market battlefield, and its entry has what it takes to get the job done. It's actually a little bigger than the standard-size Ponycar and, in many cases, more sophisticated and stylish. And, if the styling doesn't get 'em, the performance options will.

Like most of its competition, the Challenger is available in a multitude of models—both hardtop and ragtop—(nine) and in two price classes. Built on a 110-inch wheelbase, the Challenger stands a shade over 51 inches high and spans a total length of 191-plus inches. Its wide track stance is heftier than the full-size Dodge Coronet. Its suspension is conventional Dodge, with beefy adjustable torsion bars up front and leaf springs at the rear.

Unlike many new models which are usually upgraded optionwise the second year around, the Challenger was introduced with every imaginable performance option. You could purchase a standard Challenger or opt for the R/T model. Both models could be had with the super-glitzy Special Edition package which added leather upholstery and other luxury touches. The Challenger offered a wide variety of powerplants, ranging from the econo-respectable Six to the 440 tri-power and 426 Street Hemi. In between are the 318 two-barrel, 340 four-barrel, 383 and 440 four-barrel.

To win over the enthusiast marketplace, Dodge made all engines in the line available in the Challenger which meant that you could actually tailor a car to the most exacting performance standards. No maker in the industry could match Dodge's flexibility when it came to powertrain choices. It should also be noted that the Challenger was available with the accepted standard of automatic transmissions—Chrysler's excellent three-speed Torqueflite. It offered manual performance with automatic ease of operation and consistency. Interestingly enough, approximately 26 percent of Challengers built in 1970 had four-speed transmissions!

Even though Dodge was merchandising the Challenger under its Scat Pack high-performance lineup and using almost-obscene colors, the fact was that if you wanted real performance all you had to do was check off the right boxes. The standard powerplant in the R/T Challenger was the excellent 330-hp 383-incher and the options included the 335-hp 383, 375-hp 440, 390-hp 440 (this was the fantastic Six-Pack 440 with three Holley two-barrel carburetors) and the race-bred, dual-quad 426 Street-Hemi rated at 425 hp.

On the street or strip, Challengers were hard to beat. With the 335-hp option you could expect 0 to 60 mph times in the high, high Sevens and quarter-mile times of 90 mph in the mid-15-second area. If you opted for the Hemi Hummer you had the potential for 0 to 60 mph times of low,

The convertible was a sleek number, especially if outfitted with the matte-finished, twin-scoop hood. Production hit 3,173 units in the consumer series and 1,070 units for the glitzy R/T model.

Even without the Shaker hood and other high-performance options, the Challenger is a very appealing car. Production of the base hardtop hit 53,337, while the more expensive SE model accounted for only 6,584 units.

Production of R/T ragtops was quite limited (1,070) making them super-rare today. Even rarer are the Hemi and 440 tri-power convertibles.

The hinged back window louver and deck spoiler were dealer-installed options in 1970. The adjustable angle spoiler cost $34.80. The louver and dual outside sport mirrors came as a package for just $91.10. For an extra $5.00 you could replace the NASCAR hood pins with mini-locks for added protection. The good old days!

This is a Shaker hood, 440-Six-Pack setup in an R/T Challenger. This is a totally-stock original factory installation.

Under all the Shaker scoop plumbing is a brace of Holley two-barrel carbs which helped make the Six-Pack the most desirable of the high-performance daily drivers. This is a pre-production pilot installation photographed at Chrysler Engineering in June 1969. The manifold is one of the aluminum jobs.

In true sports car fashion, the main gauges were black and white and easy to read. Remember when cars had 150-mph speedometers and 8,000-rpm tachs?

For those who felt that "bigger was better" and "only the most will do," there was no substitute for the 426-inch Street-Hemi. When you opted for the Street-Hemi you got the legend as well as the motor!

low Sixes and quarter-miles at over 100 mph in the high-13-second bracket. There were few more-popular Ponycars that could match the Challenger's performance.

The Challenger is one of the most tasteful executions of the long-hood/ short-deck styling theme which became the standard of the Ponycar market. Its sleek, low, smooth and almost totally void of geegaws and other hokey styling gimmicks. It's almost impossible to beat the combination of wide, trim, wrap-around bumper, outlined sunken black grille frontal styling, clean integrated tail treatment,

imposing performance-oriented hood options, and white-lettered, black-walled 60-series fat tires on mag-styled wheels. Even the door handles are flush to preserve the sano body lines.

On the inside is a highly-stylized cockpit-type interior with high-backed buckets with built-in headrests, and a refreshing instrument cluster which puts the gauges in front of the driver. Unfortunately, unless you ordered the rallye cluster (standard on the R/T) you didn't get an oil pressure gauge, tach and trip odometer. There's lots of wood and vinyl for that sporty car touch.

A lot of engineering went into the Challenger for the express purpose of protecting driver and passengers in case of collision. There's a collapsible steering column with secondary energy-absorbing members mounted between the steering wheel and shaft. There's a transmission and steering wheel locking ignition switch setup on the column and recessed interior door handles and locks. The handles hinder accidental opening in a roll-over condition. The Challenger is an all-new car from bumper to bumper, with enough fresh ideas to give GM a run for the money.

THE PONYCAR PERSONIFIED

The Plymouth AAR CUDA and Dodge CHALLENGER T/A have become the most sought-after collector Ponycars ever built. Here's why

AAR CUDA/CHALLENGER T/A PERFORMANCE

0 to 30 mph	2.1 Seconds
0 to 60 mph	5.8 Seconds
0 to 100 mph	14.4 Seconds
Quarter-Mile ET	14.3 Seconds
Quarter-Mile Speed	99.5 MPH
Top Speed	125-130 MPH

Note: Above times recorded by auto magazine road testers in 1970 using an AAR Cuda with four-speed transmission, 3.55-to-1 rear end and closed exhausts and street tires.

Designed specifically for the T/A and AAR Cuda, the A-833 fourspeed has close-ratio gearing with a 2.47 First, 1.77 Second and 1.34 Third. Cars were also available with automatic.

ENGINE DATA

The AAR Cuda and Challenger T/A came through with only one engine, there were no engine options. The cylinder blocks used in the special 340-inch applications were stress-relieved and built with extra-think main webbing for four-bolt-main modifications at a later date. These blocks were specially-numbered. A typical Challenger 340 block has the letters TA as part of the cast-in serial number.

Cylinder heads for this application were specially-machined and have pushrod holes relocated to allow for bigger ports. The number is #3577053. Other unique goodies include longer-than-normal pushrods with special ends for rocker arm adjusting screws. The adjustable rocker arms have a special offset and cast-iron adjusting screws pre-set to adjust to Hemi engine specifications. Lifters are hydraulic with HD snap rings (Hemi engine specifications) and the rocker shafts have additional lube spreader grooves.

A-833 FOUR-SPEED MANUAL TRANSMISSION

THE MYTH & THE MAGIC

The standard rear axle in all Plymouth and Dodge models is an 8¾-inch model with 3.55-to-1 gears and the standard brakes are power disc front and 11-inch diameter drums in the rear.

All models have fiberglass fresh air scoop hoods (Plymouth #3443686, Dodge #3443685) and radio aerials mounted on the right rear quarters. The aerial cable is routed down the right side sill and spot-taped in place.

The Rallye suspension with front and rear sway bars and HD shocks is standard equipment. The rear spring camber has

149

been increased to provide ground clearance for the special side outlet exhausts and G60-15 rear tires. Standard equipment front tire is E60-15 with raised white letters; rear tire is G60-15 with raised white letters. Road wheels are 15 x 7-inch and a colapsible spare tire is standard.

Special front fenders are used on these cars (also Hemi-engined Challengers and Cudas) to accommodate the wider 7-inch wheels and fat Sixty-series tires.

The road-racing-style front spoilers were optional and shipped not-installed to dealers. According to research, the quick-steering was listed both as standard and optional. Note: All cars tested in 1970 by the author who was Editor of CARS Magazine were equipped with the quick-steering ratio—2.7 turns lock-to-lock. Sure-Grip limited slip differential was also optional at extra cost and not standard equipment. The rear springs were 150-pound/inch assemblies as used on Hemi-engined models.

Even though the models were listed for sale in 1971 dealer brochures, (Dodge-"End of the road for the do-it-yourself kit") records show that production was actually limited to one-year. Dealers did sell leftover cars into the 1971 model year. Production of the '70 AAR Cuda was 2,724, while the Challenger T/A was 2,539. The model code for the Cuda is BS23J and the Challenger T/A is JH23J.

Dodge version is called "340 Six-Pack." Engine is the same. This example has been detailed for show.

Sam Posey carried the Dodge banner to the Trans-Am wars in his Autodynamics — prepared Challenger T/A.

Air cleaner assemblies used for Cuda applications received "340 Six-Barrel" decal designation.

One-year-only Challenger T/A production hit 2,539. Only one engine was available and hood was lightweight fiberglass with large scoop.

This is the AAR Cuda (Dan Gurney's Racing Team) with unique side stripe treatment. Production hit 2,724 for one-year production.

AAR CUDA/CHALLENGER T/A ENGINE

Displacement . . . . .340 cubic inches
Bore . . . . .4.040 inches
Stroke . . . . .3.31 inches
Compression Ratio 10.5-to-1
Pistons . . . . .Autothermic, Alloy Tin-Coated
Pins . . . . .Full-floating
Crankshaft . . . . .Fully-Counterbalanced
Camshaft . . . . .Hydraulic Lifter
Duration . . . . .268/276 degrees
Lift 429/.444-inch
Intake Valves . . . . .2.02 inches
Exhaust Valves . . . . .1.60 inches
Intake System . . . . .Edelbrock Tri-Power
Exhaust System . . . . . .Dual, low-restriction mufflers, side exit

SIX-PACK INDUCTION SYSTEM

DESCRIPTION	SPECIFICATIONS
Intake Manifold	Edelbrock alloy, #3418681
Center Carb Number	3577182/183
Holley Number	R-4791A/92A
Front Carb Number	3577184
Holley Number	R-4789A
Rear Carb Number	3577185
Holley Number	R-47904
Center Throttle Bore	1½-inch
Outboard Throttle Bore	1-9/16-inch
Center Metering Jet	#62/#61
CenterPower Valve	#65

This is what the carburetion looks like, complete with Edelbrock aluminum intake manifold. This engine has been modified for drag racing. Headers are not stock.

QUICK TRIPPER FROM SCAT CITY

Dodge offers a Trans-Am twin to the Dan Gurney AAR-Cuda that has got to be the hairiest ponycar ever offered to the public

The T/A and AAR Cuda were little more than excuses for the factory to go racing. McAllister Dodge ran T/A drag car, left, and Sam Posey ran Ray Caldwell Autodynamics T/A road racer powered by destroked 305-inch, 450-hp Keith Black engine. Swede Savage ran Plymouth version in 1970 Trans-Am season. Cars were produced only for one-half of 1970 model year; none produced in 1971. Total production was approximately 5,000.

Standard engine is tri-power 340 with three Holley carbs on Edlebrock alloy manifold, .430/.445-lift hydraulic cam, 10.5 forged pistons, heads with relocated pushrods and Hemi valve springs and a four-bolt main block with full-thickness webs. Output is 290 hp at 5,000 rpm and 345 foot pounds of torque at 3,400 rpm. In stock shape car could run 0 to 60 in 6.0 seconds, 0 to 100 in 14.0 seconds and the quarter-mile at 100 mph in 14.5 seconds.

Ramcharger Dale Reeker designed the super functional hood scoop. Car came with close-ratio four-speed with 2.47 First gear, 11-inch gear drum brakes, front discs with metallic pads, quick-ratio power steering and E and G-60 Goodyear tires for that trick raked look.

the Rapid Transit system

A nitty-gritty tech spec look at the system which is helping Plymouth make it on the '70 supercar scene

Specifications:

	'Cuda					440
Engine	340	383	440	440 6-bbl.	Hemi	440
Displacement, cu. in.	340	383	440	440	426	440
Horsepower @ rpm	275 @ 5000	335 @ 5200	375 @ 4600	390 @ 4700	425 @ 5000	375 @ 4600
Torque, lbs.-ft. @ rpm	340 @ 3200	425 @ 3400	480 @ 3200	490 @ 3200	490 @ 4000	480 @ 3200
Compression ratio	10.5:1	9.5:1	9.7:1	10.5:1	10.25:1	9.7:1
Camshaft	High lift, long duration, high overlap					High lift,
Cam duration, intake/exhaust/overlap	276°/284°/52°	276°/292°/54°	276°/292°/54°	276°/292°/54°	292°/292°/68°	276°/292°/54°
Lifter type	Hydraulic	Hydraulic	Hydraulic	Hydraulic	Hydraulic	Hydraulic
Valve dia., int.	2.02"	2.08"	2.08"	2.08"	2.25"	2.08"
Valve dia., exh.	1.60"	1.74"	1.74"	1.74"	1.94"	1.74"
Carburetion	Single Carter AVS 4-bbl.	Single Holley AVS 4-bbl.	Single Carter AVS 4-bbl.	Triple Holley 2-bbl.	Dual Carter AFB 4-bbl.	Single Carter AVS 4-bbl.
Distributor	Dual-Breaker	Single-Breaker	Single-Breaker	Dual-Breaker	Dual-Breaker	Single-Breaker
Air induction (standard)	Under hood	Under hood	Under hood	Under hood	Air Grabber	Under hood
(optional)	n.a.	n.a.	n.a.	Air Grabber		Air Grabber
Exhaust system	Dual, low restriction, with cast iron headers and high-flow mufflers					Dual, low-headers
Transmission (standard)	Heavy-duty 3-speed		High-upshift TorqueFlite automatic			High-up-
Transmissions (optional)	Heavy-duty 4-speed		Heavy-duty 4-speed			
	High-upshift TorqueFlite					
Suspension Torsion bars, front	Heavy-duty 0.90" dia.	Heavy-duty 0.90" dia.	Extra-heavy-duty 0.92" dia.	Extra-heavy-duty 0.92" dia.	Extra-heavy-duty 0.92" dia.	Extra-heavy-duty 0.92" dia
Rate at wheel, lbs. per in.	113	113	124	124	124	124
Shock absorbers	Heavy-duty	Heavy-duty	Extra-H-D	Extra-H-D	Extra-H-D	Extra-H-D
Stabilizer bar, front	Heavy-duty, 0.94" dia.	Heavy-duty 0.94" dia.	Heavy-duty 0.94" dia.	Heavy-duty 0.94" dia.	Heavy-duty 0.94" dia.	Extra-heavy-duty 0.94" dia.
Stabilizer bar, rear	0.75" dia.	0.75" dia.	n.a.	n.a.	n.a.	n.a.
Rear springs, right	Heavy-duty, 4½ leaves	Heavy-duty, 4½ leaves	Extra-H-D; 5 leaves + 2 half-leaves	Extra-H-D; 5 leaves + 2 half-leaves	Extra-H-D; 5 leaves + 2 half leaves	Extra-H-D; 5 leaves + 2 half leaves
Rear springs, left	Heavy-duty, 4½ leaves	Heavy-duty, 4½ leaves	Extra-heavy-duty, 6 leaves	Extra-heavy-duty, 6 leaves	Extra-heavy-duty, 6 leaves	Extra-heavy-duty, 6 leaves
Rate at wheel, lbs. per in.	129	129	148	148	148	148
Brakes, front	11 x 3" cast iron drums; self-adjusting					11 x 3"
rear	11 x 2½" cast iron drums; self-adjusting					11 x 2½"
Optional brakes, front	Discs; full-floating calipers					Discs,
Driveshaft dia.	3.0"	3.0"	3.0"	3.0"	3.0"	3.25"
U-joints	H-D	H-D	H-D	H-D	H-D	H-D
Rear axle	Heavy-duty, Chrysler-built 8¾" dia. ring gear		Extra-heavy-duty, Dana-built 9¾" dia. ring gear			Extra-heavy-
Axle ratios	See chart					
Rim size (std.)	15 x 7"	14 x 6"	14 x 6"	14 x 6"	15 x 7"	14 x 6"
Tire size (std.)	E-60 x 15"	F-70 x 14"	F-70 x 14"	F-70 x 14"	F-60 x 15"	F-70 x 14"

GTX		Sport Fury GT		Road Runner			Duster 340
440 6-bbl.	**426 Hemi**	**440**	**440 6-bbl.**	**383**	**440 6-bbl.**	**426 Hemi**	**340**
440	426	440	440	383	440	426	340
390 @ 4700	425 @ 5000	350 @ 4400	390 @ 4700	335 @ 5200	390 @ 4700	425 @ 5000	275 @ 5000
490 @ 3200	490 @ 4000	480 @ 2800	490 @ 3200	425 @ 3400	490 @ 3200	490 @ 4000	340 @ 3200
10.5:1	10.25:1	9.7:1	10.5:1	9.5:1	10.5:1	10.25:1	10.5:1
long duration, high overlap		High lift, long duration, high overlap		High lift, long duration, high overlap			High lift, overlap, long duration
276°/292°/54°	292°/292°/68°	276°/292°/54°	276°/292°/54°	276°/292°/54°	276°/292°/54°	292°/292°/68°	275°/284°/52°
Hydraulic	Hydraulic	Hydraulic	Hydraulic	Hydraulic	Hydraulic	Hydraulic	Hydraulic
2.08"	2.25"	2.08"	2.08"	2.08"	2.08"	2.25"	2.02"
1.74"	1.94"	1.74"	1.74"	1.74"	1.74"	1.94"	1.60"
Triple Holley 2-bbl.	Dual Carter AFB 4-bbl.	Single Carter AVS 4-bbl.	Triple Holley 2-bbl.	Single Carter AVS 4-bbl.	Triple Holley 2-bbl.	Dual Carter AFB 4-bbl.	Single Carter AVS 4-bbl.
Dual-breaker	Dual-breaker	Single-breaker	Dual-breaker	Single-breaker	Dual-breaker	Dual-breaker	Dual-breaker
Under hood	Air Grabber	Under hood	Under hood	Under hood	Under hood	Air Grabber	Under hood
Air Grabber		n.a.		Air Grabber	Air Grabber		n.a.
restriction, with cast iron and high-flow mufflers		Dual, low-restriction, with cast iron headers and high-flow mufflers		Dual, low-restriction, with cast iron headers and high-flow mufflers			
shift TorqueFlite automatic		H-U TorqueFlite automatic		H-D 3-speed	High-upshift TorqueFlite automatic		H-D 3-speed
Heavy-duty 4-speed		n.a.		Heavy-duty 4-speed			H-D 4-speed
		n.a.					H-U TorqueFlite
Extra-heavy-duty 0.92" dia.	Extra-heavy-duty 0.92" dia.	Heavy-duty 0.98" dia.	Heavy-duty 0.98" dia.	Heavy-duty 0.90" dia.	Extra-heavy-duty 0.92" dia.	Extra-heavy-duty 0.92" dia.	Heavy-duty 0.87" dia.
124	124	118	118	113	124	124	106
Extra-H-D	Extra-H-D	Heavy-duty	Heavy-duty	Heavy-duty	Extra-H-D	Extra-H-D	Heavy-duty
Extra-heavy-duty 0.94" dia.	Extra-heavy-duty 0.94" dia.	Heavy-duty 0.94" dia.	Heavy-duty 0.94" dia.	Heavy-duty 0.94" dia.	Heavy-duty 0.94" dia.	Heavy-duty 0.94" dia."	Heavy-duty 0.88" dia.
n.a.	n.a.	n.a.	n.a.	n.a.	n.a.	n.a.	n.a.
Extra-H-D; 5 leaves + 2 half-leaves	Extra-H-D; 5 leaves + 2 half-leaves	Heavy-duty, 6 leaves	Heavy-duty, 6 leaves	Heavy-duty, 4½ leaves	Extra-H-D; 5 leaves + 2 half-leaves	Extra-H-D; 5 leaves + 2 half-leaves	Heavy-duty, 6 leaves
Extra-heavy-duty, 6 leaves	Extra-heavy-duty, 6 leaves	Heavy-duty, 6 leaves	Heavy-duty, 6 leaves	Heavy-duty, 4½ leaves	Extra-heavy-duty, 6 leaves	Extra-heavy-duty, 6 leaves	Heavy-duty, 6 leaves
148	148	137	137	129	148	148	
cast iron drums; self-adjusting		11 x 3" cast iron drums; self-adjusting		11 x 3" cast iron drums; self-adjusting			Disc
cast iron drums; self-adjusting		11 x 2½" cast iron drums; self-adjusting		11 x 2½" cast iron drums; self-adjusting			10 x 1¾" cast iron drums
full-floating calipers		Discs, full-floating calipers		Discs, full-floating calipers			n.a.
3.25"	3.25"	3.25"	3.25"	3.25"	3.25"	3.25"	2.75" manual, 3.00" automatic
H-D	H-D	H-D	H-D	H-D	H-D	H-D	H-D
duty, Dana-built 9¾" dia. ring gear		Extra-heavy-duty, Dana-built 9¾" dia. ring gear		Heavy-duty Chrysler-built 8¾" ring gear	Extra-heavy-duty Dana-built 9¾" dia. ring gear		Heavy-duty Chrysler-built 8¾" ring gear
See chart		See chart		See chart			See chart
14 x 6"	14 x 6"	15 x 6"	15 x 6"	14 x 6"	14 x 6"	14 x 6"	14 x 5½"
F-70 x 14"	F-70 x 14"	H-70 x 15"	H-70 x 15"	F-70 x 14"	F-70 x 14"	F-70 x 14"	E-70 x 14"

AERODYNAMICS AND THE WINGED WARRIORS

More than a decade before it was fashionable,
Dodge & Plymouth capitalized on the value of streamlining

This is one of the pre-production Charger Daytona prototypes on the Corporation's drag strip. The Charger was a '69½ model while the Road Runner Superbird carried a 1970 model designation. Key people in this program were George Wallace, Special Vehicle Engineering, Gary Romberg, Race Car Aerodynamicist and Bill McNulty Chelsea's High-Performance Supervisor.

Plymouth built 1,935 winged cars, one for every two dealers for ACCUS certification.

CHRYSLER'S racing engineers, headed by racing chief Robert M. Rodger, have learned a lot about how to improve engine performance in developing Dodge and Plymouth NASCAR stock car and drag racing successes. But race cars have not been noted for their contributions to design.

"The plain fact is that the way future cars look will have a lot to do with the way they perform. In fact, design will have more influence on performance in the future than it ever has before. We're going to see more and more body designs that emphasize the aerodynamic aspects," said Rodger, Chrysler's special car manager and chief engineer for product planning. Rodger has not previously emphasized the benefits of the race track as a means of testing cars for every day passenger car use.

"We still believe that the best way for an engineer to design a car is to develop it for the job it has to do. The cars we engineer for stock car racing are developed to perform best on oval tracks at 180 miles at hour, not on open highways at 60 or 70," Rodger said in 1971.

"But aerodynamics is the closest we've ever come to testing new engineering developments on race tracks which will have definite applications to all of our production cars," he added.

Webster defines aerodynamics as "the branch of physics dealing with the forces exerted by air in motion." To automotive engineers aerodynamics means making air flow over the body of a car with the least resistance.

Reducing air resistance on the body can improve the handling and performance of any passenger car. At 50 mph, engineers estimate, improved performance is about half aerodynamics and half chassis efficiency and engine output. At speeds above 50 aerodynamics becomes the most important single influence on performance.

Improved performance is just one of many benefits of better aerodynamics. Other important customer benefits of more aerodynamic designs include economy, safety, comfort, etc.

Reduced air resistance, accomplished by improved aerodynamics, means the same performance can be achieved on less engine power, therefore with less fuel consumption.

The car's stability, traction and ventilation can all be improved by better aerodynamics. The better stability and traction achieved the safer the car, espe-

NASCAR champ Bobby Isaac took his Daytona Charger to the Bonneville Salt Flats and on September 12, hit a top speed of 217.368 mph for the Flying Kilometer, breaking Mickey Thompson's records. He also set the 100-mile record at 194.290 mph.

This is another Proving Grounds car undergoing testing prior to introduction. On May 24, 1969, Buddy Baker became the first man to break the 200-mph barrier, setting a closed-course record of 200.477 mph in a Daytona Charger at Alabama International Motor Speedway.

Plymouth and Dodge versions of "wing decor".

cially in higher speed ranges and in certain stress situations, like cornering or passing a large truck on the open highway.

Improved aerodynamics helps to keep the circulation of dirt, dust and exhaust fumes away from the car.

"Aerodynamics is the next big step left in the performance area. We've gone so far in maximizing the use of engine power that we're looking elsewhere for improved performance, and there's a lot to do in aerodynamics," Roger said.

From the styling point of view, the emphasis on aerodynamics is a definite plus. Dodge Division's Charger Daytona, gives an inkling of what aerodynamic design can do for appearance.

The long hood and front fenders of the Daytona dip low into a wedge-shaped front end. Grille work is minimal, and headlights are comcealed—designed in the pop-up or "frog's eye" fashion. A rear horizontal and vertical stabilizer emphasizes the rounded, airplane fuselage-like appearance of the car. The entire design is strikingly streamlined. It's long, low and attractive.

Another example of the aesthetic values of aerodynamic design is the Concept 70X, a futuristic idea car introduced by Chrysler-Plymouth Division at the 1969 Chicago Automobile Show. Concept 70X features flush glass, doors extending to the roofline, and clean, uncluttered lines. Elwood P. Engel, Chrysler's styling Vice-President, said styling's goal in the Concept 70X was to create a "fully integrated, aerodynamically sound appearance with major improvements in convenience, safety and driver visibility."

Increasing emphasis on aerodynamics is good news for the drivers, engineers and fans who have made auto racing, and especially stock car racing, the nation's Number Two spectator sport. But more than that, the emphasis on aerodynamics is simply inevitable.

The latest government figures, released by the Federal Highway Administration, show that the average speed traveled on all U.S. highways in 1968 was 59 mph. Passenger cars traveled an average of 64.4 mph on interstate highways, the government report said. And for the future, the Commerce Department has studied the possibility of developing limited access super-highways with controlled top speeds of 120 to 150 mph.

Automotive aerodynamicists point out that aerodynamic design becomes an important influence on car performance, stability and safety at 40 mph. At 50, aerodynamics is as important as any other influence. At 120, aerodynamics is

Continued

157

Winged cars drew crowds standing still. This photo was taken at a popular New York speed shop in 1969.

Bob Rodger, Chrysler's racing chief at the time and one of the guiding forces behind the Daytona and Superbird projects.

vitally important.

By way of contrast, cars of the 1920s were designed for cruising speeds in the 40-mph range. As speeds increased through the 1930s, '40s and '50s, car shapes were rounded. And in the 1960s they have been lowered, lengthened, and streamlined. Some of the aerodynamic design improvements incorporated in the Charger Daytona help to illustrate how aerodynamicists think.

To an aerodynamicist, an automobile traveling at speed is boring a hole through the air approximately proportional to its frontal area. The resistance to this action is called aerodynamic drag. The amount of drag is determined by the shape, size and velocity of the car. A blunt-shaped front end, then, creates more drag than a wedge-shape, and a lower car less than a higher car.

The aerodynamicist concerned with performance at raceway speeds knows that a high amount of drag means more horsepower will be reduced, more speed will result with the same power or the same speed with less power.

At 180 mph and up—the approximate speeds attained at Daytona—about 17 additional horsepower are required to make a stock car go one-mile-per-hour

faster in the straightaway, and about 20 to 25 additional horsepower to pick up one-mile-per-hour in the curves.

Rodger predicted that the new stock car rules announced recently by the Auto Competition Committee of the United States (ACCUS)—which call for a reduction of maximum engine displacement from 430 to 366 cubic inches in 1971—will accentuate the importance of aerodynamic improvements.

The design changes incorporated in the Charger Daytona were made to "overcome the aerodynamic forces which tend to unstabilize the car and slow it down," Rodger said.

For example, the wedge-shaped nose reduces drag. The front spoiler reduces it further by counteracting front end lift. At 70 mph, tests showed the movement of air created about 180 pounds of front end lift on the Charger—or enough to lift the whole nose of the car by about one-half inch. The new design gets lift back down to zero or a slight downforce. "The front end design pierces the air lower and lets less air get underneath the car," Rodger said.

The rule of thumb is that the less air you have passing under the car the better the performance and stability. This is

especially true when the vehicle is operating at today's freeway speeds or on one of the super speedways.

The flush rear window configuration of the Charger Daytona eliminates turbulence, cuts down on wind noise and decreases the rear drag. The vertical stabilizers, like the feathers on an arrow, will tend to keep the car going straight, and horizontal stabilizers improve rear traction and stability.

The entire design makes the Daytona much less sensitive to side air pressures, such as those created by cross winds on the highway or in the drafting sensation experienced when a motorist passes a large truck at highway speeds. Similar side pressures are enormous on the curves at our major speedways.

"The design of the Daytona moves the center of pressure of the car back to approximately the center of gravity. This stabilizes the balance of the whole automobile and generally improves its handling characteristics," Rodger said.

It looks like the future in automobile engineering and design will bring form and function much closer together," Rodger added.

DURING the summer of 1970, Holly Hedrick with help from the Los Angeles & Orange County Dodge Dealers, prepped a street-driven Daytona for some very serious racing. The record books have been re-written many times since 1970, but this was truly an important effort.

In the attempt to establish a new flying mile speed record for American production automobiles, the Charger Daytona qualified as a vehicle which had been produced in quantities of 500 or more and offered for sale to the public by established Dodge dealers.

Part of the challenge was to squeeze added performance, under rules which permit only minor alterations. A protective roll-over cage, this one from Race Car Engineering, and other safety equipment are permitted, along with certain limited engine modifications. Fuel must be certified commercially-available pump gasoline, and superchargers of any type are prohibited.

Beneath the street-driven Charger's hood is a 426-inch Dodge Hemi rated at 475 hp and good for 180-mph top speeds. During the actual runs, however, power was furnished by a highly-refined version, engineered by Keith Black Racing Engines, to hit 685 hp at 7,200 rpm. That's Dyno horsepower.

Computer calculations indicated speeds between 235 and 240 mph, which would handily eclipse the present 202-mph record.

Hedrich's partner in the record hunt was "Diamond Jim" Annin, of La Canada, California. A champion driver in his own right, Annin is credited with technical contributions which include the critical powerplant design.

Hedrich, then a Keith Black vice president, parlayed his advantage into a sampling of the firm's engineering output. While opting for Pennzoil #60

WINGING IT AT THE FLATS

Super-Sano Dodge Daytona Charger Daytona gets the job done on the street and the Salt

racing oil with a Fram Dual System filter, Hedrich and Annin leaned on Keith Black for a gear-type pump and wet sump pan to round out lube chores.

Crankshaft, radiused and grooved, and gear-type camshaft drive also carry Keith Black Labels. Other goodies include 13 ½-to1 pistons plus template-ported cylinder heads.

While most of the remaining components are stock Dodge, some replacements were in order. Transmission is standard Dodge four-speed, but Schiefer forged aluminum, 11-inch clutch and flywheel now transfer

power back to a Sure-Grip 2.73-to-1 rear end which is used in conjunction with Goodyear land speed tires mounted on Cragar wheels. Cyclone four-tube equal-length headers and collectors cap the exhaust system. Simpson five-way seat belts keep the driver in his Solar Plastics bucket, while a Simpson drag chute is designed to keep the Daytona in Utah!

The Charger Daytona Hemi is driven daily on city streets. Decked out in its Pearl White and Candy Blue and Red paint by George Cerney Jr., the car's appearance alone stops traffic and turns heads.

SAM POSEY, TRANS-AM CHALLENGER

Sam Posey talks about driving his Trans-Am Challenger
on the most difficult of all the tracks
in the legendary SCCA circuit

Colorful Sam Posey was Dodge's Great White
Hope in the 1970 Trans-Am Series. He drove
the factory-sponsored Autodynamics TA
powered by a destroked 340-inch small-block
(305 cubic inches).

AT St. Jovite the immediate difficulty is not one with the race cars but with the pretty girls—it's difficult to keep one's mind on the business of racing at first. None the less once you tear yourself away from the paddock and get your racing car on the track there is plenty there to demand your fullest attention on the 2.65-mile road course.

Mont Tremblant is generally regarded by drivers as the most difficult race course in North America. It starts off tough and gets worse! The section immediately after the pits is the roughest thing anywhere. It starts with a very fast hill crest, then the road drops away from under you, snakes to the left and flattens out. The road then rushes uphill and crests with the car going into the air while the road continues to turn under you.

It's easy to come down with your two left wheels off of the road at 120 miles per hour—and there's a guard rail there to wrinkle up your car in case you make a mistake. Following the hillcrest the car plunges downhill into a sweeping right turn as you head for the second turn into a tunnel of trees with a river at the bottom of a steep bank to the left.

After the roller coaster effect of Turn One it requires considerable audacity to keep your foot flat on the gasoline

Ray Caldwell engineered the chassis at his Autodynamics complex in Marblehead, Mass. The T/A was shod with Goodyears mounted on Minilite mags. Classic Car Wax was also a sponsor. Posey finished the 1970 SCCA season in Fourth Place.

Leading the pack through a tight turn at St. Jovite in Canada, Posey proved the Dodge Challenger's worth as a real road racer.

through this section. There is a right hand kink just as the road flattens somewhat, then there is an abrupt, very sharp and very long tight right hander that empties into the extremely tight left hander of Turn Three. The combination of turns Two and Three is so difficult that no one driving at the limit puts two laps the same back to back.

In spite of the difficulties of two and three turns you have to be sure that things are gathered up sufficiently well to allow a good exit from Three because from Three to Five it is flat out for the Dodge Challenger.

The get around Turn Four flat-out requires a good exit from Three because you have to pitch the car in toward the apex and let the tires scrub off some of your speed.

They should call Turn Five "Frustration Corner" because it has been just that for many high-caliber racing drivers over the years. There are banks on both sides of the track that block your vision completely. It was at this turn in 1969 that George Folmer spun out. His car ended up sideways in the road with the result that he just got out before seven cars piled into his racer. It ended the hopes of Mustang in the Trans-Am series. Three of their four cars were destroyed.

If you can survive Turn Five, Turn Six won't be much of a challenge but Turn Seven—an expanding radius curve—will be sufficient to test any reserve confidence you might have built up! First at the entrance to Seven—where you do your braking and down shifting—the track is very rough making it difficult to decelerate the car smoothly; then this

turn always gets oily during the race and it's tough to accelerate out of it. None the less it's important that you exit well from Seven because Turn Eight preceeds the longest straight on the track.

At St. Jovite, where nothing is easy, even the straight is difficult! A hill right in the middle of the straight crests at the bend in the track (Turn Nine). At this point the car wants to leave the ground—which Jackie Oliver's titanium car did here—at the end of the straight there is an "S" bend with first a right at Ten and then a left at Eleven. For once at Mont Tremblant you can see the turns before you get to them. However, they are quite fast and the track quite narrow so great precision is called for in this area.

Leaving Eleven there is a little downhill and then the track swoops uphill, goes under a bridge and turns sharp left just as it crests. A good memory manifests itself here because you can't see the apex for Turn Twelve until you're in it. Twelve preceeds a flat out section so the exit from it is important. One is still climbing somewhat after Twelve, then the track turns right at Thirteen and starts down again to level out under a bridge. It then goes steeply uphill, crests that hill and finally twists down into a very, very tight hairpin (Fourteen) which turns the car completely around.

This hairpin is famous for trapping even the best drivers into braking too late for it—the penalty is usually a harmless spin although there is a bank on the outside that has dented the egos of quite a few drivers over the years!

The track from the Turn Fourteen hairpin continues downhill toward the start-

finish line with a little left-hander at Fifteen. It is very narrow and undulating with the car building to over 100 miles-per-hour at the start finish line.

Across the start-finish line and into One going through the gears is a Fourth gear run—the feeling of speed is terrific in this section. In Turn One Third gear has to be grabbed just before the bottom of the steep hill. Second is a must for the tight "S" bend at Two and Three turns. Accelerating from the Third turn you go into Third gear and get Fourth gear just before Turn Four even if it means shifting a little bit sooner than my usual 7,800-rpm redline. I don't want to unbalance the car here with an upshift.

For Turn Five we will go back to Third briefly and then hold Fourth gear down to Turn Seven where—depending on the way the Challenger is geared—I'll either use Third or Second accelerating out of the Seven-Eight turn.

I'll be going just as hard as I can getting up into Fourth gear for the blast over the hill and down into turn Ten. Turn Ten will call for a downshift into Third gear and I'll stay in Third gear for Eleven and for the short straight into Twelve.

Then I'll have to cross the quadrant of my four-speed gear box to get Second gear long enough to swing around the tight uphill Turn Twelve. Then I'll go to Third gear for Thirteen—and for just a moment—Fourth before going down into Second gear for the hairpin.

Although the road is cambered oddly on the way out of Turn Fourteen I'll still have my foot hard on the gas as I grab Third and Fourth gears to sweep across the start-finish line.

A HEMI FOR THE SEVENTIES

Extra-strength and increased-performance modifications highlight the updated race Hemi engine marketed by Mopar

THE TWO main modifications to the unstoppable race Hemi engine for 1970 includes a new stronger engine block with a revised, beefier lower-end and a new set of super-efficient cylinder heads. The new heads, debuted by Dick Landy, the Ramchargers and Don Garlits, are of twin-plug design. The application of two-spark-plugs-per-cylinder was accomplished without any interference with the rocker arms or pushrods. The use of twin-plugs provides improved propagation of the flame within the chamber and allows a lower spark advance. ●

Modified twin-plugs Hemi head as used by Don Garlits and Dick Landy. Twin plugs provide improved flame propagation within the combustion chamber.

New stronger Hemi race block boasts a beefed lower end for increased durability at high rpm under heavy loads. In 1970 this block was available from Chrysler's Performance Parts Services in Warren, Michigan for $385.

THE END Is NEAR!

Chrysler Corporation officially withdraws from NASCAR, the Street-Hemi becomes history and the supercar market takes a conservative down turn

A Charger with Super Bee option, motorized Ram Air induction and Six-Pack 440 power was Dodge's entry in the Supercar Sweepstakes.

CAPSULE COMMENTS

THE MOPARS have come on strong this year, both in performance car styling and in retaining live wire action for anyone who wants it. Big news at Plymouth is a Satellite line. Stand a '70 and a '71 Satellite side by side, and it's like suddenly stepping out into the future. Instead of compromising the wheel base for two different requirements, like sedans and coupes, all of the Satellites now use the shorter 115-inch platform for the coupes and a 117-inch platform for the sedans and wagons. A similar situation prevails in the Dodge lineup with the Coronet and the Charger, except that there the Coronet wagons and sedans go to a 118-inch wheelbase.

The Satellites come through with a full loop bumper design, a long thin nose and a semi-fast-back rear. Road Runner trim turns out to be unusually discreet, with a little tiny "beep-beep bird" in the center of the grille, and a racing stripe, that hoops like a rollbar over the roof (which is made of reflective tape for safety as well as looks). When Dick Maxwell, Mopar's six-foot-three drag racing expert, says, "there is room enough in the new Road Runner trunk," he proves the point by sliding in with full comfort. There is also room enough up front to pick

your own choice of engines from a Hemi or a Six-Pack 440 on to a 225-inch Slant Six. When it comes to picking hoods, there are three or them, ranging from plain to one with decorative but non-working side inlets. For the real thing, order a *shaker* scoop. It is vacuum-operated and also has a control from inside the car. Charger hoods follow a similar pattern and carry an added bonus: the sticker price is coming down within reach.

Among the small fry, some rapid fire shuffling has taken place. The Swinger moved up a notch, while a newcomer, the Demon has taken its place. It won't take you long to guess that the Demon happens to have an older brother by the name of Duster. Of course, a Demon also has a big brother, called the Demon 340. It is a pretty husky performer with floor stick three-speed (all synchro) or a four-speed. Add to this a heavy-duty suspension, and bigger brake drums, and a modest price tag. In the Plymouth Duster camp, you'll find also a 340-incher with similar equipment. An automatic and a spoiler are but a few of the options.

The '71 Cuda's nose is *wild,* with a series of fins and dividers, in body color, or silver, as you please. Headlights went

1971 HIGH-PERFORMANCE ENGINES

CUBIC INCHES	BORE	STROKE	HORSEPOWER	TORQUE	COMPRESSION	INDUCTION
340	4.040	3.310	275 @ 5000	340 @ 3200	10.50	FOUR-BARREL
383	4.250	3.380	300 @ 4800	410 @ 3400	8.50	FOUR-BARREL
426	4.250	3.750	425 @ 5000	490 @ 4000	10.20	DUAL-QUAD
440	4.320	3.750	370 @ 4600	480 @ 3200	9.50	FOUR-BARREL
440	4.320	3.750	385 @ 4700	490 @ 3200	10.30	TRI-POWER
340	4.040	3.310	290 @ 5000	340 @ 3200	10.50	TRI-POWER

Author Martyn L. Schorr, above, left, presented Dodge's Bob McCurry with CARS Magazine's Top Performance Car of the Year Award, for the 1971 Charger lineup. There was something for everybody. Bolt-on rear spoiler, above, was dealer-installed option on Challenger. Vacuum motor controlled fresh air box fixture used on Ram Air models. It was heavy, but it worked really neat and attracted a lot of attention. Super Bee with 383 Magnum engine option was neat econo-supercar.

up in number from two to four, and some slanted "hash-marks" have been added to the fender. 'Cuda or Challenger, the list of handling and engine options is impressive. Heavy duty suspension begins with .88-inch front torsion bars, a front and a rear stabilizer bar and some heavy-duty springs. From there you move an "extra heavy duty" package which has a .92-inch torsion bar, 4½-leaf rear springs with control to balance out the traction between right and left on hard take-offs, and heavy duty "everything else." This extra heavy-duty package is standard on the 440 Six-Pack and Hemi, and optional for the 340.

A series of axle packages are available with the Hemi and

Dodge Charger R/T, above, and Plymouth Road Runner, below, were Chrysler's prime movers in the supercar sweepstakes. Unfortunately, performance was starting to become a dirty word and the handwriting was on the wall.

440 Six-Pack. The top package—the Super Track Pak—has the big 9¾-inch Dana with a 4.10 gear, a limited slip, a four-speed manual or an automatic, and some extra goodies, such as a dual-breaker distributor, a seven blade torque drive fan, and a bigger radiator. Next step down is the Track Pak (no "Super") which differs only in a more streetable 3.54 rear axle. The two lower axle packages offer a 3.90 (for the 340 four-barrel) or a 3.55.

When it comes to engines, the best low-buck performance buy is a 340-incher. It comes with a steel crank and a rocker shaft that is completely deflection-free. In other words, the valve train doesn't "move around," using up valuable cam timing and lift. Valves are big, 2.02-inch intake and 1.60-inch exhausts, operated by mechanical lifters. For 1971 the 340 retains a 10.5-to-1 compression ratio and delivers 275 horses. Bigger is not necessarily better and the new '71 arrival, a 360-incher, is intended for street rather than strip. It has a cast crank instead of a steel one, a longer stroke and a smaller bore (4.00 x 3.51 instead of 4.04 x 3.31). The heads are the same basic castings as on the 340, but to make a nice streetable package, the two-inch intake valves were replaced by 1.88-inch valves. This is done to achieve a higher port velocity and a better scrubbing action of any liquid fuel traveling down the manifold. It improves throttle response and

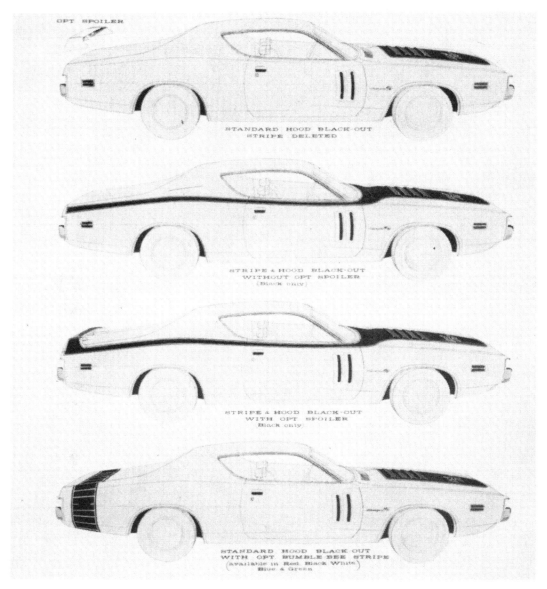

OPT SPOILER

STANDARD HOOD BLACK-OUT
STRIPE DELETED

STRIPE & HOOD BLACK-OUT
WITHOUT OPT SPOILER
(Black only)

STRIPE & HOOD BLACK-OUT
WITH OPT SPOILER
(Black only)

STANDARD HOOD BLACK OUT
WITH OPT BUMBLE BEE STRIPE
(available in Red Black White)
Blue & Green

murders top-end horsepower. The connecting rods are similar to those of the 340, but have pressed pins instead of full floating ones.

There has been a change in carburetion on the 340, with the Carter AVS being replaced by the new Thermo-Quad. The TQ base is aluminum; it has a large body made out of a black plastic and an aluminum cover. At first glance, it looks like a three-barrel since the secondary side doesn't even have a venturi between the air valve and the throttle. The TQ has quite a competition program behind it, with a lot of on-the-strip experience. This shows in details, such as being able to change jets right on the engine without removing the carburetor from the manifold. Just pop the cover and you'll find the jets, accelerator pump and metering rods, all packaged on top. Screw the jets out and put bigger ones in if your heart tells you to, but these have been carefully-calibrated for performance. As on the AVS, you have to adjust the spring tension on the air valve to get good response out of the gate.

For 1971, Cars Magazine editor, Martyn L. Schorr, presented its Top Performance Car of the Year Award to Dodge General Manager Bob McCurry for the new Dodge Charger. •

Dodge made its Charger to appeal to a broad audience which explains why so many different stripe and decal packages were available. It was the most visible supercar on the market. Vacuum-operated fresh air door on Six-Pack Ramcharger cars attracted a lot of attention on the street.

ENGINES

	Cricket 4 cyl.	Duster 198	Duster 225	Duster Twister (318-2)	Road Runner Duster Cuda (340-4)	'Cuda Road Runner (H.P. 383-4)	'Cuda GTX Road Runner (H.P. 440-4)	'Cuda Road Runner (440-6)	'Cuda Road Runner GTX (Hemi 426)
Bhp @ Rpm	57 @ 5000	125 @ 4400	145 @ 4000	230 @ 4000	275 @ 5000	300 @ 5200	370 @ 4600	385 @ 4700	425 @ 5000
Torque @ Rpm	74 @ 3000	180 @ 2000	215 @ 2400	320 @ 2000	340 @ 3200	410 @ 3400	480 @ 3200	490 @ 3600	490 @ 4000
Bore	3.39 in.	3.40 in	3.40 in.	3.91 in	4.04 in.	4.25 in.	4.32 in.	4.32 in.	4.25 in.
Stroke	2.53 in.	3.64 in.	4.12 in.	3.31 in.	3.31 in.	3.38 in.	3.75 in.	3.75 in.	3.75 in.
Displacement	91.4 cu. in	198 cu. in.	225 cu. in.	318 cu. in.	340 cu. in.	383 cu. in.	440 cu. in.	440 cu. in.	426 cu. in.
Compression Ratio Nominal	8.5 to 1	8.4 to 1	8.4 to 1	8.6 to 1	10.3 to 1	8.5 to 1	9.5 to 1	10.3 to 1	10.25 to 1
Minimum Combustion Chamber Volume	42.1 cc	53.8 cc	53.8 cc	60.6 cc	63.3 cc	79.5 cc	79.5 cc	79.5 cc	167.7 cc
Minimum Deck Clearance	.032 in.	.076 in. below	.141 in. below	.060 in.	+.045 in.	.019 in.	.051 in.	.001 in.	+.536 in.
Carburetion	Zenith	Carter	Holley	Carter	Thermo Quad	Single Holley	Single AVS	Three Holley	Dual AFB
Throttle Primary	1½ in.	1 11/16 in.	1 11/16 in.	1 7/16 in.	1⅜ in.	1 9/16 in.	1 11/16 in.	1½ in.	1 7/16 in.
Secondary	—	—	—	—	2¼ in.	1¾ in.	1 11/16 in.	1¾ in.	1 11/16 in.
Cam Duration Intake	248°	248°	248°	248°	276°	276°	276°	276°	292°
Exhaust	244°	244°	244°	256°	284°	292°	292°	292°	292°
Overlap	26°	26°	26°	28°	52°	54°	54°	54°	68°
Ignition	Single-Breaker	Single-Breaker	Single-Breaker	Single-Breaker	TorqueFlite: Single-Breaker 4-Speed: Dual-Breaker	Single-Breaker	Single-Breaker	Dual-Breaker	Dual-Breaker
Point Gap	.015 in.	.017-.023 in.	.017-.023 in.	.014-.019 in.	.014-.019 in.	.014-.019 in.	.014-.019 in.	.014-.019 in.	.014-.019 in.
Timing Torqueflite	7° BTC	2½° BTC	TDC	TDC	Single-Breaker 5° BTC	2½° BTC	2½° BTC	2½° BTC	2½° BTC
4-Speed	7° BTC	2½° BTC	TDC	TDC	Dual-Breaker 5° BTC	TDC	TDC	Dual-Breaker: 2½° BTC	TDC

POWER TRAINS

Car	Engine	Transmission	Axle Type and Ratio Non-Sure Grip	Sure-Grip
Cricket	1500 cc	Automatic 4-Speed	3.91 Standard 3.91 Standard	
Duster	198	Automatic 3-Speed	2.76 Standard 3.23 Standard	2.76/3.23 Optional 3.23 Optional
Duster	225	Automatic 3-Speed	2.76 Standard 3.23 Standard	2.76/3.23 Optional 3.23 Optional
Duster Twister	318-2 318-2	TorqueFlite 3-Speed	2.76 Standard 3.23 Standard	3.23/3.55/3.91 Optional 3.23/3.55/3.91 Optional
Duster 340	340-4	TorqueFlite 4-Speed	3.23 Standard 3.23 Standard	3.55/3.91 Optional 3.55/3.91 Optional
Cuda 340	340-4	TorqueFlite 4-Speed	3.23 Standard 3.23 Standard	3.55/3.91 Optional 3.55/3.91 Optional
RR-340	340	TorqueFlite 4-Speed	3.23 Standard 3.23 Standard	3.55/3.91 Optional 3.55/3.91 Optional
'Cuda Road Runner	383-4 383-4	TorqueFlite 4-Speed	3.23 Standard 3.23 Standard	3.55/3.91 Optional 3.55/3.91 Optional
'Cuda GTX Road Runner	440-4 440-4 440-4	TorqueFlite 4-Speed	3.23 Standard NA	3.55/4.10 Optional 3.54 Standard 4.10 Optional
'Cuda Road Runner	440-6 440-6	TorqueFlite 4-Speed	3.23 Standard NA	3.55/4.10 Optional 3.54 Standard 4.10 Optional
'Cuda Road Runner GTX	426 Hemi 426 Hemi 426 Hemi	TorqueFlite 4-Speed	3.23 Standard NA	3.55/4.10 Optional 3.54 Standard 4.10 Optional

Panel-painting treatment with billboard displacement lettering let the world know what was under the hood. Rarest model of the 1971 lineup was the convertible powered by Hemi engines. Conflicting total Hemi production figures show 108 or 114 cars with 7 being ragtops. One source shows 108 with 68 being four-speed Hemis and 40 fitted with Torqueflites.

1971—THE TURNING POINT

The accent is on small-cubes and handling rather than big-inch straightline performance

The goodies that Supercars and Ponycars are made of! Plymouth didn't forget about the add-ons that kept the youth market knocking on dealers' doors.

FOR 1971 there's a new grille treatment, based on a vertical theme with six sections formed by bold vertical bars. Last year's setup was unquestionably cleaner and more in keeping with Cuda's sano lines. The same thing goes for the blackout tape panel on the side adorned with 340 trim.

The base engine for the Cuda series is the four-barrel 383, a non-performance-oriented (adjusted compression ratio) engine which really isn't worth having if you're a performance nut as the 340 four-barrel is a not extra cost option. The cost is already dialed-in. For more bucks you can pick up on the 440 Six-Pack. The 340 four-barrel is obviously the best buy in the lineup.

What we really like about the Cuda 340 is that it's a together package. It handles and it hauls. It tracks straight, doesn't roll and offers positive steering and directional control. The lightweight engine helps out in this department. What also helps is the heavy-duty suspension package which boasts .088-inch torsion bars, HD rear springs and front and rear sway bars. There's an extra heavy-duty job that's reserved for the bigger-engined models. Add to that power front disc brakes and you've got yourself a handling and haulin street machine.

Very respectable 340 four-barrel engine pumped out an impressive 275 hp at 5,000 rpm. Shaker scoop added weight, status and dollars to basic car.

Plymouth kept the Ponycar image alive with paint treatments, a
Shaker hood and even hood pins. With 340 cubes, handling qualities
are right-on. Sales were way down from 1970 with the hottest selling
base coupe hitting just 9,459 units. Ragtops hit 1,014.

Short pistol grip stick offers good shift control, but HD Mopar
four-speed is not the easiest shifting box around. However, as far as
durability is concerned, the Mopar four-speed is the best.

Cuda models show hardtop production of 6,228 units and just 374
convertibles. With four-speed and 3.91 gears, 340 Cudas ran 91-95
mph in 14.80s. You could buy a loaded 340 Cuda for less than $4,000
in 1971!

1971—THE SCAT PACK SCENARIO

The Dodge Boys do their best to keep the
Ponycar Revolution alive

Low and lean, the R/T Challenger with 440 Six-Pack power was running proof that performance was alive and well at Dodge. They built 4,630 R/T models out of a total production of 29,883 units.

Pop-open chrome fuel filler was neat status touch on this R/T Challenger. It was detailing like this that helped keep the image alive.

WHEN THE Challenger was debuted in 1970, most dealers and press people were unquestionably impressed. It proved to be an extremely tasteful execution of the popular long hood/short deck theme, with all the makings of a winner—sexy lines, gobs of performance and luxury options, mod colors and an almost non-existent trunk. Everything the public wanted! Needless to say the Challenger made it, accounting for 13 percent of industry Ponycar sales. And, of this 13 percent, high-performance model, 340-440 and 426 Hemi—sales accounted for a fantastic 40 percent. A rather impressive record on both counts.

For 1971 all the good things were carried over including the non-existent trunk and rear passenger seating capacity. They were smart enough not to tamper with the styling, only making slight grille, tail blinker and interior trim changes. The recessed grille is split into a pair of narrow horizontal rectangles to simulate air scoops. The rectangular treatment was carried to the rear in the form of tail blinker housings. There are optional

Continued

The 440 Six-/Pack was the hot street setup in 1971. While Dodge did advertise the T/A Challenger with 340 Six-Pack power in its 1971 catalog, none was built. Leftover 1970 models were marketed as 1971 cars.

This is the real McCoy on the Indy tarmac. Note aftermarket mag wheels, steel-belted Firestones and hood pins.

With blackout trim around the tail blinkers, the Challenger R/T looked even more aerodynamic than it really was. This photo was taken on the Chrysler Corporation drag strip in June of 1970.

color-keyed polyurethane-coated bumpers for those who want to carry the mod yellow, plum, orange or blue all the way.

The single biggest improvement in the 1971 Challenger—or any other MOPAR with four-speed—is the improved transmission. The innards have not been modified for smoother shifting, but the transmission interlock and steering wheel linkage have been removed. A movable ring, which is part of the steering column, handles the locking control chores. Now, with these modifications and the use of a Hurst shifter, shifting is on par with competitive stock factory four-speed setups.

With the new four-speed, and 4.10 gears, the 440 Six Pack Challenger's performance is quite impressive. Fortunately, you can't get the package without good brakes, HD suspension and tires. The R/T dash is well laid out for performance driving and with the twin molded scoops, there's a clean view of the road on tap.

Not only does the 440 Six-Pack Challenger look and run good, it also sounds good. Its horsepower is ably backed up by a throaty exhaust note which really raps when you back off the pedal.

Dodge built a total of 23,088 base coupe and hardtop models and 2,165 convertibles. This is a rare job with non-performance equipment and a rear deck spoiler. I wonder how many of these were ever built?

Seldom-seen rear deck spoiler was spotted at the Chelsea Proving Grounds during the 1971 new model showing.

On May 29, 1971, the official Challenger Indy Pace Car started the 500-mile race. Because of an unfortunate Pace Car accident, it was to be the last time for Chrysler at the Brickyard in Pace Car capacity.

FUTURE SHOCK!

Compact Colt station wagon gets a one-of-a-kind
Weslake-head de-stroked 340-incher to keep the Dodge Boys in the limelight!

Bill McGraw took over the wheel of the Colt from Stickel & Noltemeyer
and demonstrates here the fine art of weight transfer!

The Rod Shop crew works on the Weslake-head 340 motor
during the car's initial outing. With unique injection and
heads, the Colt attracted a lot of attention.

THE COLT wagon is the brainchild
of Rick Stickel, but is actually
owned by Bob Riffle. Except for the
body, the car represents pure U.S. drag
racing ingenuity. After taking delivery
of a Colt wagon, the Rod Shop crew
and Chris Buttler discarded the engine,
transmission, rear end and front and
rear suspensions. What they were left
with was a stripped Colt body sans any
chassis or suspension components.

Chris Buttler heliarced a rectangular
tube chassis, and then fitted the lightweight frame with an Exhibition Engineering dropped tube front axle, four
coil/over spring shocks and a chopped
Mopar rear. The rear was shortened to
32 inches (width) and fitted with a
Detroit locker, mid-five series gearing
and Exhibition Engineering disc
brakes. There are no brakes up front. A

Running at the 1971 Indy Nationals, Ray Noltmeyer drove the Colt in D/Altered and posted an impressive 131 mph in 10.41 seconds. This is some station wagon!

Doesn't every econo-compact wagon have a full roll cage, spartan bucket seats and a T-handle Hurst shifter?

Sliding valve injectors and lightweight Weslake heads were originally designed for Chrysler's destroked Indy engine project executed by Keith Black.

full roll cage is employed, which is actually part of the chassis. The car is set up to run with a 319-cubic-inch engine at 2,905 pounds, but it can be lightened by 300 pounds to juggle around class entry with a 305-inch Trans-Am engine.

The real exotica in this machine lies under the hood. That's where the money is! The engine is a destroked 340 Mopar that was designed and built by Keith Black for Chrysler Corporation. That's when Chrysler decided to challenge the Indy Fords. It puts out 560 hp, will run to 10,000 rpm and cost a mere $12,000 in 1971!

What makes this wedgie worth big bucks is that it was designed on Black's dyno to run 500 miles at redline revs. It's equipped with Weslake heads with gigantic ports that offer a direct shot at

the valves for maximum efficiency and breathing. You will note in the photos that the fuel injection assembly bolts directly to the ports in the heads—there is *no* manifolding. The engine utilizes a Hilborn pump, but unlike Hilborn injection it works on a sliding valve and not on the butterfly principle. Short, polished intake stacks really work with the 8,000-rpm shift points and 9,800-rpm redline.

The super trick WRP-135-4002 Weslake heads are similar to those used on the Gurney-Ford-Weslake small-block racing engine, and are manufactured in England. Valves used in these heads are almost identical in size to those used in Z/28-LT-1 Chevy engines—2.02X1.60 inches.

The amazing part of this engine is that it was designed to run for dura-

bility at Indy and that it wasn't modified when the Rod Shop received it for their drag racing car.

Other engine goodies include a Crane 282/393-A cam, Vertex magneto and Doug Thorley headers. The lower end, which was built for racing at the 500, sports a steel billet crank, Carrillo billet steel rods and a dry sump lube system with a 3½-gallon oil tank. Backing up the engine is a slick-shift modified Chrysler Hemi four-speed with a 2.66 First gear. Between the First gear ratio and the engine's ability to rev, Ray Noltemeyer is into Second gear by the time he reaches the Christmas tree. If he's not, the engine shutoff takes over!

REQUIEM FOR THE HEAVYWEIGHTS

The Six-Packs are phased out
and the future of the
street-performance stocker looks pretty grim

Road Runner, above, still has plenty of image, but power was way off. Early plans called for continuation of Six-Pack power. New 400-inch wedge, left, was standard in Road Runner and matching Dodge. It boasted Carter Thermo-Quad and dual exhausts. With dyno tuning, engine was a strong contender on the street. Dodge Charger, below, offered same power options as Road Runner plus extra luxury features. Charger had all the makings of a genuine GT sedan. It's nice to see that Charger nameplate is still alive and used on an image car.

1972 HIGH-PERFORMANCE ENGINES

CUBIC INCHES	BORE	STROKE	HORSEPOWER	TORQUE	COMPRESSION	INDUCTION
400	4.340	3.380	255 @ 4800	340 @ 3200	8.20	FOUR-BARREL
440	4.320	3.750	230 @ 4400	355 @ 2800	8.20	FOUR-BARREL
440	4.320	3.750	280 @ 4800	375 @ 3200	8.20	FOUR-BARREL

*SPECIAL NOTE: Six-pack engines were planned for 1972 models but were pulled after initial production.

The surprise performers of the 1972 lineup ended up being the 340 four-barrel Challenger and Barracuda ponycars, available with four-speed or automatic. Superior handling qualities gave these cars an edge on the competition. The factory resorted to a lot of "decal customizing" to replace the power losses.

1972—THE HANDWRITING'S ON THE WALL

The outlook for high-performance Ponycars
is not good, but the Barracuda and Challenger hang in there
with 340-inch mini-maulers

BROTHERS under the skin, the Barracuda and Challenger received minor styling changes and an overall castration for 1972. In keeping with industry-wide performance cutback because of emission control, safety and insurance rating systems, Chrysler Corporation dropped the biggies from their Ponycar lineup. Only sheetmetal differentiates the Challenger from the Barracuda.

The nitty-gritty here is that both cars have been relatively unsuccessful—as have other competitive Ponycars—and it won't be long before they are phased out of production. The mystique of the new Ponycar seems to have faded and most buyers are not willing to sacrifice interior space and trunk space for long hood/short deck styling and high insurance rates. And, the tariff on the loaded models is really outrageous.

The Barracuda for 1972 is available in hardtop form only with a choice of standard or Cuda models. The standard model can be had with either a 225 Six or 318 V-8, both of which are of little interest to the enthusiast. The Cuda is available with the 340 four-barrel, the top engine offered in the Ponycar line. The 340 comes with the pointless electronic ignition and a Thermo-Quad carb. As in the past, a wide variety of tape stripe treatments are available. There's also a new blue vinyl roof containing reflective metallic particles.

There's a new grille on the Barracuda which sports single headlamps mounted in its outboard portions. In the Cuda series the grille is available in colors to

The Challenger looked a little front end heavy—even without the long-haired beauty. Dodge sold 18,535 hardtops and 8,123 Rallye models in the 1972 model year.

match or blend with exterior finishes. Also on the Cuda is a performance hood with simulated scoops. Gone is the ram-air *shaker* setup which proved to be heavy, clumsy, expensive and which didn't keep with the performance playdown for 1972.

Dodge offers basically the same with its Challenger line. There's an economical hardtop and a Rallye model. The engine options are exactly the same. The grille treatment is much more effective and there are dual headlights. The Challenger also offers tape treatments. The Challenger is slightly longer and wider and comes off looking like a more impressive vehicle. As far as handling and performance are concerned, the Barracuda and Challenger are equals.

While the 318-inch package is an insurance-rate-beater, it offers nothing for the enthusiast. The 340 four-barrel has potential and does offer the type of performance you would expect from a Ponycar. It doesn't offer the "animal acceleration" of a 440 Six-Pack, but it makes for a pleasant performing automobile. The 340 cars also handle and stop much better than comparable big-inch models made in 1971.

Both test cars were fitted with 340 four-barrel engines. 3.55 Sure-Grip rears, Rallye suspensions with rear and front sway bars and seven-blade clutch fans and 26-inch shrouded radiators. The

A 340 Cuda at speed on the Chrysler skid pad in July of 1971. In track tests the automatic versions were quicker and faster than the four-speed models. The car could have used a smoother-shifting Borg-Warner box.

Challenger was fitted with a Torqueflite shifter with slap-stick positive shifting console controls. The Cuda was four-speed equipped and Hurst-controlled. Under street conditions testing the automatic Challenger would get to the Cuda every time The torque multiplication factor and the consistency paid off in spades. On the strip, the stick-shifted Cuda had a slight edge. Both cars handled well but could have used healthier rubber than the F-70x14 stockers. Heftier 60-series shoes and wide wheels were not available on 1972 models.

The 340 four-barrel engine was a good choice for the Ponycar models, but the engine should have been beefed-up or the cars put on a diet. The little 340 grew to become a very important engine in drag and circle track competition.

A sporty two-spoke steering wheel which allowed for full instrumentation visibility was standard equipment on base and Cuda models. Dash was lacking a real performance feel.

A pre-production 340 Rallye Challenger about to gobble-up a Charger on the Chelsea high-speed oval.

While stock, original is the way to go, installing a bigger 440 mill in a Challenger or Barracuda is not a very difficult job. The factory built a number of these 440 cars for testing and evaluation prior to getting the word that 340 cubes was the max.

In 1972 Plymouth sold 10,622 hardtop coupe models and 7,828 Cuda high-performance jobs. Hood treatment with twin scoops offered that "clean and mean" look.

KING RICHARD, THE HEMI-HEARTED!

NASCAR's living legend has put more Plymouths in the winner's circle than all other stock-car drivers combined

Richard Petty and his '72 STP-Plymouth NASCAR stocker at the Daytona 500. It definitely pays to stay slim and trim since stockers do not have operating doors.

RICHARD PETTY, undisputed king of stock car racing and perhaps the most successful figure in all the long history of all kinds of automobile racing, has won more important races, won more prize money and established a consistently brighter winning record than any man to ever drive a big-league racing machine.

The son of Lee Petty, himself an illustrious figure in the sport and a three-time NASCAR Grand National championship winner, Richard prepared a car completely on his own for his first venture into professional racing just 10 days after he passed his 21st birthday. That was in 1958 and he ran a 100-miler on a Columbia, South Carolina dirt track. He heeded his father's advice "not to go faster than it felt good to go" and finished Sixth in the scramble on the half-mile track.

Richard scored his first win at a 100-miler at Charlotte, North Carolina and he's been winning ever since.

This past season, which gave him his third Grand National Title and an all-time mark in money winnings, saw him compete in 46 races with 21 wins. Compared to a baseball batting average this shows Petty to be hitting .456, which puts him on a par with the great Ted Williams. He was in the top five 38 times and in the top 10 a total of 41 times. He raced 12,870.88 miles and won $333,148.

His career statistics show 565 NASCAR races, 141 wins, 335 times in the top five and 98,939.28 total racing miles. His money won, up to the end of the 1971 season, totaled $1,138,133 and he started the 1972 season with a victory at the Riverside 500 which marked his first race with the STP Racing Team of Andy Granatelli.

The First Family of stock car racing—Lee, Maurice and Richard Petty. Brother Maurice builds the engines; Richard does the driving. Andy Granatelli and Richard Petty at a press conference in 1972 announcing Grand National racing program. Petty's teammate was Buddy Baker in a '72 STP-Dodge.

Although he had been named the Martini-Rossi Driver Of The Year for 1971, the honor which Petty treasures most is his President Nixon Council of Physical Fitness. He shares that honor with his new racing associate, Andy Granatelli, and Petty feels the inclusion of selected racers in the President's Council is meaningful. "It allows all to carry the important message of physical fitness to the youth of our country," he said. "I can think of no greater contribution that we could make."

"The occasion on which Andy and I met with President Nixon and other racers at the White House recently, brought home to both of us, I am sure, the new status which auto racing people enjoy in our country today."

During his years of racing, Petty's cars have always carried the number "43" which is one digit higher than the "42" number formerly carried by his father. In all but his earliest races, his cars have been painted the famous "Petty Blue" color and except for one season, he has consistently appeared in Plymouth stock cars.

This year, racing for the STP team for the first time, his mount will continue to be a Plymouth, but the colors will have STP racing red added, forming a tone tone red and blue paint job, but retaining the giant numerals "43" painted in white.

Richard's pretty wife, the former Lynda Owens, who met him when he was a high school football star and she was a cheerleader in their home town of Randleman, North Carolina, summarizes Richard's future this way:

"Richard has never lost his enthusiasm for racing. When he does, he'll quit. Right now he's thinking of a fourth championship and $400,000. Nobody's ever done that." ●

The Petty pit crew doesn't give Richard much time to rest during typical pit stop at Daytona 500 in 1968. They were able to change tires and fill the gas tank in less than 25 seconds. Richard in his Superbird stocker, below, at speed on the tricky Riverside, California, race track.

SOX & MARTIN, PLYMOUTH'S DYNAMIC DUO

Ronnie Sox & Buddy Martin did more for Plymouth's supercar sales and image than all that company's advertising campaigns combined!

FROM a grandiose dream in 1962 to a multi-million dollar reality in 1972, Sox & Martin, Inc. has evolved from a little-known Burlington, North Carolina based racing operation to a teeming business venture.

The name Sox & Martin is nationally known now. And, at each strip visited by the famed duo, the red, white and blue Plymouth machine is the car to beat even though it wasn't always like that. It took some ten years of building by partners Ronnie Sox and Buddy Martin to establish the name among the elite of automobile racing.

The Sox & Martin brand of racing comes on a quarter-mile asphalt strip and since their first venture in 1962, the dynamic duo has become expert at winning national meet races.

Sox "just grew up around cars" in Burlington and had soon established himself a reputation among drag racing cliques. Martin, a Greensboro, North Carolina native, became a hobby drag racer and soon ran up against Sox, a driver he couldn't best on the strips dotting the Carolinas.

The adage "if you can't beat them, join them" soon became true for Martin. In 1962 Sox & Martin, Inc. was formed and the combination soon became one of the toughest in the country when it came to winning.

Sox & Martin hit the big-time with their first major triumph in 1964 when Ronnie drove a Mercury Comet to a NHRA eliminator crown.

In 1965 the Sox & Martin team began campaigning a Hemi-powered Plymouth Belvedere under the Chrysler Corporation banner. The Plymouth, nicknamed the "Paper Tiger" because of its light weight, was one of the first Funny Cars. In 1966 S & M switched to a fuel-burning Barracuda which was pitted against other professionals mainly in match races.

Then in 1967, Sox & Martin returned to the stock classes and Ronnie won the NHRA's Springnationals at Bristol, Tennessee, Suddenly, it seemed that the magic formula for winning had been discovered and in 1968 Sox & Martin annexed one NHRA triumph and three AHRA titles.

And with the winning trend came success of the Plymouth SuperCar Clinics. This performance program called for Sox & Martin to tour Chrysler-Plymouth dealerships to hold seminars on drag racing and automotive preparation.

"I guess the clinics are among the more satisfying things we do," says Martin. "We average about 50 appearances a year and sometimes the attendance is as high as 2,500. There is a good deal of interest in performance among the kids and it's a pleasure to work with them".

By 1969, personal rewards for both Sox and Martin began flowing in their direction. That year the S & M team scored five major events wins and headed into 1970 riding the crest of their most successful season on the quarter mile.

And, it was 1970 that emerged as the Super Sox & Martin season. With Memphis, Tennessee racer Herb McCandless joining the team as a second driver, 17 major triumphs were recorded (13 of them by Sox).

Last year wasn't exactly like 1970's win column, but the Sox & Martin team won 15 national championship events, set two National records (NHRA and NAAR), appeared in 125 cities in 32 states, presented 40 SuperCar Clinics, had a winning rate of 75 percent in major events and represented drag racing at President Nixon's reception for motor-sports figures at the White House, plus numerous personal awards for Ronnie, Buddy and master mechanic, Jake King.

Now Sox & Martin, Inc. has become a flourishing car building and high performance parts business. Expansion of the facilities in early 1972 has enabled Sox & Martin, Inc. to increase its payroll to 25 employees and to become the Chrysler drag racing parts outlet for the eastern United States in addition to being the only complete facility of its type to build complete stock-bodied drag cars for its customers. •

THE RAMCHARGERS

A scientific and businesslike
approach to drag racing helps position
Dodge as the King of
Super/Stock competition

*Shortly after Ramchargers got Hemi engines
sorted out, they had one in a fuel digger.
First runs netted them with 191.98 mph
in 7.59 seconds. Not bad!*

THE RAMCHARGERS is a group that has fluctuated in number from 10 to 30 (now 10) of Chrysler Engineering staff employees who share a strong mutual interest in high performance automobiles. They come from many different facets of engineering operations such as the engine laboratory, sheet metal shop, even styling. There is but one exception to the rule and that person, though an outsider, is on permanent assignment to Chrysler Engineering Staff and the team from Holley Carburetor Company.

Their backgrounds vary from theoretical research and design through the development stages of engineering. Included is everything from master mechanic to an English subject Cambridge graduate.

The group was formed in the summer of 1958 and became a chartered National Hot Rod Association club shortly thereafter. Meetings are held twice a month either at Chrysler Engineering or at the club speed shop in Ferndale, Michigan, a Detroit suburb.

Activities include technical discussions, racing car construction, drag racing, and family and social gatherings. Officers are elected once a year. Membership is limited to those who work at Chrysler Corporation's Engineering Staff. Membership becomes inactive when a member goes into the service or to another industry or competitive manufacturer.

Candy-striped Dodges campaigned by Ramchargers were unbeatable in Super/Stock. They bowed out of S/S racing after the 1964 NHRA Indy Nationals after they set a new record at 130.05 mph in 11.23 seconds. It was almost 2 mph faster than A/FX record!

During the Seventies the Ramchargers branched out into Funny Cars and the "Club" image had all but died out. Their rail was the first to run the new-style Hemi.

The original purpose was to provide a meeting ground for interested people to discuss their hot rodding hobby and ideas. At first, activity was confined to members' private cars. By 1959, however, a club project was undertaken. The Ramchargers built a C/Altered, a '49 Plymouth powered by a 1956 Chrysler 300 engine. This car established several C/A records and started a new movement in American hot rodding—raising the center-of-gravity to gain weight transfer on a wide-open throttle start.

At the same time, several members' private cars were top contenders in their respective classes—NHRA C, E & G/Gas. Then early in 1961 the '49 Plymouth, called the "High and Mighty", dropped an exhaust valve and was retired.

At this time the Super/Stock era of the Ramcharger club activity began. The club acquired a '61 Dodge Dart which became the David among competitive Goliaths at the NHRA Summernationals in Indianapolis on Labor Day, 1961. The white and candy apple red-striped Super Stock activity continues apace, as innumerable trophies attest now the Ramcharger Dodge is a label well recognized throughout drag racing circles.

Early in 1963, the hard-core members incorporated into the Ramchargers Maximum Performance Corporation to put the operation on a businesslike basis. Making sets of headers,

Jim Thornton was President of the club and chief shoe of the S/S car. He literally owned the Super/Stock class for a couple of years and proved to be one of the most consistent drivers in the history of the sport.

souvenir photos and decals for sale helps provide additional revenues.

These refreshing enthusiasts lend considerable new face to the field of automotive performance. Time was when stock car ovals and drag strips were frequented by questionable characters. Movies, book and magazine stories emphasizing undesirable black leather-jacketed sorts amplified this impression, unfairly stigmatizing all enthusiasts out of proportion to reality.

That once unsavory image now is fast fading. Emerging in its place is that of a healthy, clean-cut, well-rounded familied American sportsman. The Ramchargers are typical of the welcome more wholesome type. The change is attracting new friends and gentlemen participants. Now there are perhaps 100,000 pro and amateur autophiles helping to turn automotive high-performance into the number two or three American spectator sport. An annual paid attendance of over 32,000,000 at all types of contests, trials and rallies throughout the US now attests to this.

Who are the Ramchargers, personally and individually?

Founding members include: Thomas M. Hoover, physicist, of Farmington, Michigan, one of seven members with master's degrees, presently racing coordinator for Chrysler Corporation's Engineering Staff (his wife "Marge" is secretary-treasurer of the Ramchargers); Herman Mozer, of Detroit, chemist, a Ramcharger driver, vice-president and board member, who supervises construction of Chrysler Corporation turbine cars; Richard Maxwell, mechanical engineer, contact engineer for the Mound Road Engine Plant; and Dan Mancini, coordinator and expediter and assistant to Hoover supervising special parts and test car procurement, a master carburetor mechanic and former Ramcharger driver, of Roseville, Michigan, and vice-president of the group and a board member.

President and board member, James F. Thornton, of Royal Oak, Michigan, another Ramcharger driver, is assistant racing coordinator under Hoover at Chrysler Engineering Staff, and formerly was a steering and suspension engineer.

Others are: Jerry Donley, a master experimental mechanic and test driver, of Garden City, Michigan; Dan Knapp, a mechanic-technician and Ramcharger board member, of Wyandotte, Michigan; Hartford (Mike) Buckel, mechanical engineer, of Madison Heights, Michigan, who is a development engineer working on engine performance and a board member; Thomas T. Coddington, a mechanical engineer, who works on advance fuel metering, and lives in Madison Heights.

Gary Congdon, of Detroit, a carburetor specialist, is exceptional in being something of a "ringer," though every bit a part of the tight "family." He is now on protracted loan-out from his own company but he pitches in nightly and weekends with all the rest. He, too, is a board member. ●

The Ramchargers and their '65 Dodge race car, left. Left to right Jim Thornton, Herm Moser and Mike Buckel at their top, favorite play, and, below, labor of love. Like all Ramchargers they worked an eight-hour-day as engineers before working on race car projects.

There were also Ramchargers behind the scenes, right. All are engineers, master mechanics or technician-specialists at Chrysler. Far left, Tom Hoover; far right, Dan Mancini. Top two, Dick Maxwell and Dan Knapp; below, Tom Coddington, Jerry Donley and Gary Congdon.

A BLAST FROM THE PAST!

Looking back at where Chrysler came from, what they accomplished and why Dodge & Plymouth engines and powertrains ruled the roost

CHRYSLER was achieving things on the racetracks back in the early Fifties, when Ford and Chevy were running obsolete Flathead and Six-cylinder engines. The early V-8 Hemi, introduced with 331 cubes in 1951, was the basis for performance development by Chrysler in those days. They finally achieved 440 hp with fuel injection and alky, and this engine in a Kurtis broke the Indianapolis lap record in tire tests. A high-performance street version of this engine dominated NASCAR racing in 1955 in the Chrysler "300." (the first use of Holley high-performance four-barrel carburetors in the "300" dual-quad setup for NASCAR.) In the 1956 and 1957 seasons the lighter Dodge D-500s did well in NASCAR with a smaller "Red Ram" version of the Hemi.

MoPar Super/Stocks started winning on the drag strip in 1960, when those "ram-type" dual-quad manifolds were developed for the new 413-cubic-inch wedge engine. These manifolds were inspired by ram-tube research done on the 1953 Indy engine.

They flipped over the long cast iron ram tubes that looped over the top of the engine—30 inches from carb to valve! There was upwards of 500 ft-lbs. of torque at medium revs where the bouncing pressure waves in the long tubes "tuned in."

In 1962 we saw a new all-out competition version of the 413 wedge with big-port heads, solid cam, cast iron exhaust headers, and a radical new "cross-ram" dual-quad manifold. Short ram passages crossed over the top of the engine, from carb plenum chambers over the opposite bank, and the major boost tuned in the 5000-6000 rpm range. Result: over 450 horses at 6000 rpm on pump gas, enough to push those early Dodge and Plymouth SuperStocks to ets in the 12's at over 110 mph. A new "Stage III" version of this engine in 1963 had cleaner head ports, an improved cam and the 426-cubic-inch block. At least 500 horses were available in super-tuned form.

Chrysler domination of Super/Stock drag racing dates from these big-port 413 and 426 wedge engines of the '62-'63 period. They appeared to be stronger than equivalent 409 Chevy and 427 Ford SS engines, because of the cross-ram manifold (Ford and Chevy were still using the old in-line manifolds).

But the MoPars would still have been competitive on the strips with *less* horsepower, because of the TorqueFlite transmission. With upwards of 500 hp and the tires available at the time, the Super/Stocks could turn better ets with a fluid-drive transmission. They could jump off the line quicker. Chrysler wisely put their money on the TorqueFlite while Ford and Chevy bet on the four-speed. We know now that Chrysler was right.

The 426-Hemi engine burst on the racing scene in 1964. Chrysler used the basic 426 wedge block but beefed it up with cross-bolted main bearings, hardened crank, forged pistons, stronger rods and a high-flow lubrication system. The block was cast with extra stud bosses at the top to receive Hemi cylinder heads with inclined valves and double rocker shafts. The engine combined fantastic breathing with excellent strength and durability. With 2.25-inch intake valves the volumetric efficiency was nearly 90 percent at 5500 rpm, and the bottom end would take 6800 rpm all day—or 7500 to 8000 for quarter-mile runs.

Chrysler's new 426 Hemi was an immediate success on both the drag strips and the speedways. With one big Holley four-barrel under NASCAR rules, they were pulling 550 to 575 hp and 600 hp or over with the dual-quad cross-ram carburetion.

Nobody could touch this performance. By then GM was officially out of racing and the 409 Chevy engine was obsolete. And Ford's hi-riser 427 was in the 500-550 hp range. The Hemi MoPars dominated on both the strips and NAS-

CAR tracks to the extent that NASCAR officials banned the engine in the 1965 season—saying it was a hand-built racing engine and not "stock." This was quite a blow to the Chrysler people, after spending so much money on development of the Hemi engine, and it almost put them out of racing.

The NASCAR ban was a blessing in disguise because it forced Chrysler to tool up the 426 Hemi engine for volume production (around 5000 units a year) in order to satisfy NASCAR that it was a legal "stock" engine for the 1966 season. And this, of course, brought us the "Street Hemi" engine that was offered for $900 extra in Dodges and

image. And they cost too much. Chrysler made the mistake of putting their high-performance engines in fancy bodies so the price was out of reach.

Chrysler got smart in the early Sixties. The new B-block wedge engine made a beautiful base for high-performance equipment combinations. Certainly the most popular combination used the 383-cubic-inch block, with hot 268-degree hydraulic cam, big Carter four-barrel carb and dual exhaust and was rated 330 hp. Similar goodies were offered with the big 413 and 426 blocks for ratings of 365 and 375 hp. Nothing exotic or expensive here, just solid big-inch performance en-

Plymouths in the Spring of 1966. The Hemi was de-tuned with lower compression, milder cam, cast iron headers and a clever in-line dual-quad manifold with heat brought up through tubes from the right exhaust manifold. It wasn't what you would call a "smooth, flexible" street engine, but it was driveable in all kinds of weather and it gave you enough brute power and torque to blow the doors off practically anything you would meet on the street.

Early Dodge and Plymouth Super/Stock models (Furys, D-500s, etc.) were not popular with the young market in the Fifties. They had reasonably competitive performance, but no

gines with relatively mild tuning and very smooth, flexible street performance. And the key was that Chrysler offered these engines as factory-installed optional equipment in any Dodge or Plymouth. You didn't have to pay $5000 extra for a fancy model name and special trim that didn't help performance at all. (In fact, the extra weight would hurt it.) In the 1962-'65 era you could drive out of the showroom in any one of these cars for under $3000.

In later years Chrysler gave us improved 340, 383, 440 wedge-motors which offered more-performance-per-dollar-spent than any competitive car maker. ●

THE KIT CAR CONCEPT

In 1974 Chrysler showed enthusiasts how to go short-track racing on a budget and win

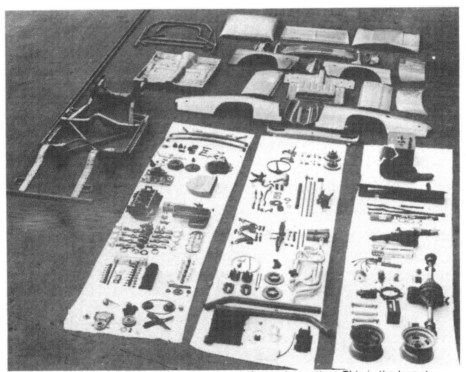

All the goodies you need to go racing—just put them all together. This is the layout offered in the first Chrysler Kit Car in 1974.

To launch the program, Pete Hamilton built a pre- production Kit Car around a Dodge Challenger and proceeded to race it and break the track record at Carraway Speedway in North Carolina.

COMPONENTS for a race car that can be assembled do-it-yourself fashion for low-dollar independent round track enthusiasts was first made available by Chrysler Corporation in 1974.

The Kit Car is a performance-engineered version of compact '74 Dodge Dart Sport 340 or Plymouth Duster two-door models on a 108-inch wheelbase.

"It's called a Kit Car because anyone can purchase the packaged components and assemble them, just as youngsters put together scale models from a hobby shop kit," said Larry Rathgeb, then manager—stock car programs for Chrysler.

"All the right parts are in the kit, and directions are explained very simply in black and white," said Rathgeb. "The buyer will be responsible for welding the parts and most will assemble their own engines. But, the beauty of the program is that we have taken the mystery out of building a stock car."

The kit car components, depending on a buyer's preference, could be adapted to a choice of short track racing forms—either late-model Sportsman, or late-model Modified cars. Or the components can be incorporated into a body an owner may already have.

Rathgeb said deliveries in response to early orders began in March, and that the initial build program through 1974 called for 60 units.

"But the potential is much greater," he said. "The Kit Car program is ideally suited to the needs of thousands of owners who race weekly on nearly 2,000 tracks in the U.S.

The parts were originally merchandised through Petty Engineering in Randleman, North Carolina, and later by Performance Parts Warehouse in Detroit.

Initially tagged "The Saturday Night Special," the Kit Car enabled almost anybody to be competitive in a much shorter span of time than in the days when a racer might spend weeks or months trying to locate, install and experiment to get the right pieces. But the nickname is a misnomer in that the kit car embodies engineering experience that comes from years of involvement in stock car racing by Chrysler.

"We know which parts can withstand the punishment and which ones can't," says Rathgeb. "And we put all the right parts in the kit to make a straightforward car that most people can understand, many can put together, and lots of people can win races with."

Grand National champion Pete Hamilton worked as a test driver as Chrysler engineers refined the kit car design in a pre-prototype, and the car broke the track record at Carraway Speedway, North Carolina in July 1974.

Though Hamilton's car was a Dodge Challenger and the actual Kit Cars were Sports or Dusters, Rathgeb said the prototype Challenger was built to represent the average performance levels of the Kit Car.

And in a stock Sport or Duster, the front frame rails are too close together, so the Challenger front frame section was used, which is as nearly stock as possible. For Kit Car purposes, tying the front and rear suspension and the basic X-frame together is one of the most important design areas.

To achieve better suspension geometry, upper control arm pick-up points were altered from stock and rear spring mounting points were also changed. But all the dimensions are indicated in print for the independent builder when he begins putting the pieces together from the boxes in which they're shipped.

The components came in five major groupings: the frame, the front and rear suspension systems, roll structure, body panels, and the drive line.

The Kit included everything except
Continued

Later the Kit was expanded to include an ATL fuel cell. At the time the complete Kit was priced at $8,880.00 and available from dealers, Richard Petty and direct from Chrysler's Performance Parts Division.

Powerplant is 340-incher with single four-barrel, headers and other goodies for short-track racing.

Steering column installation in actual Kit Car showing steering linkage in relation to the wheel.

Much like a hobby model car kit, the Chrysler Kit Car goes together easily and unlike the toy version, when completed is ready for some serious racing on short-tracks throughout the country.

Front sheet metal is fastened by four quick-release pins for easy removal at the track. Everything fits: every-thing works.

The web of tubular steel ties the roll cage together, neatly showcasing the quick-change rear.

tires and fuel. All special fluids for critical areas were included. To insure standardization, the frames were built with Detroit-designed assembly fixturing.

In putting the components together, the front and rear suspension structrues simply are bolted onto the X-frame.

The front suspension includes basically stock, independent, lateral, non-parallel upper and lower control arms, torsion bars, fully adjustable front sway bar and single Monroe Blow-off type shock absorbers. Grand National-type parallel, longitudinal leaf springs are used in the rear suspension, along with single shocks, and lowering blocks to make the car hug the ground.

The driver's seat is nested in a central roll cage which includes tubing

that ties into the front frame rails for added driver safety and chassis strength.

Putting the body panels together is much like assembling a jig-saw puzzle, one piece positioned by another, said Rathgeb. Panels include front fenders, hood, roof, quarter-panels, rear deck and doors. One the A-pillar is in place, that sets the edges of the windshield opening, which subsequently locates the edges of the cowl and the upper edges of the roof, and so on. This positioning is also done for the lower panels off the sill, which is part of the frame.

All front end sheet metal is held together by four quick-release pins, which permit easy access. Front sheet metal is heavily supported with roll-bar tubing that also ties onto the frame.

The location of body foundation to

frame has been altered for optimum car lowering. Chopping, channeling and other operations are done. All the customer has to do is weld it together.

The only other major step is installing the driveline which includes the 340 CID four-barrel engine, standard three-speed manual floor-mounted transmission, straight tubular driveshaft and a quick-change rear axle.

Disc brakes have been adapted to the quick-change Franklin rear so that there are discs at all four wheels, and they're controlled by an adjustable proportioning valve.

Some of the under-the-hood features include a single Holley, four-barrel carburetor, Edelbrock manifold, Hooker tuned headers and Chrysler electronic ignition.

THE SENSIBLE SUBSTITUTE!

The Direct Connection has found the substitute for cubic inches

---

355 W-2 KIT CAR ENGINE

GENERAL SPECIFICATIONS

Type	90° Overhead Valve V-8
Bore	4.050
Stroke	3.46
Stroke/Bore Ratio	.854
Combustion Chamber Volume	65 to 68 cc
Gasket Compressed Thickness	.033 in.
Gasket Allowance Volume	7.0 cc
Compression Ratio	12.5:1
Cylinder Numbering	1-3-5-7 (Left Bank)
	2-4-6-8 (Right Bank)
Firing Order	1-8-4-3-6-5-7-2
Dry Weight	568 Lbs.
Length — Back of Block to Front of Fan	32.00 in.
Width — Without Oil Filter	26.37 in.
Height — Bottom of Pan to Top of Manifold	21.45
Coolant Capacity Block and Heads	8.7 Qt.
Carburetor	4-BBL Holley (4788)
Tappet Lash	.028 Intake, .032 Exhaust
Ignition Timing	36° Max. @ 7200 RPM
Spark Plugs	N57R
Size	14 mm
Gap	.022
Oil Pressure w/SAE 30 at 120°F.	20 PSI Min. at 500 RPM
	70 PSI between 2,000 to 7,000
Oil Capacity	10 Qt.
Add 1 Qt. w/Filter Change	

TORQUE SPECIFICATIONS FT.-LBS.

Cylinder Head Bolts ½-13	100 ± 5 Retorque After Warm-Up
Main Bearing Cap Bolts ½-13	100 ± 5
Connecting Rod Cap Bolts	70-75 With Oil
Camshaft End Bolt ⁷⁄₁₆-14	40-45 With Loctite
Crankshaft Screw ¾-16	100 ± 10
Intake Manifold Bolts ⅜-16	30-45
Spark Plug 14 mm	30 ± 5
Rocker Shaft Bolt ⅜-16	40-45
Rocker Screw Adjusting Nut ⅜-24	20 ± 1
Windage Tray ¼-20	95 In-Lbs.

CLEARANCE DATA

Main Bearing Clearance	.002-.003
Crankshaft End Play	.002-.007
Connecting Rod Bearing Clearance	.002-.003
Connecting Rod Side Clearance	.015-.020
Crank Damper Hub Fit On Crankshaft	.001-.003
TDC Location of Piston With Respect to Block	.025-.035
Piston Pin Clearance In Rod	.0008-.0012
Piston Pin Clearance In Piston	.0008-.0012
Piston Pin End Play	.000-.010
Piston Skirt Clearance at Center Line of Pin	.0065
Piston Ring Gap	.016
Piston Ring Side Clearance	.0015-.003
Camshaft End Play	.002-.010
Camshaft Bearing Clearance	.001-.003
Valve Tappet Clearance in Block	.0015-.0025
Intake Valve Stem Clearance	.0016-.0036 ⎫
Exhaust Valve Stem Clearance	.0026-.0046 ⎬ .0005-.0010 With Bronzewall Guides
Valve Spring Installed Height	2.00" at 105 Lbs.
Valve Spring Load Minimum	105 Lbs.
Oil Pump and Distributor Drive	.005-.014

THE INCREDIBLE W-2/355

You know the names and reputations of the stock car stars who have proven the 355 cid Mopar with new W-2 heads . . . on NASCAR superspeedways, USAC miles, and short track ovals across the country . . . stars like Petty, Stott, McClusky, Marcis, and Cushman. Their track wins, backed by Chrysler factory engineering and testing, bring you immediately the benefits of a development program many months and much money in the making. It's all standard — at no extra cost — in every Chrysler Kit Car . . . and it's all there for the asking at Dodge and Chrysler-Plymouth dealers.

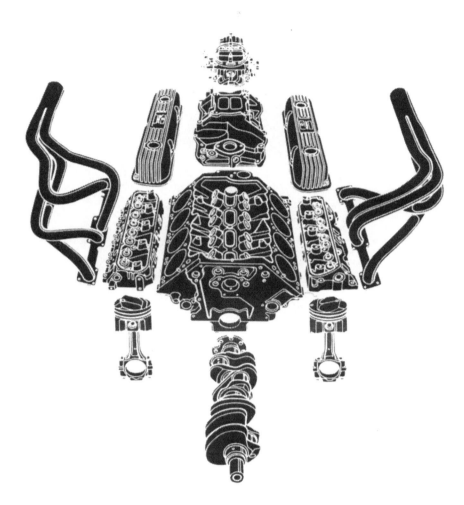

355 Engine Features

- Stress-relieved, 340 block — long-lasting and reliable.
- Special F-77 tri-metal crank and rod bearings for race-finishing endurance.
- Magna-fluxed connecting rods made from double shot-peened, polished, heavy-duty forgings, with 7/16" SPS nuts and bolts. Floating pin.
- Pistons machined from bullet-proof TRW forgings. 12½-1.
- Dyno and track-tested cam with mushroom lifters.
- Gebler Headers with 2" tubing for outstanding low-end performance.
- Special Holley aluminum intake manifold, designed for high-output W-2 heads.

W-2 Head Features

- Advance-design ports for improved air flow and better breathing. Extra material around large, oval intake ports permits optional porting.
- Valve seat cut for 2.02" intake and 1.60" exhaust, semi-finished for installation of trick race valve seat.
- Intake pushrods inclined at very steep angle to allow maximum intake porting.
- Exhaust valve guides are wet for better cooling. Machined lower for high-lift cams and greater valve seal clearance.

- Rocker shaft pedestals have extra material and large radius next to head for added strength.
- Valve spring seat has large diameter for Hemi-style 2" length springs.
- Extra material added to exhaust side at each end of head (in head bolt area) for added strength and rigidity.

THE ULTIMATE BEEP-BEEP!

Plymouth's follow-up act to the
Dodge Charger Daytona revolutionizes
the supercar street scene

FOR 1970, production of "winged thing" cars was taken over by Plymouth with a Superbird version of the ultra-successful Road Runner. The Superbird has a 19-inch-long aerodynamic nose cone and stretches the overall length of the car to 221 inches, 17.2 inches longer than the standard Road Runner 203.8-inch length. The rear stabilizer fin sits 25 inches over the rear deck.

While the Daytona Chargers were essentially converted Charger R/T models, the Superbirds were built from scratch by Chrysler using current-model Plymouth GTX intermediates fitted with Dodge Coronet front fenders and hoods. Unlike the bargain-basement-priced Daytonas, Superbirds listed for $1,000 over the cost of a comparably-equipped Road Runner.

Of the total of 1,935 Superbirds built, 1,084 were 440-cube four-barrel-powered; 716 440-cube tri-power and just 135 cars were factory-equipped with Street Hemi powerplants.

PONYCAR SCOOP SCIENCE

There's more to fresh air induction than just 'sucking wind.'

Original Barracuda Shaker hood scoop is more than just a dress-up accessory. It can be made to work on strip cars, too.

Unique limited production Trans-Am fiberglass scoop as on T/A and AAR/Cudas was used successfully on road racing cars and is dynamite for the street.

Ronnie Sox campaigned this Hemi-Cuda in 1970 with his own design hood scoop.

FRESH AIR systems and hood scoops can provide real performance gains if they are properly designed and executed. However, they can also result in no-gains or, in some cases, even a loss. There are many different styles of aftermarket hood scoops available. We will limit our discussion to scoops that have been used on Chrysler production cars and Chrysler developed add-on scoops. They can be used on most makes for street or strip.

Most of the 1966-'71 426 Street-Hemi engines were built with a hood-scoop-type fresh air system as standard equipment. Hood scoops have also been used on the 340, 360, 383 and 440-inch models from 1968-'74 in the "A," "B" and "E" body cars. Some of the "package" cars in 1969 and 1970 had integral fiberglass scoops and hoods.

The hood scoop and fresh air intake systems for production cars began in 1963 with the 426 Max Wedge cars. The fresh air systems were carried along on the 1964 426 Max Wedge, the 1964 Race Hemi and the 1965 Race Hemi package cars.

The '67 Belvedere and Coronet package cars were the first Street-Hemi cars to use hood scoops. All of these 1963-'67 scoops were made of steel or aluminum and were attached to standard hoods. The fresh air system available on the 1968-'69 Road Runner and Super Bee cars with 383 or 426 Hemi engines utilized inlets that were integral parts of the standard hoods.

The '69 Road Runner and Super Bee 440-Six-Barrel cars were the first production cars to use all-fiberglas hoods. This hood was a pinned lift-off design. In 1970 the Plymouth AAR-Cuda and Dodge Challenger T/A 340 cars also used an all-fiberglas hood and scoop. These hoods were hinged and not of the lift-off design.

In 1970, shaker hood PN 3462249 (scoop only) was introduced on the Barracuda and Challenger models with the 340, 383, 440 and Hemi engines. Some of the Challengers with 340, 383 440 and Hemi engines also used the '70 T/A fiberglass hood. In 1970 and 1971, the Road Runner and Charger models used an "Air-Grabber" fresh air system that consisted of the trap door in the center of the hood that could be opened and closed from inside the car.

The 1973 and '74 340/360 Dart Sports utilized an add-on scoop (PN 3672605) attached to the standard hood. There are holes cut in the hood panel, but the air cleaner is not sealed to the hood so this scoop is more decorative than functional. The 1968 Race-Hemi Cudas and Darts had a lift-off fiberglass hood and scoop as a standard part of that package. These complete hoods are no longer available from Chrysler.

The Pro Stock craze brought on a new type of hood scoop, first developed by Chrysler's John Bauman. This is a Challenger with a built-up and sealed scoop.

Several of the fiberglass hoods discussed are available from your Chrysler/Plymouth or Dodge dealer. They are as follows:

1969—440-6 Barrel Road Runner—PN 3412055

1969—440-6 Barrel Super Bee—PN 3412056

1970—340-6 Barrel AAR Cuda—PN 3443686

1970—340-6 Barrel Challenger T/A—PN 3443685

In cases where the car did not come with a fresh air system and a good hood scoop is desired, several important items should be kept in mind. Although shaker hoods and Air Grabbers can be purchased through your local dealer, a conversion to these types of systems can be expensive and quite complicated. Shakers and Air Grabbers work fine as a fresh air system but, because they are complex and expensive systems, they are not recommended for the "bracket racer"

When Sox & Martin went Pro Stock, the scoop on the Hemi-Cuda was changed to meet the latest specs.

Lee Smith's modified C/Altered Barracuda was fresh air inducted with a Pro Stock-style scoop.

The legendary Motown Missile driven by Don Carlton. Note massive hood scoop treatment with a ramp-like base.

Factory racer Don Grotheer used a modified '68 S/S Hemi-Cuda scoop on his racer.

type of custom installation.

Once the decision to install a hood scoop has been made, one of the fiberglass add-on scoops is considered the best choice. They are easy to attach to a standard steel hood and are quite inexpensive. One of the best choices in this category is the 1969 440-Six-Barrel scoop (PN P3412057) because it has a wide flange which can be used to pop-rivet the scoop to the hood. Before installing a scoop, the carburetor inlet hole should be cut in the hood. It should be located directly over the carburetor and away from any hood braces if possible. The hole can be either round or square but should be at least six inches across. The scoop should be facing forward. The best installation procedure is to pop-rivet

the scoop to the hood and then fiberglass over the pop rivets and the edge of the flange. The fiberglassing helps seal the scoop to the hood and improves the appearance of the installation.

There are four fiberglass hood scoop styles generally available. All four scoops will deliver cold air to the carburetor so your selection should be based on which one would look the best on your car. The scoops are described by the car they were originally used on.

1967—Hemi Super/Stock Style—P3549782

1968—Hemi Cuda/Dart Super/Stock Style—P3549783

1969—440 Six-Pack Style—P3412057

1972-'73—Pro-Stock Style (Two-Piece)—P3690153

The most important consideration with any of these hood scoop designs is that the carburetor *must* be sealed to the scoop. If the scoop is sealed to the hood, then the carburetor can be sealed to the underside of the hood by using foam rubber. If the carburetor is not sealed to the hood, the engine will pull hot-air from inside the engine compartment and the hood scoop will be useless.

For an all-out race car in Pro-Stock, Modified-Production or Formula Stock, the "Bauman boundary layer bleed-off" scoop (PN P3690153) should be used. It is *imperative* that the carburetors be well-sealed to the hood scoop. It is also very important that carburetors be depressed .50-.75-inch below the scoop. That's the hot scoop setup.

Breinigsville, PA USA
16 December 2009
229358BV00002B/4/P

9 780982 173312